THE CIVIL WAR AND THE WEST

Recent Titles in
Reflections on the Civil War Era

Decision in the Heartland: The Civil War in the West
Steven E. Woodworth

True Sons of the Republic: European Immigrants in the Union Army
Martin W. Öfele

Weary of War: Life on the Confederate Home Front
Joe A. Mobley

The Civil War at Sea
Craig L. Symonds

Politics and America in Crisis: The Coming of the Civil War
Michael S. Green

The Confederacy: The Slaveholders' Failed Venture
Paul D. Escott

The Black Experience in the Civil War South
Stephen V. Ash

The Civil War in the East: Struggle, Stalemate, and Victory
Brooks D. Simpson

Civil War Journalism
Ford Risley

The Civil War in the Border South
Christopher Phillips

American Civil War Guerrillas: Changing the Rules of Warfare
Daniel E. Sutherland

THE CIVIL WAR AND THE WEST

THE FRONTIER TRANSFORMED

CAROL L. HIGHAM

Reflections on the Civil War Era
John David Smith, Series Editor

AN IMPRINT OF ABC-CLIO, LLC
Santa Barbara, California • Denver, Colorado • Oxford, England

Copyright 2013 by Carol L. Higham

Library of Congress Cataloging-in-Publication Data

Higham, C. L.
    The Civil War and the West : the frontier transformed /
Carol L. Higham.
        pages cm. — (Reflections on the Civil War era)
        Includes index.
        ISBN 978-0-313-39358-7 (hardback) — ISBN 978-0-313-39359-4 (ebook)
        1. West (U.S.)—History—1848–1860.   2. West (U.S.)—History—Civil
War, 1861–1865.   3. West (U.S.)—History, Military—19th century.   4. Frontier
and pioneer life—West (U.S.)   5. Indians of North America—West (U.S.)—
Government relations—History—19th century.   6. Migration, Internal—United
States—History—19th century.   7. Federal government—West (U.S.)—
History—19th century.   I. Title.
    F593.H54   2013
    978'.02—dc23   2013018983

ISBN: 978-0-313-39358-7
EISBN: 978-0-313-39359-4

17   16   15   14   13   1   2   3   4   5

Praeger
An Imprint of ABC-CLIO, LLC

ABC-CLIO, LLC
130 Cremona Drive, P.O. Box 1911
Santa Barbara, California 93116-1911

This book is printed on acid-free paper (∞)

Manufactured in the United States of America

CONTENTS

Series Foreword   vii
Preface   ix

Chapter One: The International Frontier   1

Chapter Two: The Army of the West   21

Chapter Three: The Indian Frontiers   43

Chapter Four: Statehood and Crisis   67

Chapter Five: The Region Responds   87

Conclusion   109
Notes   115
Bibliographic Essay   137
Index   147

SERIES FOREWORD

"Like Ol' Man River," the distinguished Civil War historian Peter J. Parish wrote in 1998, "Civil War historiography just keeps rolling along. It changes course occasionally, leaving behind bayous of stagnant argument, while it carves out new lines of inquiry and debate."

Since Confederate General Robert E. Lee's men stacked their guns at Appomattox Court House in April 1865, historians and partisans have been fighting a war of words over the causes, battles, results, and broad meaning of the internecine conflict that cost more than 620,000 American lives. Writers have contributed between 50,000 and 60,000 books and pamphlets on the topic. Viewed in terms of defining American freedom and nationalism, western expansion and economic development, the Civil War quite literally launched modern America. "The Civil War," Kentucky poet, novelist, and literary critic Robert Penn Warren explained, "is for the American imagination, the great single event of our history. Without too much wrenching, it may, in fact, be said to *be* American history."

The books in Praeger's *Reflections on the Civil War Era* series examine pivotal aspects of the American Civil War. Topics range from examinations of military campaigns and local conditions, to analyses of institutional, intellectual, and social history. Questions of class, gender, and race run through each volume in the series.

Authors, veteran experts in their respective fields, provide concise, informed, readable syntheses—fresh looks at familiar topics with new source material and original arguments.

"Like all great conflicts," Parish noted in 1999, "the American Civil War reflected the society and the age in which it was fought." Books in *Reflections on the Civil War Era* interpret the war as a salient event in the hammering out and understanding of American identity before, during, and after the secession crisis of 1860–1861. Readers will find the volumes valuable guides as they chart the troubled waters of mid-19th-century American life.

John David Smith
Charles H. Stone Distinguished Professor of American History
The University of North Carolina at Charlotte

PREFACE

For most students of American history, the Civil War represents the single most important conflict in 19th-century American history. It pitted brother against brother and consumed a nation. The nation it consumed, though, did not include the American West. In the 1860s, westward immigration and pursuit of statehood consumed the few trans-Mississippi states, meaning those west of the Mississippi River. Though some states, like Minnesota, produced units to fight in the Civil War and others, like Kansas and Oregon, became deeply involved in the fight over slavery, the Civil War did not affect the West in the same way it did the East. It remained a far-flung conflict, beyond the bounds of most western communities, who had more important problems at hand: Indian conflicts, internal state politics, the pursuit of statehood, the restriction of immigrants.

For Western historians, the Civil War is not the fulcrum of the 19th century that it is perceived to be for the South and even the North. In 1860, only Arkansas, Louisiana, Missouri, Texas, Iowa, Minnesota, California, and Oregon of what would become the 25 western states had entered the Union. The rest remained territories in various states of flux. Utah and Kansas actively sought statehood, but became embroiled in national politics which prevented them from making it through Congress. Colorado had just begun its immigration boom thanks to the discovery of gold and silver. Montana and Wyoming experienced a similar boom during the Civil War. Other territories, like New Mexico and Washington, still fended off international challenges to their existence as a U.S. territory. For most of the western states, Indian wars dominated the headlines and the worries of settlers. The Civil War seemed a far removed controversy. As Elliott West points out, "I know we should put our foot down and not allow the Civil War to continue behaving as it does now in our texts and histories, sitting there like a gravity field, drawing to itself everything around it and bending all meanings to fit its own shape."[1]

For Western historians, like Elliott West and Robert Athearn, the question of the frontier drives their study of the West. In 1892, historian Frederick Jackson Turner declared the American frontier closed based on the U.S. census revelation that no more free land existed. All land west of the Mississippi belonged to someone: the federal government, individuals, railroads, or other industries. Whereas the federal government owned little land east of the Mississippi, it owned vast amounts west of the Mississippi as Indian reservations, land grants, and territories. To many today, the West remains a bastion of federal control, for better or worse. This reality seems in conflict with the great myth of the West: the control of the individual frontiersman or pioneer and his family, heading west, breaking the sod, and creating success out of his own labor. The conflict between these two historic images of the West represents the crux of the debates and conflicts that shaped the U.S. West before and through the beginning of the Civil War. The constant tensions between the rights of individuals and the importance of a federal presence shaped the West and its responses to the Civil War. And outbreak of the Civil War affected and shaped the West through the tensions between the individual and the federal government, as neither one could exist without the other in the West.

The topics most associated with the West in the pre- and Civil War periods by Civil War historians often represent Eastern concerns about the West rather than what concerned Westerners. Civil War historians focus on the debates in Congress about the extension of slavery that erupted every time a new territory or two asked to enter the Union. Congressional leaders, from the 1830s until the beginning of the Civil War, saw the West as a canvas for greater issues within the American political system. Lines on a map over territory only inhabited by Indians would help resolve tensions between the North and South. The East, as also both North and South, saw the West as a safety valve with which to relieve the political pressures that threatened the Union.

Westerners did not see these debates through the same lens. When they asked for states' rights, they wanted the right to choose who settled and what institutions could be moved into their new states. They worried more about security and safety on the frontier than the political issues of how many states came in as free or slave. Westerners wanted federal intervention and support, wanted to limit black and other non-white immigration and secure the new territories for a white Manifest Destiny. To much of the white western population, slavery existed only as an economic threat to Jefferson's yeoman farmer. Thus, slavery motivated Westerners to act, but not for the same reason or in the same way that Easterners did.

This conflict between Eastern desires and Western interests appears in the push to create a continental railroad. Not that Westerners would not eventually welcome and need the continental railroad, but the debates of the pre-war period circled around routes and connections with very little input from Westerners, since most did not have representation in Congress as they were just territories and not states. Eventually, the biggest Western interest to express an opinion about and desire for a connection to the East by rail would be Californians, though they argued about whether a northern or a southern route would best serve their interests. So, though most textbooks carry "the war no farther west than Arkansas and Missouri," as Robert Athearn points out, "The very existence of the West becomes important when causes of the war are considered."[2]

This book argues that the Civil War transformed the West from a region of international conflict into an American region ruled by the federal government. It explores how these international and internal conflicts, combined with the diverse population of the West, opened the West for the dominance of the federal government, eventually leading to the closing of the frontier. The book argues that the Civil War affected populations in the West not through warfare but through dilemmas and choices. Some groups, like the Sioux, tried to use the Civil War to try to sever their relationship with the U.S. government, while others, such as Germans in Minnesota, used it as a chance to chart their own path and develop their own societies. Others, like the settlers in Kansas and the Five Civilized Tribes in Indian Territory, got caught up in the politics of the Civil War. The Civil War dramatically altered the U.S. government's presence in the West, including the military and Indian agents, destabilizing the government's relationships with Indians and the relationships between Indians, emigrants, and other groups. By the end of the Civil War, the stage had been set for the creation of the Plains states and the opening of Indian territories from the Mississippi River westward for white settlement. In many ways, the Civil War predicted Turner's thesis and the closing of the frontier in 1890, a mere generation after the end of the Civil War.

Chapter One examines these diverse populations in the West and the settlement traditions they brought with them when the United States forcibly incorporated them. It uses 1848 as a turning point, the point when the West became solidified as U.S. territory. Chapter Two explores the establishment and structure of the military in the West, how that changed with the beginning of the Civil War, and how that change affected relations in the West. The federal government stationed the U.S. Army in the West to protect gold fields, emigrants, and to reign in or control the Indian population. When the regular army withdrew to the East and volunteers replaced them, dramatic changes occurred.

Chapter Three looks at how the Civil War affected the choices of the Five Civilized Tribes in Indian Territory and the choices of the Sioux. All these Indian nations faced ultimatums during the Civil War. Their choices highlight the stakes at risk during this period. The outcomes of these choices affected the West in the post–Civil War period, in more dramatic ways than Reconstruction in the South. Chapter Four examines westward migration during the Civil War. The pace of emigration did not slow during the four years of the Civil War, as people continued to flow west in search of opportunity. It also looks at the conflict within Bleeding Kansas, one of several states that entered the Union during the Civil War.

The final chapter looks at the introduction of the federal government in the West and how it affected the diverse populations of the West. It traces the changes occurring in the most populated Western territories and states: California, Texas, Oregon, Utah, Minnesota, and the Indian Territory. Their responses to the outbreak of the Civil War tell us much about how the West was beginning to coalesce as a region and how people outside the conflict viewed the causes and effects. It provides a window into more diverse understanding of the issues around which the Civil War erupted.

ONE

THE INTERNATIONAL
FRONTIER

When the founding fathers inked their signatures onto the U.S. Constitution, the trans-Mississippi West, the land west of the Mississippi River, remained under the control of three empires: the Spanish, the English, and the French. These three countries claimed control and rights over large territories in the West, as well as economic rights, with the hundreds of Indian nations who lived there. Yet, none of these European empires dominated the West with settlements, a fact that would make the arrival of the Americans after 1848 all that more shocking to the Western Indian and *mestizos*, people of mixed Indian and European descent, populations. They used alliances and intermarriages with the Indian nations that resided in the West, many of whom did not view themselves as conquered or as part of these European empires. Between the 1770s and the end of the Mexican-American War, these empires would be forced out of the West through internal and external conflicts. But their presence and the populations they left behind created a West with different interests, beliefs, and a different racial mix than the East.

NORTHWEST COAST

In the late 1700s, the Spanish controlled the most territory, stretching up the Northwest Pacific Coast and across the Southwest.[1] "Controlled," though, may be an overstatement. The Southwest Indians had dealt with the Spanish since the 1500s, driven some of them out at the end of the 17th century, with the Pueblo Revolt of 1680, and then been reinvaded at the beginning of the 18th century.[2] But when the Spanish returned, they came seeking accommodation to better secure what they termed their "Far Northern Frontier." In the Southwest, after the Pueblo Revolt, the Spanish rebuilt their bureaucracy by incorporating local strong Indian nations into it. They used Southwestern tribes' political structures in the Spanish system, making Pueblo chiefs tax collectors and local petit bureaucrats to expand the empire, since Spanish settlers considered the Far Northern Frontier a place of exile and a punishment.[3] Additionally, the Spanish government gave the Hopi, Navajo, and Pueblo nations official land grants, simply giving the tribes formal Spanish rights to their own land. The Spanish held onto their territory in California, not through the massive immigration of the Spanish settlers, but through the mission system and trade with the Indians. Spanish missions in California and the Far Northern Frontier not only spread Christianity, to varying degrees, but also language and political structures in these same territories.[4] In much of the Spanish territory, their cultural and political influence reigned, but the Spanish had co-opted or melded with the local populations. In what became California, New Mexico, and Arizona, a growing *mestizo* population of both Spanish and Indian descent inhabited the region. On paper, the Spanish believed they controlled a third of what would become American territory. In reality, Indian and other European nations disputed that claim.

The Northwest Coast demonstrates the international tensions that gripped the trans-Mississippi West before the Mexican-American War. By the 1790s, the English and the Russians began to make inroads into Spanish territory on the Northwest Coast, leading to a conflict between the Spanish and these interlopers for control of the region's otter pelt trade and its links to inland trading routes and Columbia Plateau Indians.[5] Though the Spanish had considered the Northwest Coast theirs since 1528, in the eyes of the Russians or English, they had not laid any claim to it. The Spanish had neither planted settlements there nor had they extended their bureaucratic control over the region, unlike California and New Mexico. Aware of their lack of presence, the Spanish began sending scientific expeditions up the coast from Mexico and Southern California to map the coastline, peruse the resources available, and demonstrate their control.[6] At the same time, the Russians began trading with Indians as far south as Northern California. The British, who saw the region and its trade as an unclaimed resource, began to establish trading posts along the coastline, shipping otter pelts to their ports in China and India.[7] In 1792, the Spanish arrested several British commanders for trespassing in Nootka Sound, one of the largest trading ports in present-day British Columbia. Negotiations between the British and the Spanish led to the Spanish ceding the territory to Britain in 1794.[8] Even as the British took control of the region on paper, new challenges presented themselves. The Russians continued to trade with the Indians along the Pacific Coast. And, soon,

American whaling ships and explorers made forays into the region, drawn by the otter pelt trade and access to Asian markets. As late as the 1830s, the British still considered the Northwest Coast theirs.[9] French and Russian traders, continued to make their presence known, either working for the British or the Americans, or working independently, still inhabited the area, intermarrying with local Indians.

The tensions over the Pacific Coast between England, Spain, and Russia illustrate important differences between the Pacific West and the United States at the turn of the 19th century. England, Spain, and Russia sought trade and connections on the Pacific Coast to help increase their trade into Asia, not to Europe or the United States. They and the Indians, with whom they traded, looked west, not east. Trade goods, like ceramic and textiles, came from China and India into the Pacific Coast, not from Europe or the United States.[10] Additionally, the European groups sought trade, not settlement. They hoped to lure Indian groups into agreements without expending the expense of troops or settlers. European and some American traders wanted to link into established trading systems, not create a new society. The Indian populations came to expect goods and autonomy, not settlers and cultural assimilation.

While the British tussled with the Spanish for control of the Northwest Coast, the French also saw their empire waning in the trans-Mississippi West. Pushed west by the French and Indian War, ending in 1763, French traders and trappers, including the soon-to-be-famous Toussaint Charbonneau, who led Meriwether Lewis and William Clark on their voyage, still plied their trades in the West. But the loss of Louisiana to the Spanish after the war made the vast French territory in the West less alluring and profitable for France. Without control of the mouth of the Mississippi River, the French lacked an easy outlet for their trade. They had to transport furs overland to Quebec or link into American and British trading systems, which some did. Despite these setbacks, the French maintained some influence through their few remaining missions along the Mississippi River. The French territory remained a paper empire, with few settlers or proof of control on the ground in the West.

France sought to remedy the situation in 1800 with the Treaty of San Ildefonso, which transferred Louisiana back to France from Spain. This treaty reopened New Orleans for French trade and effectively blocked the American westward expansion, or so the French hoped. France quickly closed the port of New Orleans to American citizens. As Talleyrand, Grand Chamberlain to Napoleon, wrote, "The power of America is bounded by the limit which it may suit the interests and the tranquility of France and Spain to assign here. The French Republic . . . will be the wall of brass forever impenetrable to the combined efforts of England and America."[11] France hoped this wall of brass would protect their empire and stymie the British and American desires for it. Such moves did not make the nascent United States happy. President Jefferson, seeing his moment, sent Robert Livingston to pressure Napoleon to sell the land to the United States. Jefferson threatened to side with the

British in any conflict with France, something France could not afford. In 1803, with the swipe of a pen, the United States doubled as it added the Louisiana Territory, shattering the French wall of brass.

As Spain and France had learned previously, adding a territory on paper and controlling that territory are two different things. In 1804, Jefferson dispatched Lewis and Clark to explore the resources available in this new territory. After wintering on the Missouri, where they met up with Toussaint Charbonneau and his wife, Sacajawea, a Shoshone who had been taken by the Hidatsa, Lewis and Clark traveled to the West Coast and back. The fact that they needed Charbonneau and Sacajawea as guides demonstrates the difference between having a territory and controlling it. Charbonneau and Sacajawea knew the territory and spoke the languages of the Indian groups that controlled it and its trading networks. Until the 1830s, the Louisiana Purchase territory remained in the hands of the Plains, Columbia Plateau and Northwest Coast Indians who traded with whoever appeared, be they French, British, or American. The United States did not succeed in settling the edges of the territory itself until the 1830s, when they clashed with the British over control of parts of it and sent settlers there. So, by 1805, the Spanish had seen their territory reduced, leaving them California, New Mexico, and Texas, the British had expanded their western empire on the Pacific Coast, the French had lost theirs, and the United States had expanded on paper.

THE DECADE BEFORE
THE MEXICAN-AMERICAN WAR

Between 1792 and the late 1830s, the Indian populations in the West continued to fight over territorial control with each other. For the Northwest Coast and Columbia Plateau peoples, the arrival of Lewis and Clark in 1803 represented just another group who wanted resources, and even after Lewis and Clark paddled down the Columbia the area remained, at least on paper, in British hands.[12] Though the otter pelt trade collapsed by 1810 due to overhunting, American whaling ships had joined the trade, prompting some historians to argue the inevitability of an American takeover.[13] The 1830s, though, brought change, unlike what they had experienced before in the form of American settlers. The Columbia Plateau peoples, in the interior of Washington and Oregon, had dealt with the French and the English for nearly 100 years by the time the Americans moved in during the 1830s. They had survived several bouts of diseases, adopted certain European goods, and been exposed to Christianity.[14] Neither Lewis and Clark nor the presence of American whaling ships made the territory American nor is it proof of their inevitable takeover. The French, not Americans, began to settle the area as a French Indian population arrived, drawn by trade. They even tried to establish a Catholic church, writing to Joseph Provencher, Bishop of

Juliopolis in Manitoba, requesting a Catholic priest in 1835. He could not supply one until 1839, by which point the Americans had already arrived.

In 1834, Jason and Daniel Lee arrived in the Oregon Territory to establish a Methodist mission. Two years later, the Whitmans and the Spaldings, sponsored by the Congregationalists, strode over the mountains into the Willamette Valley. Though they came to convert the Cayuse and Umatilla to Christianity, they soon brought with them settlers from the East Coast in an effort to secure the land from British occupation.[15] These settlers came to create farms out of the land and expose the Indians to farming techniques and civilization. Marcus Whitman, the leader of the group, made several trips back to the East Coast over the course of 10 years, bringing more and more settlers.[16] As they disrupted the lives of the Cayuse, Umatilla, and Nez Perce, they also disrupted the local and international economies. The Indians in the Columbia Plateau found themselves under assault from within, as their land became fenced off, livestock ate their crops, the presence of white farmers scared away game or they hunted it, and disease spread through the valley.[17] The arrival of Americans was not new; the new settlers' inability to incorporate or be incorporated into local economies and society was.

The settlers posed an international problem, as well. The United States and Britain had yet to settle where the boundary between their two territories ran. The Hudson's Bay Company manned posts in the region and traded with the Indians, helping the British maintain a presence. These traders provided a counterpoint to the American settlers who came in and appeared to take over. In 1846, the United States and Britain entered into negotiations to try and set a boundary between British territory and U.S territory. Known as the Oregon Controversy, President James Polk pushed the resolution of using the 49th parallel, because he sought to secure the northern border before working on securing the southern one in Texas. Though Washington and London resolved the issue, the Indians in the region still felt squeezed by the immigrants and continued to trade with the British.

The Cayuse, Nez Perce, and others became frustrated. Although they had received goods and other useful items from the French and from the previous English and American invaders, in addition to the disease and disruption, now they seemingly received nothing of use.[18] In 1847, they revolted, killing the Whitmans and most of the settlers.[19] The one survivor, Henry Harmon Spalding, accused the French and then the British of orchestrating the massacre to clear the valley of the illegal American population.[20] The U.S. Congress immediately sent troops to establish a garrison in the Oregon Territory, half a nation away from the rest of the country.[21] Negotiations frothed between the British, who still claimed it as their territory, and the Americans, who now claimed it as theirs with a force of men.[22] Journalists and politicians saw it as an international incident, because it illustrated tensions between the United States and Britain.[23] Nobody seemed to see it as belonging to any of the various Indian groups, except for them. The Whitman Massacre, though, did lead to an Indian war that prevented the interior of Oregon from being settled until 1859.[24]

The American foray into Oregon and Washington illustrates several western tensions in this period. Just because Americans came to a territory did not mean they controlled it. Settlement or squatting did not equal ownership in the eyes of the European or Indian groups, who already resided there or considered it their territory. And, American immigrants imposed their rules and assumptions on a new territory, with little exchange or interaction with the previous group. Finally, Americans came to settle and transform the territory into the United States, both culturally and on paper.

TEXAS

After 1805 and the loss of New Orleans, the Spanish empire began to struggle to maintain its control of Texas. "The region had existed as a classic borderland long before Mexican statehood."[25] The arid climate and hostile Indian nations hampered Spanish settlement from 1600s onward.[26] The Spanish succeeded in briefly establishing missions and settlements along the eastern edge of the territory, near Louisiana, to prevent the French from gaining the territory and access to mines further west.[27] Even these missions did not last long in Texas, as Indians drove them out and the Spanish populations fled. West Texas remained outside Spanish control.

The 1820s represented a time of change and turmoil for Texas and Mexico. Mexico revolted against the Spanish in 1821. By the 1830s, the Mexican government became concerned enough about American squatters and Eastern Indians moving into *Tejas* that they contracted with Americans to act as *empresarios*, or agents, for the *colonias*. Stephen Austin became one of the most influential, quickly attracting settlers to the area. He also became one of the biggest critics of how Mexico ruled the far-flung province. Some of the Southern immigrants brought slaves, though Mexico had abolished slavery in 1820 and freed the slaves in 1824. Like the Spanish before them, the new settlers sought to transport their own culture and ideas into the province, including slavery and ignoring the requirement for raising their children as Catholics. Americans in Texas flaunted both these rules, setting up the conflict that would arise a decade later. In frustration, the Mexican government banned further American immigration in 1830, galvanizing the American desire to separate.[28] Until 1846, when the United States annexed Texas, "emigrants from the southern US especially, but also from eastern US cities, Ireland, Germany, and other parts of Europe flocked to the area," drawn by land agents called *empresarios* to the *colonias*.[29] By luring in settlers from the United States and Europe, offering hundreds of thousands of acres to sets of families in exchange for following Mexican law (and raising their children as Catholic), the Spanish, and then the Mexican government, hoped to secure the territory from takeover by the United States.

As the population diversified, including Mexicans, Anglos, Indians, both from within Texas and immigrant Indians from the Southeast, and blacks, both free and enslaved, a movement grew to separate into their own nation. The Anglo-American settlers who came in soon dreamed of grandeur and sloughing off Mexican rule as did *Tejanos*, descendants of early Spanish residents of the province, who wanted to be free of Mexican rule.[30] The ability to import and use slaves became one of the key issues for the split from Mexico. "By 1836 North Americans outnumbered Mexicans by perhaps seven to one in Texas, and they and their Mexican allies were successful in their revolt for independence."[31] In 1836, Texas declared its independence from Mexico and President Antonio López de Santa Anna. The United States recognized the new nation of Texas in 1837; but Mexico did not recognize the new nation and sent troops in to quell the rebellion. At first, Mexican forces drove the rebels east toward U.S. territory in Louisiana, captured the Alamo (where they executed 300), and seemed to be winning. As the Americans ran east, many of their slaves ran west and south to freedom in Mexican territory. But at San Jacinto, the tide turned, and the Texans pushed the Mexicans out and succeeded in establishing a slave-owning republic.[32] Now Texans, including Anglo-Americans and Tejanos, controlled not only the territory, but also their own country. For eight years, Texas existed as an independent nation, much to Mexico's irritation. Independence, though, had its problems. Financially shaky and under constant attack from the Mexicans, who raided the border, and Comanches and other Indian groups, who raided from the North and the West, the Texas Republic struggled. They requested annexation from the United States, but it wasn't until 1846 that the United States agreed. When Mexico cut off the Republic of Texas from trade, the United States declared war and the Mexican-American War began.

CHEROKEE

At the same time that Whitman brought settlers to Oregon Territory and Austin brought them to Texas, new groups of settlers began invading the Great Plains. Instead of Euro-Americans, they consisted of Eastern Indians, like the Cherokee and Sac and Fox, forced west by the growing United States to the East and its influence on their nations, both politically and culturally. Though some of these Indians, small groups of Cherokee for instance, moved by choice, most moved as the result of a new U.S. Indian policy: removal. The period from 1830 to 1848 saw an influx of non-Western Indians into the western territories, causing conflict, reshaping relationships and power, and setting the stage for revolt during the Civil War.[33]

Removal policy was born out of several desires and beliefs of the U.S. government. In 1806, Zebulon Pike declared present-day Kansas, Oklahoma, and Nebraska, the Great American Desert because of its lack of rainfall. He deemed this part of the Louisiana Purchase too arid for farming and white settlement, but fine for the Indians and bison he saw there. His misinterpretation of the land stemmed from standard ideas about farming at the time, which would influence land policy and the debate about slavery. He believed that a certain amount of rainfall was necessary to grow crops on a standard farm of 160 acres. He ignored or did not see the small plots of farming that some of the Plains Indians did in this very area. His definition of the area as a desert led policymakers to decide it would not suit white settlers, but would suit Indians removed from the East. This solution to the Indian Problem in the Northeast and Southeast ignored the Indian populations already living in the Great Plains.

Unlike the Northwest Coast and the Columbia Plateau, the Great Plains Indians had little contact with European empires at this point. Those on the western edge of the Great Plains avoided contact with Europeans until almost the 1830s. In the 18th century, the Eastern Great Plains Indians had contact with French traders, trappers, and missionaries, who fanned out from missions and trading posts along the Mississippi River. The traders and trappers, like the Chouteau family of St. Louis, built on traditional Great Plains trading patterns and established themselves through intermarriage and trade. They also created a growing *métis* population of the children of French men and Indian women. The French Catholic missionaries introduced Christianity and lived with many of the groups. The Eastern Great Plains Indians pursued their own empires and agendas until the late 18th century and early 19th century, when the British and then the Americans forced more Northeastern groups, like the Ojibway (Anishinabe), west into their territory.[34] Other Northeastern groups, like the Sac and Fox, had fought their way west and continued to do so to gain territory and shore up alliances to better stand against the U.S. government. Conflict came to the Great Plains from the East, before it became official U.S. policy.

In the 1820s and 1830s, the U.S. government moved from negotiating with the Indians and treating them as nations within a nation, to removing them ahead of the white population. The Indian Removal Act, passed under President Andrew Jackson, sought to remove most of the Eastern Indians, like the Cherokee, into Indian Territory, consisting of present-day Oklahoma, Kansas, and Nebraska. For policymakers, removal solved several problems. It opened land for settlement in the Northern and Southern states. It would limit Indian and white contact and conflict. And it would use the land deemed the Great American Desert, while settlers passed through it to the better areas of Oregon, Washington, and California. Moving the Indians into the territory secured it for the United States. But the Great Plains Indians did not see these advantages.

Beginning in the 1830s, the U.S. government forcibly removed Eastern Indian nations to Indian Territory. As groups like the Five Civilized Tribes crowded into the new federally designated Indian Territory, they settled on land that the Comanche, the Osage, and other Great Plains groups considered theirs. The Five Civilized Tribes (Cherokee, Choctaw, Chickasaw, Creek, and Seminole) viewed the Plains Indians as barbaric and savage, an opinion they shared with white Americans working their way into the territory. Many of the Southern Plains groups relied on raiding and hunting for their survival, and they saw the Cherokee, Choctaw, and others as interlopers and squatters the same as they saw nascent American settlers. Army Lieutenant R. C. Carter observed, "Noticing that 'our two savage chiefs from the Texas Plains gazed with equal curiosity' at the Cherokee with their plentiful demonstrations of 'independence and good thrift,' that, 'the two types seemed as wide apart as the two poles of the world.'"[35] During the 1830s, thousands of Eastern Indians flooded into the Great Plains, often bringing their own political and economic struggles. By 1848, Great Plains Indians also began to experience an American invasion of their land as American settlers moved into Minnesota and Iowa, following the riverboats up the Mississippi, the gold rush in Iowa, and the farming frontier that expanded out of the Northwest.[36] For the Great Plains Indians, this expansion represented an international conflict, as Americans invaded their sovereign territory. As Cherokee and the other Five Civilized Tribes plowed fields and built schools, the Great Plains attracted other settlers from Texas and Arkansas.

MORMONS

As the Whitman Massacre exploded and increased fears about the stability of the West, another group of immigrants traveled through the Great Plains into the Great Basin region: the Latter-day Saints, known more colloquially as the Mormons. The Great Basin Indians who occupied Nevada and Utah remained isolated from European incursions, barring the occasional Spaniard who wandered into their territory. Beginning just before the end of the Mexican-American War, though, the Paiute, Ute, and Bannocks encountered their first group of Anglo-European settlers, who came over the Wasatch to create a new Zion and to escape the American government, all at the expense of the Great Basin Indians.[37]

Founded in the 1820s in upstate New York by Joseph Smith, the Latter-day Saints had continually migrated west in search of a place where they could establish communities and practice their religion. Based on Christianity, the *Book of Mormon*, which Mormons use in conjunction with the Bible, focused on how God dealt with the early inhabitants of the Americas, meaning the Indians, "plural marriage," known to critics as polygamy, and "condemned all forms of human bondage."[38] The *Book of*

Mormon declared that the Lord "denieth none that come unto him, black and white, bond and free, male and female."[39] All these views shaped the Mormon response to their trek to Utah.

Mormons opposed slavery throughout the 1830s, but avoided being labeled as abolitionists.[40] Even as early as the 1830s, people in the United States reviled abolitionists as radicals and the Mormons sought to avoid any hint of association. In a resolution written in 1835, the Mormon Church made its position clear: "We do not believe it is right to interfere with bondservants, neither preach the gospel to, nor baptize them, contrary to the will and wish of their masters." Additionally, the resolution laid out support for the government, stating that "Such interference we believe to be unlawful and dangerous to the peace of every government allowing human beings to be held in servitude."[41] These two statements absolved the Church from converting African Americans held in bondage and supported the government without judging the morality of slavery. The Church would continue to parse similar positions throughout the Civil War, in an attempt to avoid conflict with neighbors and governments.

Soon after the founding of the Church, the Saints first settled in Ohio, but the locals drove them out violently. Local Gentiles, as the Saints call non-Mormons, blamed the Saints for the bank's failure and drove them out to Missouri, where they ran into a different conflict which led to a violent response by local authorities. Missouri allowed slavery, something many Saints felt uncomfortable with, though they did not welcome African Americans into their church.[42] Their leader, Joseph Smith, tried to soften tensions between the Saints and the Missourians by issuing some proslavery statements.[43] But Missourians still saw the Saints as different, not only because of their religious practices, but also for their perceived antislavery beliefs and potential as abolitionists. Eventually, in 1838, Missouri drove them out. The Missouri governor "sent militiamen against Mormon settlements, killing 18 Latter-day Saints, and driving more than 15,000 members of the Church out of state."[44] Soon, the issue of slavery and questions of loyalty would follow them to Utah.

From Missouri, the Latter-day Saints fled to Nauvoo, Illinois, where the situation seemed promising. There, they quickly drained the swampy land and built a temple, homes, and businesses. And they limited the political and civil rights of the blacks within their community. In addition to banning interracial marriages, the Nauvoo city charter "permitted only 'free white males' to vote, hold municipal office, or belong to the militia."[45] At this point, the Mormon Church also banned blacks from entering the priesthood. These rules may have been an attempt to curry favor with the local population. But conflict dogged them, and in 1844, a mob killed Joseph Smith and his brother Hyrum while the state held them in protective custody. After the state of Illinois revoked the Mormon community's Nauvoo charter in 1845, mobs torched and fired cannon at the temple. By 1846, the Saints had left Illinois and settled, at least temporarily, in Winter Quarters, Nebraska.

At this point, their new leader, Brigham Young, decided that the Saints needed to move somewhere without a Gentile population to harass them. They decided to leave the United States for Mexican Territory, specifically Utah. They hoped by being beyond U.S. law they could practice their religion in peace, and saw Utah, Deseret to the Saints, as an isolated promised land. They, then, organized a rather spectacular migration as most of the immigrants pushed handcarts from Winter Quarters, Nebraska, to Deseret. They went in waves, as groups leapfrogged along the trail, providing supplies to those that followed. The wave of first migrants established businesses and irrigation systems to help the next wave settle. Just as they began their trek, the Mexican-American War exploded and Mexico turned a blind eye to their settlement. Utah remained in Mexican hands only on paper.

Mormon missionaries had success recruiting converts in the British Isles, and these Saints joined their brethren for the 1,000-mile trek from Winter Quarters to the Wasatch Mountains. There, as the new settlers passed through the Wasatch Mountains into the Salt Lake Valley, they must have felt they had reached the "promised land," or Zion, with a shimmering lake, a biblical desert landscape, and mountains shielding them from an intolerant American population. They quickly built canals, farms, and towns, and became an important stopping point for immigrants to the West Coast territories for supplies. The Mormons chose Utah for a variety of reasons. Having settled in Illinois and Missouri, only to be driven out, the Mormons chose Utah Territory because it lacked another white population which could cause them problems. They moved into Mexico, which was where Utah Territory resided. Young, their leader at this point, also felt the Wasatch Mountain range would shield them from the United States and its rules. But while eschewing the United States, the Mormons still remained involved with it. Despite the *Book of Mormon*'s seeming clarity on bondage and black rights, slavery and attitudes toward African Africans shifted with the national political winds over the next 30 years.

The Saints had learned some valuable lessons as they moved west. The Saints figured out that establishing their own economic power helped them build businesses quickly. This pattern helped them build their community in Utah, as their leaders planned a settlement that relied little on outside trade and supplies, perfect for the harsh conditions Utah offered. Besides realizing that they need to be isolated from the Gentile population, they also better understood how to play politics to protect their right to practice their religion.

Young, the new leader of the Latter-day Saints after Nauvoo, made such a political move during the Mexican-American War. He volunteered a Mormon battalion to help fight the war for the United States. It served two purposes. One, it made the Latter-day Saints seem loyal and patriotic.[46] Two, from the perspective of the federal government, the Saints provided men to fight the Mexican-American War and helped secure future U.S. territory. Additionally, "Rather than giving outright aid to the Mormons for their trek, government authorities allowed Colonel Kearney [of the U.S. Army] to recruit five hundred to one thousand Mormons to his army."[47] For the U.S. government, this arrangement made sense. They gained men to fight the war and secured contested Mexican territory for the United States, should they win the war, without officially sanctioning the Mormon settlement. And the U.S. government offered aid to the Mormons.

While the U.S. government seemed tickled by the arrangement, Mormon men had some concerns. Though they would earn wages and use army transportation to move west, they feared working for a federal force which had failed to protect them in Missouri or Illinois. Army officers recruited Mormon men by arguing that "California as yet only sparsely settled and therefore not hostile to their unconventional beliefs offered them a rich new land."[48] The Mormon Battalion, as it became known, straggled into San Diego in 1847 "shoeless, hungry and nearly naked."[49] Utah became part of the United States in 1848 and the federal government created the territory of Utah in 1849.[50] But relations with the federal government did not remain cordial. Like other Americans in the West before the Mexican-American War, Mormons acted as settlers. The decade before the Mexican-American War represented one of rapid change, with Americans moving into Oregon, Washington, Texas, and Utah territories, all areas that did not actually belong to the United States at the beginning of the American settlement. These American squatters and their development of the land led to conflict with the British, the Spanish, the Mexicans, and various Indian nations, and brought with them cultural norms, like slavery and farming, which dismayed and disrupted the local populations.

MEXICAN-AMERICAN WAR

After the War of 1812, foreign invasions of the United States ceased in the Northeast and Southeast. On the other side of the continent, the trans-Mississippi West, remained at the center of several international conflicts. The Mexican-American War ended 70 years of contestation for control of the western two-thirds of central North America. The international conflicts before the Mexican-American War demonstrated economic and political patterns, unlike those in the United States at that time, including an economy focused toward Asia. The international conflicts left behind foreign populations, who did not always or rarely welcomed annexation by the nascent United States. If the Europeans and the Indians in the trans-Mississippi West shared one desire it was to keep the Americans out of their respective territories. More so than the Louisiana Purchase, the Mexican-American War opened Indian and non-U.S. territories to an immediate expansion by the United States.

Even as legislators and writers portrayed the tensions between the United States and Mexico as the freeing of a downtrodden people from the Mexican empire, Western populations saw it as an old-fashioned war of empire. The conflicts between 1835 and 1845 "revolved around American desires to expand trade, agriculture, and political sovereignty."[51] Additionally, Americans in Texas pushed back against Mexico outlawing slavery and freeing the slaves.[52] Setting the stage for war and annexation, in 1845, James K. Polk ran on a platform of Manifest Destiny or the belief in a "preordained mission of the American republic to expand over the whole continent."[53] Polk wanted California, New Mexico, and Texas, thus opening a route to the riches of the Asia trade. Mexico felt differently about these territories, which they considered Mexican.[54]

The United States provoked Mexico in 1846, starting the Mexican-American War, or the Mexican War. Tensions between Mexico, Texas, and the United States had never settled down after the Texas Rebellion. While Texas struggled to stay afloat, Mexico continued to cross into the territory and harass the population. Polk and others saw expansion as the United States' God-given right and set their sights on Mexican territory. The United States tried to buy California and New Mexico in 1845. Mexico refused. In 1846, his predecessor, John Tyler, annexed Texas, adding the vast territory to the United States, and Polk saw his chance for expansion. He used the pretext of a Mexican invasion to justify sending U.S. troops into Texas. The Mexicans responded by sending troops into the territory they still considered Mexican. The resulting conflict became the Mexican-American War.

Just as the Mexican-American War began, the Bear Flag Revolt erupted just north of San Francisco in California. The men leading the revolt hoped to recreate what Texas had, a separate nation, free from Mexican rule. John C. Frémont, there on an exploratory expedition, led the Bear Flag Revolt, and helped captured Sonoma and its commander, Mariano Vallejo. Though the revolt only lasted a month until the U.S. Navy appeared and raised the U.S. flag, it set the stage for further threats of separation by western territories during the antebellum period and the Civil War. These rebellion leaders viewed the Bear Flag rebellion as an American tradition of resistance against outside domination. As Jose Marie Amador, a large Mexican landowner in California, stated, "Independence would likely translate into Yankee domination in one form or another."[55] Manifest Destiny had come to California.

U.S. troops invaded Mexican territory from Texas, California, and the Mexican coast. California fell early, with the *Californios*, Mexicans, and *mestizos* who lived in California signing the "Treaty of Cahuenga on January 13, 1847, in which they pledged to put down their arms and were, in turn, promised the full exercise of their civil liberties and property rights" while the United States occupied the territory.[56] In 1848, the Treaty of Guadalupe-Hidalgo effectively ended the war. The United States agreed to pay Mexico $15 million in return for California and the new territories of

New Mexico, Arizona, Utah, and Nevada, taking the Rio Grande River as the border between the two nations. It stripped any Indians, including those in California, of their rights, identifying them as savage tribes.[57] Additionally, it failed to protect *Californios'* land titles.[58] By the end of the Mexican-American War, U.S. troops and the federal government viewed and treated the *Californios* and the Indians as losers and a "mongrel Indian race."[59] It appeared that rights and responsibilities would certainly change under the American government, and not for the better for native and resident populations.[60] The U.S. military governed California until it became a state in 1850. The United States effectively stripped the rights and responsibilities from the *Californios* and the Indians even as they expanded American territory and rights westward.

The Mexican-American War lasted two years and resulted in the United States gaining the territories that would become California, New Mexico, Utah, and Colorado. Including the annexation of Texas, this war added 900,000 square miles to the United States for settlement and resources extraction. It became the first war fought by the United States in foreign territory. It trained many of the generals, including Ulysses Grant, who would fight in the Civil War. Yet, it did not come without costs. The war split parts of the United States. Some Northerners thought Polk started the war simply to be able to extend slavery, already a contested issue with the rise of abolitionists. Others felt the move to be morally wrong, using war to gain territory from a sovereign nation. James Kent in New York condemned it as "causeless & wicked & unjust."[61] The South and the frontier states expressed support for the war as they saw new lands opening up for development.[62] Thus, the Mexican-American War exposed differing views of expansion between the North and the South and within those regions.

Unlike the War of 1812, the Mexican-American War involved an alien population of Spanish and Indian descent, who were Catholic and non-English speaking. Kent bemoaned that "the acquisition of large Mexican Territory would ruin us & destroy our institutions. I view the project with horror."[63] While wanting to spread American institutions and democracy into the new territories, critics like Kent feared the expansion would weaken the United States. The war fed into the more racist and exclusionary aspects of the burgeoning American society and the concept of Manifest Destiny.

Part of Manifest Destiny rested on the idea that the Americans represented an ideal society that illustrated the pinnacle of mankind. Just before the Civil War, European and American anthropologists and scientists began to toy with ideas of monogenism—the belief that all humankind descended from Adam and Eve—and polygenism—the belief that humankind had multiple beginnings and species.[64] While supporters argued violently over whether humankind descended from one set of ancestors or several, both sides agreed that the Europeans and Americans represented the zenith of what humankind could achieve. For Americans, though, they believed they held an edge over Europeans, as they had entered the wilderness of the Indians in North America and had bested it. Manifest Destiny often revolved around the idea of the fading European empires and the rising American one, as argued by historians about the Spanish empire.[65] The West seemed to present the evidence of this trend, as the British, French, and Spanish empires appeared to fade before the American invaders.

Not only did the Mexican-American War feed this ideal, but the Gadsden Purchase, which brought 32,000 square miles of former Mexican territory under U.S. control, did as well, representing "the culmination of the widespread and swelling popular conviction that it was the unmistakable, pre-ordained mission of the American republic to expand over the whole continent."[66] Americans believed they embodied exceptionalism, a uniqueness that let Americans succeed where others failed, something that the world had not seen before and that exceptionalism came with the great responsibility of taking care of and directing those populations that could not genetically rise to the occasion. In other words, westward expansion allowed the Americans to succeed where the Indians had failed, and slavery became a responsibility.

Mexico and her population fit this description of a fading group. Oft portrayed as a hybrid nation by the English and the Americans, made up of the bastard children of the Spanish and the Indians, the United States viewed the Mexican population as worthy of conquest and sought to keep them disenfranchised. "American supporters of the Mexican War wished to see Mexico as inherently flawed, their society sliding toward dissolution, this created an opening for Americans to take control."[67] Texas provides an example of the shift. The American story of the Texas Revolution featured a small band of Americans wresting territory from Mexico, formerly part of the Spanish empire. But in many Americans' minds, the hybrid Mexicans could not compete with the transformed and exceptional Texans. Yet, many of those exceptional Texans had intermarried with Mexican families, absorbed some of their culture, and built alliances with Mexican/Spanish families who sought independence from Mexico. The story of Manifest Destiny, though, did not recognize this process. Its American supporters built on the ideal that white Americans conquered and transformed *Tejas* into Texas alone.

The Mexican-American War never existed as just a defense of the Texans. Congress sought to extend U.S. territory all the way to the Pacific Ocean along the southern half of the United States to access the riches of Asia. As early as 1828, the director of the Baltimore and Ohio Railroad Company declared that, "We are about opening a channel through which the commerce of the mighty country beyond the Allegheny must seek the ocean. . . ."[68] This drive to build a transcontinental railroad, which started in earnest in the 1830s, informed this decision. Like other Congressional decisions in this period, it relied heavily on the interests of those in the East and required little to no understanding of the actual contours of the West. Though the Southern route for a railroad posed fewer physical problems, the planners appeared unaware of the large Mexican and Indian populations in those regions. While Anglos outnumbered *Tejanos*, as the Mexican residents called themselves, in Texas, Mexicans remained a significant population, especially in the New Mexico Territory and California, at least until the gold rush of 1848. Additionally, they possessed land grants from Spain as did many of the Indian nations, which would complicate American expansion. Americans built their expansion on the idea that without title the land was available for the taking and for development. During and after the Mexican-American War, Americans encountered non-white peoples who did have legal title to their land. The Americans then needed to separate Mexicans and Indians from those titles. Arguing that they did not possess the means to exploit it, as God and destiny intended, helped justify the displacement of the populations in the Southwest.

The Mexican culture and race concerned Congress and policymakers more than their land ownership. Policymakers and newspapers portrayed the Mexican population as backward and barbaric. According to their American detractors, their practice of Catholicism made them superstitious.[69] Writers invoked all the racial epithets of the day, damning the Mexicans as half-breeds born of Catholic Spanish aristocrat fathers, who raped and pillaged the countryside, and Indian women who possessed loose morals. U.S. soldiers used the fact that Mexicans recruited runaway slaves and free blacks for their military as evidence of their social and racial inferiority. "Any progress that the latter country had made toward racial tolerance became an incitement to American soldiers to reinforce their native standards" of racial hierarchy toward blacks.[70] Powerbrokers wrung their hands in fear of what would happen to the United States once this population became part of the country. For Southerners, Mexicans represented "the dangers of unchecked miscegenation that [which] . . . would, result from the abolition of slavery and the open transgression of racial and class boundaries."[71] Americans not only feared the Mexican and Indian cultures but also transposed these cultures into their burgeoning ideas about race-mixing and its deleterious effects. The perceived moral laxity would require colonial structures to guarantee the safety of future settlers and make sure that the Mexicans did not revolt and return the land. And it was all about land, to Mexico.

The rise of nativism became an underlying theme of the Mexican-American War, as Americans claimed to see themselves as a unified nation and/or race. Even after the Mexican-American War, Senator John Sevier proposed that the Mexicans in the new territory be subject to naturalization laws and an oath of allegiance. In this way, only those willing to adopt American norms would gain American rights. But this logic only worked for those residents of the East Coast. Western residents, mainly

Indians, Mexicans, and others, found themselves being used as evidence of the right of Manifest Destiny. According to those in the East, they needed the Americans to rule them to guarantee their land for them, to protect them from themselves. Though some of these arguments had been made in the debate about slavery that blacks could not care for themselves but needed whites to do it for them, for the Western populations it took on a new form. Many of those who argued for expansion into the West did not support slavery but did see race as an indicator of success and power. The Mexican-American War shaped the Free Soil movement, which sought to prevent the expansion of slavery into western territories. This same political movement did not want blacks, Mexicans, or Indians there either.[72] Free Soilers and others voted for laws which would exclude black settlers in new western states. They sought to corral Indians in Indian Territory, thereby opening the land to the rightful and more productive American settlers, and they sought to restrict Mexican land use and power because of their hybridity.

The Mexican-American War left several legacies behind. It created tensions between Texas and New Mexico and between that state and territory and Mexico. It left Mexico angry and frustrated with its loss of land. The loyalty of the Mormons during the Mexican-American War granted them a temporary reprieve from violence and scrutiny. The Mexican-American War became a "pivotal event in westward expansion and, as such, was critical in shaping the new exploitive social relations that would characterize 'free labor' and American capitalism."[73] While adding land, it also extended U.S. racial attitudes west, which shaped how the West viewed labor, property, and individual rights. And the success of the land grab only fed the idea of Manifest Destiny. Consequently, the war left a lasting presence and legacy of military involvement in the West. Manifest Destiny might mean a transcontinental railroad and riches for those on the East Coast, but it meant colonial rule for the populations in the West.

GOLD RUSH

In an almost unbelievable coincidence, in January 1848, John Sutter found gold at his mill in California. As the Mexican-American War wound down, the gold discovery suggested huge riches awaiting the Americans. It took several months for the news to spread to the East. But once it did, the gates opened and a flood of miners and settlers flowed west from the United States, north from Latin America, and east from Asia. This influx of miners and the wealth that came with the gold rush shaped the debates in California over statehood and slavery. The gold rush sped up the adoption of ethnocentric or whites-only ideas within the state constitution, legally sanctioning discrimination.[74] Thanks to the gold rush, California became a state barely two years after the discovery.

With the sudden discovery of gold, the population of California exploded. Immigrants from within the United States and outside flooded into the territory, overwhelming the current Indian, Hispanic, *mestizo*, and white populations. Both Southerners, with experience in the gold fields in Georgia and North Carolina, and settlers from the Old Northwest entered the territory of California.[75] As in other places, their experiences elsewhere would shape their response to the Civil War.

These immigrants mixed with Latin Americans, Chinese, and European miners. But the American miners always presumed that the territory would become a state, preferably one that excluded non-whites. Just as boosters for the Mexican-American War expressed their belief that the mixed or mongrel races of Mexico could not handle democracy, so they argued that California should remain for whites and Americans. "To justify the claim to both the mineral resources and productive land of California, interested and powerful groups established social biases between 'foreigners' and 'U.S. citizens' that drew upon previous racial, class, and gender hierarchies of U.S. culture at mid-century."[76] Rather than being outliers in the culture, the U.S. immigrants brought with them the racial tensions of the East. In short order, the territorial government moved to exclude Mexicans and Indians from mining and settlement.

Three important populations flooded into the territory: American miners, foreign miners, and African Americans, either free or slave. As news spread about the strike, soldiers used their enlistment as a way to reach the goldfields, bearing with them ideas about race and Manifest Destiny. "In 1849 and 1850, as the excitement over California gold reached a frenzy, desertions emptied entire barracks in the West."[77] In the first year of the California gold rush, "fully forty percent left their posts."[78] These desertions placed new strains on the military, as it was not easy to replace men and it left the California frontier vulnerable even as the population exploded.

Other American miners came by boat or overland. The increased traffic on the overland trails led to rising tensions and conflicts with the Plains Indians and other Indian nations along the route. In turn, this development increased the responsibilities of the military in the mountain and coastal West even as they lost men to the gold rush. The public expected the army to "assert its authority" over the new territory, in addition to their jobs of "protecting, controlling, fighting, and assisting" the various groups that lived or moved into the West.[79] These demands only complicated the military's role in the West, as they finished one war and faced internal territorial conflicts within the gold mining areas.

The American miners arrived with tools, desire, and xenophobia, or a fear of outsiders. Encountering Europeans, Latin Americans, and Asians in the gold fields as well as Indians and *Californios*, many of the American miners believed they had a distinct and specific right to the gold. Extending their ideas about Mexicans to all Latin Americans, the American miners viewed them as a mongrelized race. The American miners sought "to exclude them from over-crowded mining regions and to justify Yankee claims to mineral wealth, land, and political power."[80] The Americans quickly codified their beliefs into law, enacting the Foreign Miners' Tax in 1850. The territorial government levied the monthly tax "primarily against Mexicans, Californios, Chileans, Peruvians, and Chinese. Often collected by unauthorized individuals, the tax was widely viewed as unjust in conception and practice."[81] The $20 tax became a way to exclude foreigners from the gold fields and justified vigilantism against foreigners.

Foreigners did not solely bear the brunt of nativism. Both African Americans and Indians found themselves under attack in the gold fields. The territory of California sought to restrict African Americans' civil rights almost immediately after the Mexican-American War. Lawmakers in the territory even tried to bar African Americans from entering the state.[82] Indians in California found themselves also facing exclusion as American miners sought to drive them out of the gold fields and out of much of California. At the beginning of the gold rush, many Indians worked as paid labor beside miners. Quickly, though, American miners fought against this pattern seeing it as giving *Californios* miners an unfair advantage, not unlike slavery. As miners poured into the Sierra region, which had been left "largely to Native Americans" when Mexico ruled, "the displacement and murder of Native Americans increased dramatically."[83] These actions led Indians to fight back, increasing conflict within California. The non-Indian population quickly overwhelmed the Indian population, numerically. That American population demanded that the army protect them from the Indian attacks, largely generated by white intrusion and violence. At least one general "blamed the violence on whites who first trespassed on Indian lands and then demanded military protection. But suggestions that civilians restrict their movements during the heady gold rush days in Oregon and California went unheeded."[84] Sure that Providence granted them the gold, American miners and others spread up the Pacific Coast, looking for gold and silver and clashing with Indians. The discovery of gold on the Pend d'Oreille River a few years later led to violence and the eventual cession of all Cayuse, Palouse, and Walla Walla land in Oregon.[85] Gold quickly became the justification for the pacification and removal of Indians.

Whereas the California gold rush often appears as a grand adventure that happens to propel California to statehood ahead of its neighbors, in terms of the West and the antebellum period, it represents a sign of things to come. Over and over again, throughout the West, resources would be discovered, be they gold, silver, timber, or farmland, and settlers would follow. Attempts would be made to exclude other groups, including African Americans and foreigners, from sharing in the wealth and freedom of a new territory. Indian populations would be displaced. And the military would be caught between joining in and stopping the violence. The military constantly found themselves entering the fray after greedy whites stirred up conflict with the Indians. Rather than approach the various Indian nations as nations and negotiate with them, as the military had been trained to do, they consistently engaged militarily with Indian groups. These conflicts drove up costs and frustrations for the U.S. Army. Rather than secure California after the Mexican-American War, the army quickly found themselves fighting new battles they had not begun. While producing wealth, the gold rush just as quickly ate it up through military needs.

TWO

THE ARMY OF THE WEST

Even after the end of the Mexican-American War, the West remained an area in play. The majority of the West existed as territories, with Indians, immigrants, and residents struggling to define how each territory would become a state and a player within U.S. politics. The recent exit of foreign powers, rapidly growing populations, and the constant tensions with Indian and Hispanic residents led the U.S. government to establish and expand its military presence in the trans-Mississippi West. And by the end of the Civil War that presence would have grown considerably, expanding its influence and power and making the federal government one of the main influences in the West.

After 1848, the trans-Mississippi West rested in U.S. hands, but not as a united region. Texas, the Southwest territories called the Mexican Cession, and the Oregon Territory, which included Washington, had diverse populations with little incentive to "relinquish their use (of land) to newcomers." Texas, after a brief period as an independent nation, still viewed itself as a nation and straddled the line between the West and the South, instituting slavery, which had been banned under Mexican law and causing tensions between the Anglo and Hispanic population. The population of 85,000 Mexicans/Hispanos in Texas and the Mexican Cession did not choose the end result of the war. They woke up one day as Americans, living under American law. Additionally, more than 200,000 Indians lived west of the Mississippi, broken into nations and alliances, and they also did not see themselves as willing partners or members of the United States. New challenges faced each of these internal regions. Some, like California, found themselves on the way to statehood with the large burst of gold rush miners. Others, like Kansas and Nebraska, found themselves invaded by immigrants and their own debates. Meanwhile, the Mormons had established the state of Deseret, eventually Utah, which they hoped would remain independent.[1]

In charge of these diverse and contentious populations was the military, which consisted of the regular army. They came to the new western territories to guard the gold routes, to tame the Indians, to protect the growing numbers of settlers heading west, and to secure the territory for the United States. As political and military tensions rose in the West, volunteers joined their ranks, increasing the numbers and muddling the mission. Historians often view the military in the West during the antebellum period as a training ground for future Civil War officers and as a police force, or constabulary, focused on domestic issues.[2] But much of what the army engaged in during this time represented international issues. From the Pig War in Washington Territory, to tensions on the Texas-New Mexico-Mexican borders, to most of the conflicts and treaty negotiations with the various Indian nations in the West, the military fought not domestic but foreign issues, making the West a region of international conflict.[3] Additionally, the military in the West drove the economy, boosted local development, and served as the only form of settlement in certain regions, making it the forefront of the federal government, ahead of settlers and others.

FROM MILITIA TO REGULAR ARMY

To understand the Army of the West and its role by the beginning of the Civil War requires, first, understanding the conflicts and tensions that shaped it from before the Mexican-American War until the edge of the Civil War. The very existence of the Army of the West represented a change in policy for the U.S. government. The founding fathers did not want a large standing army, which they felt would lead to power struggles between the military and civil government, as had happened in Europe, and could create an imperial class of hereditary soldiers.[4] Instead, they hoped that a small standing army would protect against international and external conflict, while militias, raised by the states and with short-term volunteers, would handle domestic or other internal issues.[5] In 1804, the government established West Point Academy to produce 50 officers per year to join a force of no more than 20,000 soldiers, who would protect a U.S. population of 15–20 million from the threat of Indian wars and attacks.[6] That same year, the United States faced several external enemies: Spain, France, and England. The government saw the various Indian nations as external and international threats as well, including the Eastern Indian nations, such as the Iroquois, Cherokee, Choctaw, and other Civilized Tribes.

From the beginning, though, conflicts emerged between the militias, the standing army, and the volunteers, who joined the standing or the regular army in times of war.[7] Locals within the states raised militia groups, forming them around local and regional communities, religions, or local politicians. The men elected their officers and voted on their rules and discipline, making each group different. During the first half of the 19th century, Americans viewed the militias as a democratic or citizens' army.[8] The very democratic nature of the militias, though, led to some of their greatest problems. Often, militias spent more time on ceremony than actual training, including spending much of their money on elaborate uniforms. Units could be driven by a cult of personality or created as fiefdoms by local dignitaries. Perhaps, the greatest problem came from the homogeneity of the units. Formed around ethnic or community associations, militias often "created an atmosphere that justified racial violence," particularly during the Mexican-American War when they encountered a non-Anglo foe. These militias helped reinforce racial ideas about exclusion, even as they helped expand the trans-Mississippi West. For all their democratic principles and independence, militias received federal recompense for their time served.[9] In other words, the federal government paid for their service, but local authorities oversaw their development and management.

The regular army provided an antithesis to the militias. Regular army recruits tended to come from the East and included more immigrants than the militias did. Between 1840 and 1849, 40 percent of the regular army recruits were immigrants.[10] Europeans "represented half or more of the men in the ranks," with Germans and Irish making up the largest proportion.[11] Many immigrants and recruits used the army as a means to get to the frontier for agriculture or gold, such as the Mormons had. Additionally, a third could not write their name, and the U.S. Army rejected another third of all applicants because they were too old or too young, drunk, or lacked the ability to speak English.[12] Known for its strict discipline, with a professional yet isolated officer corps, the regular army struggled until the 1830s for recognition as a valuable asset for the protection of the United States.

Politicians despised the regular army, seeing them as a "degraded class who fought for pay and not out of patriotism," generally unlike the militias.[13] Enlisted men "were society's flotsam and jetsam" to the 19th-century observers. To many, "only the lazy and shiftless, . . . joined the professional army, a haven for loafers."[14] Until the Mexican-American War, the regular army continually fought for funds and expansion.[15] Many in Congress believed that the regular army should be small, with reserves set out at strategic points.[16] From 1812 until the 1830s, the regular army lacked mounted cavalry because Congress deemed it too expensive. By the 1830s, after encounters with the Sioux and other horse cultures of the Great Plains, Congress funded small units of cavalry.[17] Yet Congress and Americans, in general, still viewed the regular army as degraded and suspicious, or as one observer put it, they "consisted generally of the refuse of society, collected in the cities and seaport towns; many of them broken down with years and infirmities."[18] As the United States expanded westward into what became the Old Northwest, including Illinois, Indiana, Michigan, and Wisconsin, new calls arose for a larger standing army as more of the conflicts fell along the boundaries of the United States. Senator Thomas Hart Benton of Missouri stated that a larger military "was a measure of western origin and eminently called for by the present and prospective condition of the West."[19] The expansion of the regular army did not last. The Second Seminole War, from 1835 to 1842, with its high casualties and cost, convinced Congress that a larger, more professional army was unnecessary. Additionally, a fear arose that the army's involvement in Indian removal from the Southeast and the Seminole War "made the West ripe for a pan-Indian alliance" against the United States.[20] The blame for bad Indian policy landed on the military, seen by Congress as agitators of future Indian conflicts. Consequently, the army saw its budget cut and its new cavalry units disbanded.[21]

Poor funding also led to other challenges facing the army in the period before the Civil War including—poor pay, between $5 and $6 a month, with a one-year contract. Officers earned $25 a month, which barely covered frontier expenses.[22] Almost a third of the regulars deserted for work on the canals or railroads in the antebellum period.[23] Desertions cost the army over $1,000 per person, including the cost of his training and transport. Also, deserters took "weapons and field kit; the dragoon or cavalry deserter often escaped on his horse."[24] Regulars suffered from a higher disease rate and a higher rate of accidental death than did militia members or volunteers.[25] All these factors led to a poor moral culture, with a high rate of drinking, gambling, and fighting amongst the enlisted men. To offset these problems and improve the moral culture, without spending any money, the War Department banned the traditional whiskey allotment, prohibited the sale of alcohol at forts, and reduced the enlistment period from five years to three. Yet, despite these troubles, the officer corps began to professionalize, as evidenced by the rise in the length of the median career from 10 to 20 years.[26] This change proved useful and important by the beginning of the Mexican-American War, as more officers had more experience with frontier missions and combat by the start of that war. Army officers soon became the experts on the western territories and the frontier.

The Mexican-American War brought big changes to the regular army, not the least of which was the rise in the number of volunteers serving with the regular army. Before the Mexican-American War, volunteers could be called up for skirmishes and short wars but not in the numbers needed for the Mexican-American War. President James Polk, at the beginning of the war in 1846, called for 50,000 volunteers, asking them to serve a three- to six-month enlistment. The majority who answered this call came from the South and the West, in this case Texas and Louisiana.[27] The federal government declared that the militias were in a "deplorable condition" and lacked training in military basics. Therefore, the federal government and the army requested volunteers, who would work for the federal government, not for the states, and remain under federal control.[28]

Volunteers for the regular army came from a different group than the recruits did, leading to class tensions.[29] Whereas the regular army consisted of the lower class and immigrants, the volunteers came from a higher class and represented fewer immigrants.[30] Additionally, volunteers, used to the militias, thought they would be able to elect their own officers, serve with people similar to themselves, and negotiate their terms of service as militiamen did.[31] But the army, in a democratic manner, saw them as part of the army and expected them to follow army regulations and obey officers assigned to them. Regular army recruits came from the East, whereas volunteers tended to come from the frontier states and territories closer to the battlefields in Texas, Louisiana, Mississippi, and Arkansas. Despite the proximity, and also because of it, one of the problems facing the military became the short enlistment period for the recruits. An enlistment of three to six months barely got the volunteer units from their home states to the battlefield, where they promptly disbanded and began the long march home. Their proximity also led to a higher rate of desertion. Local militias questioned the legality of the existence of volunteers, which weakened their ability to recruit members and transferred authority to recruit to the federal government. The lingering fear that a strong standing army would unbalance the U.S. government led many militias, who saw themselves as the inheritors of the founding fathers' intentions, to push back against the federal mandates.

The problem of the short enlistment period led to a push for a one-year requirement, beginning in November 1846.[32] Yet the army still lacked the number of volunteers needed for the Mexican-American War.[33] In 1847, the army introduced the Land Bounty which offered 100 acres of federal land to privates with a one-year service or $100 in Treasury scrip, or $30 over the current top pay for an enlisted man.[34] It served several purposes: attracting more recruits, extending Manifest Destiny by guaranteeing an Anglo population to settle any lands wrested from the Mexicans, or eventually, the Indians. The U.S. Army "envisioned itself as the sharp edge of Manifest Destiny."[35] Additionally, it created a conflict of interest which failed to bother anyone at the time. The men hired to subdue the Indians and to settle the international conflicts directly benefited through land taken from those conflicts.

Volunteers entered service for the Mexican-American War cocky and sure that the war would be short and victorious.[36] They served alongside an officer class with a very different expectation, having served in the War of 1812 and subsequent Indian wars, including the brutal Seminole Wars, around the new territories of the United States.[37] By the end of the war, the army underwent yet another transformation as the volunteers returned home and the officers headed farther west into new conflicts. The high number of officers trained at West Point meant they lacked innovative methods of warfare. Officers joined the regular army for "middle-class reasons: free education, military glory, frontier adventure, personal honor, and economic security."[38] A West Point education and the resulting commission often supplied these goals, but left the graduate with specific and limited training. While traditional methods worked in the Mexican-American War, this problem became more apparent as they began to fight the Western Indian nations in earnest.[39]

Several differences between volunteers and regulars emerged during the Mexican-American War, shaping the postwar Army of the West. First, the problem of the short enlistments of volunteers meant the regulars fought the first two battles of the Mexican-American War while they waited for the arrival of the volunteer units.[40] Many volunteers used their whole short-term enlistment by simply getting to Texas or California. Second, army officers discovered that regular army recruits were good for battles, garrisoning cities, and fortifying positions. While volunteers lacked the discipline for the first task, their racial attitudes and belief in Manifest Destiny helped them succeed at the second. They worked best at intimidating and policing the civilian populations.[41] Finally, as General Winfield Scott learned, once they defeated Santa Ana, the volunteers wanted to start for home immediately, unaware and uninterested in the aftermath of war and conquest. They viewed the conflict as over and their role complete. Yet, the army needed to secure the new territories. Even though the battles appeared to be over, the military responsibilities were not.

The Mexican-American War became the United States' first foreign war, fought in foreign territory, and which led to its first major expansion through warfare. For many volunteers, fighting the Mexican-American War meant extending the United States and its mission of Manifest Destiny. It did not entail them staying permanently in the West. Few volunteers extended their enlistments during the Mexican-American War, preferring to head back home as soon as they had served their time. By comparison, during the Civil War, it was common for soldiers to extend their enlistments. Because of the volunteers' attempts to leave, Congress permitted the temporary creation of 10 new regular army units in 1847. Additionally, the desertion rate for both volunteers and the regular army dropped during the Mexican-American War, though some desertions still occurred. Only about 6.5 percent deserted, whereas the regular rate before this time fluctuated between 20 and 30 percent.[42] The front, once it moved to Mexico and California, existed too far from home to easily escape; but one could leave at the end of one's enlistment. By the end of the war, it became clear to Congress that a volunteer army was expensive and temporary and that to maintain the large new territories a larger standing army would be needed.[43]

In addition to the experiment with use of volunteers, the army saw other changes immediately after the Mexican-American War. By the 1850s, foreign-born noncommissioned officers outnumbered native-born ones and made up 70 percent of the regulars, partially driven by the Land Bounty. The army became an important means of immigration to the West for foreigners. More and more commissioned officers came from West Point, with 64 percent in 1850 rising to 74 percent in 1860.[44] This continuity limited innovation in how to fight in new territories and with new populations like the more martial Apache and Sioux.

Between 1815 and 1848, the U.S. Army underwent a transformation as the federal government struggled to define the military's role without granting it too much power. Originally conceived as an army of demand, not a standing army, and as the 1830s progressed, it became clear that a standing army could be called upon to help pursue national interests, such as Indian removal and creating a "Permanent Indian Frontier."[45] But the cost of creating a standing army and a memory of those types of armies' roles in Europe still gave pause to Congress. As the United States began to add new territories, the question arose of who would protect and manage those territories. The army answered that call but not without reservations and problems.

CHANGING ROLE OF THE ARMY ON THE FRONTIER

The founding fathers intended the standing army to protect the borders of the United States from foreign intrusions. They essentially became the protectors of the ever-changing frontier of the United States. As the United States added new territories, both before and after the Mexican-American War, the government expected the army to secure and protect these frontiers. The term "frontier" better illustrates the area than "border" or "boundary." Often, the places the War Department sent the army to did not officially yet belong to the United States or had not yet been settled by an American population. In some cases, the land belonged to the United States on paper, yet the populations that resided there, be they Indians, English, or Hispanics, did not necessarily want to be part of the United States. So the army, especially the wing that would become the Army of the West, found themselves protecting and patrolling a shifting frontier from a changing enemy, being pushed by settlers from behind and non-U.S. citizens from the front.

The standing army served three roles from 1830 to 1848: protecting the frontier, building and maintaining infrastructure, and exploring and mapping new territories. Originally very small, numbering between 8,000 and 12,000 men, the federal government charged the army with protecting the frontier, in this case the frontier of the Old Northwest and the Old Southwest of Louisiana, Arkansas, and Mississippi.[46] In addition, they allowed the army to rent men out for building projects, and expected them to build and maintain roads and other infrastructures. The army created a branch to explore and map the new territories, giving them immense power over the destiny of these territories. It was on such a mission that Zebulon Pike declared the Great Plains "the Great American Desert," inspiring the policy of removing Indians into that area as well as keeping settlers out. Therefore, the army not only protected the frontier, but also mapped, defined, and developed it.

Policymakers in the 1820s viewed the frontier as one long, uninterrupted line between the Indians and American civilization and settlers. At that point, the U.S. government began moving Eastern Indians from both the North and the South over this line into the territory deemed the Great American Desert and Indian Territory. Perceived as uninhabitable, read "unable to be farmed," by whites, the territories that became Minnesota, Iowa, the Dakotas, Nebraska, Kansas, and Oklahoma became the dumping ground for the Indian nations of the Southeast and Northeast. Military conflicts pushed some, like the Iroquois, Miami, and Sac and Fox, west of this line. For others, like the Five Civilized Tribes, federal law shoved them west. The rising populations of Indians did little to assuage the fear of settlers on the eastern side of this magical line. In 1835, the citizens of Clay County, Missouri, sent a memorial to Congress asking for the creation of a line of military posts from the upper Mississippi over to the Missouri River and down to the Red River for protection, effectively establishing a permanent and secure frontier.[47] While taking advantage of the newly opened land, settlers expected a federal presence to preserve its security.

In 1836, to help resolve this problem, Secretary of War Lewis Cass proposed an 800-mile military road. Along it, the federal government would build eight or nine forts to guard the road, creating a permanent frontier. The very nature of a frontier, according to Frederick Jackson Turner, requires it to flow and move. But Congress wanted a wooden curtain that would keep Indians on one side and settlers on the other, with trade and far western settlers flowing between. The cost, though, proved exorbitant—$100,000 (or $2.2 million in 2006). The breakdown of the cost points to one of the great problems facing the military over securing the frontier. Thirty-five thousand dollars would go toward building the road, but $65,000 would pay for the nine forts at $7,222 per fort.[48] In other words, frontier security proved damned expensive. Cass argued that with 253,870 Indians on the frontier of which he considered 15,000–30,000 as dangerous, the current number of troops, 6,300, would prove too small to regulate the current frontier.[49] "The savage tribes which border upon our settlements, from the Canada line to Louisiana, are more dangerous to the lives and property of our citizens than the whole civilized world."[50] The bill passed and the wooden curtain went forward.[51] The onus now fell on the War Department to make it happen.

From the other side, the manager of the Indian Problem, the Commissioner of Indian Affairs Carey Harris, presented an even grimmer picture of the frontier in 1837. He reported that 231,806 western tribes lived within striking distance of the frontier, joined by more than 51,000 others the federal government had removed to the West. Additionally, fewer than 37,000 Indians still needed to be removed to the West, leaving a little over 12,000 in the East.[52] This accounting brought the number of Indians around the frontier to over 300,000, dwarfing the 6,000 plus troops in charge of the frontier. At the same time, a report came to Washington containing letters of recommendation from Colonel Stephen Kearney of Fort Leavenworth and Brigadier General Henry Atkinson, also the head of the Western Division of the army, two men who knew the frontier intimately. This report proposed a slightly different plan than Cass's, creating six or seven exterior forts to preserve the frontier between whites and Indians, eight interior posts to serve as a refuge for settlers in times of conflict, four supply depots to reduce the cost of supply, and 5,000–7,000 troops.[53] Both Kearney and Atkinson served in the West and understood the dual challenges facing the army: protecting the international boundary challenged by the Indians and protecting settlers from domestic and external threats. Charles Gratiot, chief engineer of the army, proposed the perpendicular double fort line because it "expanded the Army's western presence and pumped hundreds of thousands of dollars into the borderlands economies."[54] The reasoning exposes one of the constant tensions for the frontier army. The government expected them to provide economic development as trading centers, road builders, and buyers of goods, as well as security for the settlers and peace on the frontier. Closer to the Civil War, these various needs often were at odds with each other. Congressmen liked Gratiot's plan because it appeared more able to repel European and Indian invasions, still a concern barely 25 years after the War of 1812. Despite the advantages of both plans, Congress and the War Department implemented neither.

By 1840, the apparent peace of the frontier and spiraling costs ended plans for a military road or the wooden curtain along the frontier. As the threat of Indian wars appeared to fade, the military and Congress viewed the Indian menace differently. They became more concerned about rising alcoholism among borderlands Indians and trying to settle Indians in specific lands to stop raiding and intertribal warfare. The purpose became "one of protecting Indians against themselves and against ambitious whites."[55] This change foreshadowed future problems for the Army of the West. Trained to wage war, time and again the federal government called upon the army to act as peacekeepers in the West: between groups of Indians, between Indians and whites, and eventually between groups of whites.

By 1845, the idea of the wooden curtain between the Indian nations west of the Mississippi and the nascent white settlements to the east became obsolete as settlers moved to Oregon along the Oregon Trail. The 6,000 emigrants headed to Oregon, forced the military and the government to reconceptualize the frontier again.[56] It could not be a north-south barrier between whites and Indians. Transcontinental settlement required a line of communication and security for the settlers, a way by which problems could be reported and help could be dispatched.[57] In October 1847, just months before his death, Marcus Whitman wrote a memorial to Congress asking for more protection on the Oregon Trail and, in Oregon, to protect the growing number of settlers.[58] In the back of everyone's minds there arose a fear that the Indians might unite into one or two major groups, becoming a formidable force.[59] More than anything else, Congress believed that national security, a term which included threats from European forces and the Indians, depended on the security of inland transportation.[60] This assumption made the creation of strings of forts, which would stretch inland and across any new territories, like modern telephone lines, of the greatest import.

From the 1840s until the beginning of the Civil War, the number of forts west of the Mississippi both grew and receded. The first forts followed the trade and settlement routes: the Oregon and Santa Fe Trails. The army proposed that each of these forts would have 500 mounted troops along the trails, enabling them to be dispatched at the first sign of trouble. Those at the forts on the Santa Fe Trail would also begin an offensive against the Comanche, who harassed traders in the southwest territories of Texas and New Mexico.[61] These suggestions demonstrate the complexity facing the military in the antebellum west: secure the frontier and launch an offensive against marauding Indians with few men in isolated posts. Economic and political considerations, rather than practical ones, influenced the placement of forts throughout the 1840s. Fort Smith in Arkansas provides an example of these tensions. Built in 1817 to prevent war between the Osage and the first wave of Cherokee, who moved west to avoid cultural change, it eventually closed because of expense. Reopened after local leaders and business men demanded it for political and economic reasons, it became a supply depot for forts farther to the west, guaranteeing economic interactions on the frontier. Eventually, it became the starting point for the southern route to California and the goldfields, furthering its economic importance to the local community.[62] Fort Smith cycled through all the roles of forts in the West: security, economic engine, political outpost, and supply depot.

The end of the Mexican-American War added 1.2 million square miles that needed to be protected.[63] Forts spread in the Pacific Northwest to try and secure the territory from the British and stop Indian uprisings, like the Rogue River Revolt. In California, the government built forts to oversee the mining frontiers and keep miners and Indians apart. With the end of the Mexican-American War, forts expanded into the new territories to stabilize the new areas and frontiers. In the Southwest, the forts now had to quell rebellion and discontent within a resident Hispanic population as well as make treaties with the Indians. Some forts, like Fort Buchanan in New Mexico, moved into old Mexican forts in this region.[64]

When one thinks of a fort, one thinks of a walled space with large buildings, corrals, and housing. Forts on the western frontier did not resemble those in the East or in the public imagination, as they were not enclosed or, in many cases, even fortified. Some were not even permanent. Temporary forts on the far edge of the frontier, beyond settlement, consisted of Sibley tents, inspiring little confidence in the settlers or fear in the Indians.[65] The army placed more established forts near settlements where the soldiers lived in irregular collections of rough adobe or log huts.[66] In some cases, like Fort Buchanan, the government encouraged the soldiers to occupy existing buildings.[67] In others, the soldiers built housing out of the available materials. The accommodations were small, poorly heated, and badly ventilated. They had canvas or dirt floors and roofs, congested sleeping quarters, and bedbugs and fleas for company.[68] Despite the hope that the government would staff forts with 500 men or more, most forts consisted of fewer than 100 men and a handful of buildings. Such small posts inspired neither fear nor respect from the Indians. Most of the Western Indians considered warfare an economic process and these small forts with their limited resources offered little economic opportunity for the Indians.[69] Yet, temporary or permanent, all these forts possessed some similar problems, including location, cost, and mission.

The spread of forts across the West not only followed the trails and settlers, but they also branched into areas where international conflict threatened. This impetus might mean establishing forts along borders with other Euro-American nations, like Mexico, or within territory considered in play by specific Indian nations. Fort Buchanan in Arizona territory provides an example of the international and settlement role of forts. In 1856, fully six years after the end of the Mexican-American War, the War Department issued an order to establish Fort Buchanan, influenced in part by petitions and complaints from the residents of Tucson who felt isolated and vulnerable to Indian attacks.[70] Securing the territory as American and protecting the existing American and Mexican population from Mexican and Indian incursions represented the fort's main role. While that sounds straightforward on the surface, in reality, the mission represented great complexity.

Tucson, the major settlement, existed in an isolated area with several very small settlements around it in a harsh desert climate. The War Department ordered the unit to occupy the existing buildings, in this case the Mexican presidio, if possible. At the same time, the War Department charged Major Enoch Steen with choosing a location "best calculated to protect that place and the surrounding settlements." Upon arriving, he established a temporary fort on the Mexican border to make his presence known to the local Mexican, now American, population. Six months later, Steen built a permanent fort, not in Tucson but in Calabasas. He chose that site because its location positioned him for protecting settlements, possessed good grazing and water for the horses, proximity to timber for buildings, and availability of supplies from the nearby trading areas.[71] Thus, he felt the location served his main purpose: instituting an American presence in an area previously contested by the Mexicans and currently by the Apache. He, therefore, resolved the problems of location and mission.

Steen's choice of Calabasas because of its proximity to timber, grass, and trade points to the biggest hurdle facing the western forts: cost. The military shipped in nearly everything they needed. As A. B. Bender puts it, "To supply the scattered frontier army with subsistence and other necessities presented no small task." Anything perishable, like food or hay, or needed immediately, like timber, the fort purchased locally, which made the establishment of a fort an attractive economic boon for the local community. "Clothing, blankets and other quartermaster's equipment were purchased on the Pacific Coast or East Coast, and were shipped to the nearest military ports and stations."[72] Additionally, many of the items shipped from the Pacific Coast had already been shipped around South America to the Pacific Coast. In short, all these shipped items cost much more than at forts on the East Coast. Anything that could come from the local population saved money for the government.

The western forts served roles beyond simply security. After the Mexican-American War, the military used the static post system, with only one or two companies garrisoned at it. While providing a permanent appearance of security, the system limited the effectiveness of the military against "disorderly frontiersmen, and skillful, stubborn and elusive Indians."[73] There were no palisades at the frontier forts nor were they enclosed, making them both more vulnerable and more open to the non-military population. Their design suggests that "as a physical manifestation of the Federal government, forts executed power and influence through their very existence." Yet, they also represented an image of the American government unlike any other position on the frontier. Their role as communication links to Washington and the East Coast through "supply lines, written orders and frequent personnel movement" represented not the military, "but a broader Anglo-eastern culture." They were not designed or meant as a wooden curtain anymore but rather as a doorway through which American civilization and order could enter the perceived chaos of the West, physically expanding Manifest Destiny. The forts and the military that built and occupied them presented model American settlements, promoting civilized society through example.[74] "By supplementing the work of the explorer, the missionary, the Indian trader and the engineer," soldiers "helped bind the Far West—the 'Last American Frontier'" to the rest of the continental United States.[75] They represented both the federal government in the West and the civilized East, establishing an American consciousness and Manifest Destiny before settlers and others arrived, entrenching the government in the West.

ROLE OF THE MILITARY IN THE WEST

Once the U.S. government established forts and their presence in the West, the day-to-day tasks of the military and its soldiers emerged. These tasks evolved over the course of 25 years from the 1830s until the beginning of the Civil War as the West evolved. In the beginning, the military went west of the Mississippi to protect the wagon trains and build roads. Remember, from 1815 until 1846, the United States military did not fight a foreign power and the standing military consisted of just over 7,000 men.[76] These men occupied more than "100 scattered posts and stations" along the East Coast, the Great Lakes, and the western frontier, creating a very thin layering of protection.[77] Even during the Mexican-American War, the army needed to blaze roads through "Chihuahuan Desert, Gila Mountains, Sonoran and Mojave Deserts, and Sierra Nevada to San Diego and Los Angeles, California."[78] The military's role consisted more of civil engineering than security.

By 1836, the need for a bigger military able to handle more roles became apparent to those in Washington. Secretary of War Lewis Cass wrote that the military should exhibit "to the Indians a force well calculated to check or to punish any hostilities they may commit and in adding to our geographical knowledge of those remote areas."[79] The military needed to contain the Indians as well as explore the West and protect trails headed west. At the same time, it oversaw the removal of the Indians from the East into the West, a process which began to generate new tensions between the Great Plains Indians and the newcomers from the East.[80] These rising tensions between Indian nations led to the creation of new forts west of the Mississippi to protect the trails, including Old Fort Kearny, which Congress funded with a Congressional act on July 2, 1836.[81] Now, the army not only tried to keep Indians and whites apart, but Indian nations apart as well.

At the same time, the military continued one of its traditional roles: building roads. The U.S. military built 2,500 miles of roads, between 1815 and 1831.[82] These responsibilities exploded after the Mexican-American War, as both new territories and new resources came under the command of the U.S. military. Prior to the Mexican-American War, West Point graduates became increasingly in charge of managing canals and railroads.[83] The growing desire in Washington to build a transcontinental railroad drove much of the surveying and internal improvements.[84] John C. Frémont and others mapped out various routes, both north and south, for the potential railroad, adding to the knowledge of the West and the army's growing responsibilities.[85] Even as politicians fought over the potential routes, the military continued to scout those routes in the West, gaining knowledge about the terrain and landscape that would prove valuable later.[86] From a military perspective, it came down to strategy. A southern route would be more vulnerable if the Union came apart. A northern route would guarantee access to the goldfields and other western resources.

Surveying the railroad routes became an important revenue stream for the army, always under attack because of expenses in the West. In the 1850s, the Army Corps of Engineers became responsible for "extensive surveys of western rivers, the Great Lakes, international boundary lines, and emigrant routes."[87] Congress then granted $15,000 to survey various transcontinental and Pacific Coast railroad routes. These funds helped underwrite other projects as well, like scouting fort locations on the way. Railroads became increasingly important to the military. As Secretary of War

Jefferson Davis worried about the efficacy of small, isolated forts, he encouraged the military to locate them along railroad lines, even future ones.[88] Even without a transcontinental railroad, the military did well in securing the frontier, allowing the railroads to eventually be built.[89]

Guarding the caravans and wagon trains became one of the military's primary roles, until the Mexican-American War. The government thought such escorts would impress Great Plains Indian nations with "proper ideas of the power of the United States."[90] Escorting and protecting the wagon trains secured the emigrant frontier, limiting conflict between settlers and Indians, and established a visible military presence in the West for both Indians and settlers. It also took immense time and manpower away from a military with not a lot of either. The military became the economic, political, and social federal presence in the West.

The Mexican-American War only increased these tensions and responsibilities. With vast new territories open in the Southwest, the military now had more routes to protect from a greater number of Indians. Forts in the West after the Mexican-American War followed a daily routine of drill and guarding the fort as well as escort duty, protecting surveying parties and emigrant trains, fighting Indians, stopping smugglers and filibusters, or "private citizens who set out to invade foreign territories," and erecting buildings and roads.[91] For example, Fort Buchanan's garrison of men, in Arizona, needed to "protect communications with California and block Pinal and Chiricahua Apache raids into Mexico." The government and settlers also expected them to protect the Comstock Lode in Nevada and push the Shoshoni and Paiute back from that territory.[92] These tasks required man and horse power not necessarily available to the garrison, and represent the large and somewhat unrealistic expectations of settlers in the West and the government in the East.

In 1848, El Paso, Texas, asked and received a garrison for reasons similar to those of Fort Buchanan in New Mexico. Originally, the government sent the military there in defense of the new boundary with Mexico, to protect settlers against the Apache, protect California migrants, and maintain law and order. James Magoffin, a successful local trader and husband of Susan Magoffin, a famed diarist, lobbied for creating a garrison at El Paso closer to his property. He argued that the lack of one left major routes through the Pass of the North unprotected, exposed U.S. citizens to Indian depredations, endangered property (mainly his) worth $300,000, and exposed the community to bandits.[93] Eventually, the federal government built the post at Magoffinsville on Magoffin's ranch.[94] Local settlers expected the army to provide a sense of security, as they edged farther past the boundaries of the U.S. frontier.

International tensions almost appear to come to a head at the end of the Mexican-American War. The first responsibility of the army, immediately after the Treaty of Guadalupe-Hidalgo in 1848, was to establish forts and maintain the new boundaries.[95] After years of tensions between the military and foreign forces, which still saw new

U.S. territory as theirs, both the Mexicans and the British seemed to back off. Additionally, on the southern border, the treaty guaranteed that the U.S. government would prevent Indian raids into Mexico.[96] To the south, filibusters, bandits, and Indian raids increased the tensions and problems along the nascent border with Mexico. Filibusters posed a unique problem. "Their land piracy, if successful, promised to irritate the explosive issues of territorial annexation and slavery."[97] Although the Indians and bandits affected the local population, filibusters could potentially create an international incident. This reduction in tension proved to be temporary. By the end of the 1850s, tensions in Washington Territory had risen between the British and the U.S. Army.

The garrison in El Paso also provides an example of the international tensions that drew the military in, as well. The army went out to protect the border with Mexico. Yet, in the end, it came between Texas and its imperialistic desire to expand its territory into New Mexico. The U.S. military and the hostile Indians, who kept the Texas Rangers and the military busy during the 1850s, helped prevent this expansion. In 1850, New Mexico the Union entered as a state with a constitution and an established boundary line, thanks to the pressure of federal army posts.[98] Originally, in the 1840s, Washington built posts in the Washington Territory to protect the Canadian frontier from the English and from the Hudson's Bay Company.[99] By the 1850s, those international responsibilities had not ebbed. Similar tensions and responsibilities existed in Washington. In 1859, the Pig War erupted between the United States and Britain. It began simply: a pig belonging to a Hudson's Bay Company employee ate the potatoes of an American living in the territory. The American killed the pig. The Hudson's Bay company employee demanded payment. The American refused and demanded protection from the U.S. government. The Hudson's Bay Company alerted soldiers and commanders at his fort. This incident occurred on an island whose status had never been resolved during negotiations between the United States and Britain. The incident "triggered a minor arms race off the coast of Washington Territory," with 450 U.S. soldiers, 14 cannons, and a hastily erected fort against 2,000 British sailors on five warships. Sent to watch over settlers and settle the Indians in Washington on to reservations, the military found itself embroiled in an international dispute where they were sorely mismatched.

Not all the international tensions arose from national incursions into other's territory. In some cases, individuals created international incidents. In Mexico, the rise of filibusters, or independent military expeditions set on invading foreign countries, created tensions between the two nations. So, while the western forts sought to create a sense of the U.S. government in the new U.S. territories, they also served to settle the continuing international frontier that seethed around the edges of the West.[100] For Westerners in these areas, the East Coast debates about slavery and which territories might accept it seemed academic, when they worried about their day-to-day security.

As the military performed physical duties, like building roads, and traditional duties, like protecting borders, they also acted as frontier constabulary dealing with civilians and government agents. Back when Congress debated the role of the standing army and whether there should be one, many opposed it because of the fear that the military would be used against the populace.[101] After the Mexican-American War and as the West became more settled that is exactly what happened. The federal government called upon the military to act as a frontier constabulary, or police force. And, though the federal government sought to avoid sending troops against citizens, but comfortably sent them against Indians and other nationals, they did feel comfortable using troops to quiet conflict within the territories, just outside the limits of the United States and in the grey area of where citizen's rights stopped and began.

While some communities courted forts for the economic advantages, if there were not economic advantages to forts, civilian communities resisted having the military nearby. Boomtowns, in particular, viewed the military as a damper on their lives. On the whole, "remote garrisons had better relations" with the civilian population "than those in desired land."[102] Where security and economic support were needed, the civilians appreciated the military. In some cases, like Fort Gibson in Arkansas, the government suspected whites of ginning up conflicts with Indians just to ensure the economic trade with the forts.[103] The tensions between the civilians and the military went both ways. Military officers often blamed settlers for the violence that occurred on the frontier, particularly with Indians.[104] Settlers saw themselves as the rightful heirs to the land, thanks to the growing belief in Manifest Destiny, and though military officers often believed in it as well, they resented having to resolve conflicts created by civilians.[105]

Not all settlers were created equal. In the Southwest, Hispanic settlers viewed the U.S. Army with distrust and as conquerors. Prior to the Mexican-American War, the settlements in New Mexico, one of the farthest northern areas of Mexico, found themselves with little protection against Indian raids as Mexican forces focused on other issues.[106] After the Mexican-American War, new tensions arose between the New Mexicans and Colonel Edwin "Bull Head" Sumner, commander of the Army of the West. He declared the New Mexicans "thoroughly debased and totally incapable of self-government," and he recommended arming them, withdrawing the army, and letting them fend for themselves.[107] Such interactions did not endear the U.S. military to the New Mexicans.

By 1858, just 10 years after the Mexican-American War, the U.S. military acted as a frontier constabulary against U.S. citizens in three territories: the Mormons in Utah, the political conflict in Kansas, and conflicts with the Bureau of Indian Affairs (BIA). During the Mexican-American War, the U.S. Army recruited the Mormon battalion to aid in the war.[108] Colonel Kearney, for whom the fort in Nebraska would be named, recruited between 500 and 1,000 men to serve in the battalion. While helping the Mormon exodus west, many Mormons viewed this aid with suspicion. Where had the U.S. government been when the residents of Missouri and Illinois violently drove them out? Though the battalion was filled, this gesture by the government only added to the Mormon distrust of the U.S. federal government.

In the 1850s, the Mormons established Deseret in what would eventually become Utah. They envisioned it as a Latter-day Saints' theocracy. The federal government tolerated this vision for a while, but eventually wanted to enforce their power over it as the Oregon Trail ran through the Great Salt Lake Valley.[109] "Church president Brigham Young had been named Utah's first territorial governor, but his Gentile subordinates recoiled at the church's theocracy, resented the enormous power held by local probate courts, and ridiculed the practice of polygamy."[110] In 1857, President Buchanan removed Young from office and ordered the army to occupy Utah, thus sending the U.S. military against their own civilians, something the founding fathers had feared if a standing army was established. The Mormons responded by retreating from Salt Lake City, scorching the earth as they went, and harassing the military at every turn.[111] From a military perspective, the invasion of Deseret, a U.S. territory, in an attempt to enforce federal law on U.S. citizens represented a startling turn of events, and expanded the military's role and presence in the West.

At the same time, the army found itself in the middle of a political conflict on the prairie. Kansas erupted over the issue of being a slave state or not in 1857. Between votes, dueling territorial legislatures, and raids on towns with opposing views, the state earned its title as "Bleeding Kansas." In an effort to try and stem the violence, the government ordered the army in. At the end of 1857, one-seventh of the entire U.S. Army, which equaled 1,900 regulars, patrolled the Missouri border with Kansas and oversaw polling stations. In addition to stretching an already thin military thinner, the situation in Kansas required the army to serve as peacekeepers between different factions of the civilian population, never a popular role among army officers. The army found this development dismaying as "Almost to a man, soldiers resented having to referee the contest that pitted citizen against citizen, and they blamed radicals on both sides for making the army a scapegoat for their problems."[112] Babysitting civilian conflicts also forced the army to withdraw from more traditional ones with Indians, which officers viewed as a more productive and a better use of their talents.[113]

Little prepared the 1850s U.S. Army to serve as peacekeepers to civilian conflicts. Accustomed to using force against the Indians, they quickly ascertained that they could not do the same against American civilians. They could not campaign against civilians, though they essentially did in Utah, nor threaten or fire upon them. "During the interwar years, the United States was unwilling and unable to prosecute a vigorous war on other white Americans."[114] The public approved of the army firing on Indians, Hispanics, and the British, but not white Americans. They moved from acting as protectors of the international boundaries to peacekeepers.[115] The military became the policemen of the territories.

Some see the military's role with the Indian frontier or actually "frontiers," as each individual group or tribe saw themselves as an entity equal to the United States, as an extension of the frontier constabulary.[116] Antebellum military officers would disagree with that characterization. They viewed their conflicts with the Indians as war and ably used force to quell Indian conflicts. Additionally, forts were placed in hostile territory "on land the United States had not legally obtained from the people who lived there."[117] On the other side, Indians would not view it as a constabulary because they believed they protected their homeland from invading forces: settlers, military, miners. Indians would consider it, as some historians and some officers at the time do, as an international conflict. Finally, the U.S. government did not see the Indians as equals, either as humans or as potential citizens, at least not before the Civil War, as they failed to offer Indians citizenship rights in treaties at this time.[118]

Evidence of this intertribal nature of Indian and U.S. military relations exists in one of the other roles the antebellum military played in the West—that of treaty negotiators.[119] In 1849, Congress created the Department of the Interior and moved the BIA into it from the War Department, much to the frustration and anger of the army.[120] Prior to that, the military negotiated treaties with Western Indians, and in some cases, such as the Laramie Treaty of 1851, continued to do so.[121] Many in the military "acknowledged that covetous Anglo frontiersman triggered most of the wars with western Indians."[122] But their inability to regulate those relations created frustration. Nevertheless, the U.S. military still subscribed to the belief that "American Indians had to make way for the mark of Euroamerican civilization."[123] Additionally, the military tried to root out corruption over annuities and prevent the militarization of the Plains Indians.[124] Charged with protecting the frontier, the military saw these roles as integral to working with the Indians to try and maintain peace. Prior to the Civil War, peace with the Western Indians did not necessarily mean corralling them on reservations. It meant finding means, through treaties and other arrangements, to reduce tension between Western Indian nations and those settlers crossing their territories. For instance, just before the Mexican-American War, the military sought to tamp down conflict between the Otoe, Omaha, and Pawnees on one side and the Sioux on the other through the building of Fort Kearney (the first one).[125] But they built the fort too far east to be effective since the government also expected them to protect the Overland Trail. Commanders thought creating peace between the Otoe, Omaha, Pawnee, and Sioux would create peace on the trail. Military officers recognized the integrated nature of their role on the frontier.

While building forts and roads, providing economic growth to frontier communities, escorting and protecting explorers and settlers, mapping the new territories, and securing the new borders of the United States, the military in the West spent most of their time engaging with the Indian nations. This role increased dramatically after the Mexican-American War. Between 1840 and 1849, there were 42 combat engagements between the military and the Western Indian groups, and during the 1850s, there were 121.[126] At the same time, army casualties skyrocketed to 443 in the 1850s from 112 during the 1840s.[127] By 1860, less than 7 percent of the army served in the East. While the army sought out a variety of methods for dealing with the Indians, an essayist in 1894 pointed out, "As the Supreme Court is the final means of settlement of all constitutional questions by peaceful methods, so is war a final refuge when all peaceful methods have failed."[128]

By the end of the 1850s, many Western Indian groups pushed back against settlers, miners, and the military: Shoshone, Paiute, Navajo, Sioux, to name a few.[129] These eruptions led to increased tensions between settlers, miners, and other new American Westerners who expected and demanded protection from the military. The rise in conflict and warfare would shape how Westerners viewed the Civil War. Western decisions over whether to join the North or the South, or stay out of it all together, revolved around security, not slavery. If the U.S. Army pulled out of the West, it left many settlers vulnerable to rising Indian attacks as well as smugglers, bandits, and others who sought to take advantage of a reduced security force. As early as 1855, locals near Fort Buchanan in Arizona feared the withdrawal of the military because it would expose them to Indian depredations. Both Mexicans and Americans in the community wrote to the U.S. federal government requesting that the fort remain where it was.[130] Settlers in El Paso faced the same fear.[131] The government chose to penetrate the frontier with 300 forts, to better protect trails and settlement rather than "a concentration of forces at fewer, larger posts from which troops could venture forth on longer expeditions."[132] By penetrating the West, the federal government created fingers of stability and security that, much like the presidio system in the Spanish empire, became difficult to withdraw. Though the government may have expected settlers to take the lead in establishing a peaceful frontier, the settlers expected the military to enforce it. For Westerners, be they Americans, Indians, or Mexicans, "The military was, in fact, the clearest representation of the U.S. government" in the West.[133]

THE EVOLUTION OF THE MILITARY IN THE WEST

The U.S. Army underwent profound changes from 1815 until the Civil War. The frontier in the West drove many of these changes as did the Mexican-American War. Both spurred the growth of the army and the establishment of posts west of the Mississippi. Both drove the development of tactics and strategies when dealing with vast amounts of territories and hostile residents. But more subtle changes occurred, as well. The army became more professionalized. Commanders stayed in the field longer. The army redivided the units several times to provide better coverage and administration over the vast western territories. Certain responsibilities, like the BIA, went to other arms of the government, in some ways streamlining what the army needed to do: practice war. Several commanders, including Bull Sumner and General William Harney, gained invaluable experience fighting Indians, providing security, stopping filibusters and bandits, which they applied in the Civil War.

The army developed a vast arsenal of skills. Beginning as early as 1803 with the Louisiana Purchase, "the Army penetrated the Indian country, explored the new region, and attempted to pacify the tribes by peace treaties or by punitive expeditions."[134] By the time of the Civil War, the army had created a group to explore and map new territories, had patrolled several international borders, acted as a frontier constabulary, and a security force for settlement. They learned to deal with supportive, unsupportive, and violent civilian populations. They practiced negotiation with the Indians of the West; and when that didn't work, treated them as equal combatants in the struggle over the frontier.

The army became engaged in more contact with civilians than they had in the East. "Between the Mexican-American War and the Civil War they protected the emigrant, the frontier settler and the overland mail."[135] They helped secure and protect frontier towns, like Tucson and El Paso, while establishing the power and the culture of the East.[136] The forts were not defensive, but rather open to the various communities to help demonstrate the power of the federal government and the hierarchy of the powerful army.[137] Forts provided aid, comfort, and economic boosts to the surrounding communities, aiding the survival of many of them.

Just as the forts encompassed multiple functions, so did the army. As the government and the frontier required the army to cover more and more territory, more tasks fell on the army.[138] When the government considered the creation of a transcontinental railroad, they asked the army to scout routes. When the government needed a safe road to California from Texas, they asked the army. The army protected lines of communication, dealt with international incidents, and invaded Utah to quell disobedience. They performed these responsibilities with a small force, spread over thousands of miles, with little specialized training, long and expensive supply lines, and hostile populations. Yet, because of these tasks, the army knew more about the western frontier than most other entities at the time, creating documentation and knowledge that helped settle the West. The army knew where the rivers and other resources lay.

Because of these vast functions, the army also influenced Western life more than other entities, and probably more than the army had done in the North or South during earlier periods. It provided a trailblazing presence that created much of the West as the United States came to know it. New settlers became addicted to the idea that the army provided security and power, a consideration for western communities as the Civil War arrived. The question that faced the West was not slave or free but protected or exposed. For many states and territories, even those whose population would eventually support the Confederacy, the fear that the withdrawal of the federal troops would expose them to Indians, bandits, and international conflict gave pause to these decisions. "As the regulars restored peace in Kansas, established federal authority in Utah, patrolled international borders, and chased Indians, their country was breaking apart."[139] While the army provided security for the western frontier, the East exploded, eventually drawing the standing army into conflict, leaving the West at the mercy of volunteers and failed Civil War commanders.

After the Mexican-American War, Congress began to scheme how to protect its new territories and provide safe passage for the wagonloads of people headed West and the goods and gold coming East. Congress's underlying assumption rested on the fear of invasion from foreign entities. While the United States considered these new territories (those in the Southwest, California, Oregon Territory, the territories of the Great Plains), American in reality, they were not more American than the territories to the north in Canada. Congress sent the military into the trans-Mississippi West to quell the non-American resident populations, like the Hispanics that resided in the former Mexican territories, and stave off new attacks from non-American governments, like the Mexicans, British, and Indians. "The interwar frontier was a civil-military gray zone, neither entirely at peace nor at war."[140] Yet, despite all their different duties, the military remained a weak link. "Year after year, the United States deployed its Army, underfunded, undermanned, and ill-trained, into frontier war zones and demanded the work of a legion from a mere battalion."[141] Often historians do not consider the Indians as foreign threats, because they do not see them as foreign governments negotiating for territory. Yet, two facts belie this assumption. First, the United States grew the military to use it to protect American interests from non-American attacks. Second, from the perspective of Western Indian tribes and nations, they sought to protect their territories, societies, and peoples from a foreign invasion from the United States. Until the Civil War, the BIA resided in the War Department, suggesting that the government saw the Indians as hostile entity. And throughout the period leading up to the Civil War, military commanders clashed with Indian agents and civil Indian reformers over policy and treatment of the Indians. Military commanders bemoaned the corruption and turnover in the BIA, the use of patronage to fill those positions, and the lack of experience and long-term planning that came with patronage appointments. Ironically, the army itself had just left a similar system behind and could preach the value of professionalization, though when it came to Indian Affairs, it fell on deaf ears.

THREE

THE INDIAN FRONTIERS

While historians often focus on the Civil War as a battle between the North and the South, for the Indians residing west of the Mississippi in 1861, the Civil War represented an international conflict, an intertribal conflict, and an intratribal conflict. Neither the Union nor the Confederacy grasped the complexities of Indian nations in the West. For the Cherokee and the Western tribes, the Civil War was a continuation of the internal and external fights over nationhood and sovereignty, not over slavery or states' rights. In this way, the Five Civilized Tribes shared something in common with many of their western neighbors: the Civil War might not be their fight directly, but it certainly opened up and reinforced regional fights and debates.

In the 1820s and 1830s, the federal government began pursuing the policy of removal with the Eastern Indian nations to Indian Territory west of the Mississippi. Beginning in the Northeast, the Pawnee, Shawnee, and Iroquois, as well as others, signed treaties that moved them West, into other groups' territories or what the U.S. government considered Indian Territory. Through the push of settlers, Indian wars, and treaties, the majority of Northeastern groups ended up along the Mississippi River. Then, the federal and state governments turned their attention to the Southeastern Indian nations. Economic pressures and interests grew around the land and resources of the Five Civilized Tribes (Cherokee, Creek, Chickasaw, Choctaw, and Seminole). Though national rhetoric often portrayed the Five Civilized Tribes as only recently redeemed savages, an idea which justified their removal, in reality they represented a form of Southern elite rather than a poor group of nomadic Indians. The removal of the Eastern Indians into the West created international and inter-tribal tensions that shaped the responses of both Western Indians, and those recently removed, to the Civil War.

RESHAPING THE WEST WITH INDIANS

The 1820s saw a shift in Indian policy in the continental United States. The federal government forced Eastern Indian groups to the West, like the Iroquois and the Delaware. Immediately behind these removals came settlers, sometimes leaping ahead. The U.S. population rose to 23 million in 1850 from 7.5 million in 1815, creating stress on the land and the Indians who occupied it. In contrast, the Indians east of the Mississippi dropped to a few thousand in remote areas, like the mountains of North Carolina, from 200,000 in 1815. This pattern also created tensions, as Indian groups removed from the East fought to protect their new land in the West from other Indians and from settlers. As groups like the Miami and the Iroquois moved, they bumped into Western groups, like the Sac and Fox, creating intertribal conflict. Resources became strained as more settled groups moved into areas with more nomadic groups. Extractive frontiers, like the lead frontier in Iowa, also drew settlers into territory recently granted to Indians.

The push for removal ran headlong into the push for acculturation. To enhance the case for removal, settlers accused Indians of theft, trespassing, and violence. While some Indians, like the Cherokee, thought or hoped that acculturation would strengthen their case for sovereignty and recognition, others resisted. Indians fought removal through negotiations with federal commissions, including promoting mixed-race members to leadership roles, petitioning the government, and in some cases, like the Kickapoo and the Seminole, war against state and federal forces.[1]

As the Indians struggled against removal, whites differed over the future of the Indians. Some believed the Indians could become acculturated and part of the United States. Others believed the Indians could become acculturated, but only if they were isolated from the baser aspects of U.S. society. Still others saw Indians as a weaker race, whose presence and intermarriage weakened other races, an attitude reflected in the Mexican-American War. Americans expanded their fear that the Mexicans could not handle the responsibilities of democracy to Indians as well.[2]

By the 1830s, the U.S. government established Indian Territory as a permanent Indian frontier. This move created a defensible line between whites and Indians for the military. The conflicts between removed Indians and whites had inspired Lewis

Cass's and others' ideas about a line of military forts to keep the settlers and the Indians apart. The creation of an Indian Territory achieved this result. Additionally, it created a safe haven for acculturation. But the government planners assumed that the settlers would respect this line, and that the United States would not move farther west, and that the Indians would choose to acculturate. These misunderstandings led the government to design "muddled and unsuccessful federal programs" for the 19th-century Indian nations. By the end of the 1840s, with the conclusion of the Mexican-American War and the beginning of the gold rush, American settlers squeezed Indian Territory.

Tensions between the Americans and the Indians exploded in the 1840s as miners, timber cutters, fishermen, and farmers poured into the future states. In many of these areas, Indians went from being labor to competition in a few years, making them the target of the military and vigilantes who sought to exterminate them.[3] In California, these tensions led to increased violence against the Indians and a plummeting population. In Oregon, it meant the Whitman massacre, as the Cayuse and Nez Perce attempted to push back the settlers, and the Rogue River War, as settlers squeezed Indian groups out of their territories.

The United States was not settled East to West as Frederick Jackson Turner suggested in his seminal essay on the closing of the American frontier.[4] Instead, the West Coast settled earlier than the Great Plains and the Mountain West, which saw their greatest immigration of settlers beginning just before the Civil War in the 1850s. The military frontier, though, did grow from East to West, as it attempted to secure the cross-country routes of immigrants to the West Coast. Indians in these regions remained independent even as the military frontier extended farther and farther into their territory. The military often treated these Indian groups as nations, as foreigners, and conflicts as war and not peacekeeping.

The acquisition of Texas, California, and Oregon after the Mexican-American War challenged the idea of leaving a boundary between the Indians and the Americans. It began to look as though Americans would eventually want the territory granted to the Indians and that they would want the territories between the Great Plains and the Pacific Coast. Driven by overland emigrants' complaints of Indian raids and Indian complaints of overland migrants' depredations, the U.S. government, with the help of the military, negotiated the Fort Laramie Treaty in 1851, which "specified tribal lands in the West for the first time."[5] And efforts to resolve tensions in the center of the West stopped there until after the Civil War, leaving open areas of conflict and tensions that flared up as the federal government turned its attention back east to the conflict brewing between the states. Removal solved nothing and instead created new areas of struggle.

THE CHEROKEE

The Cherokee and other Five Civilized nations occupy a unique place in the history of westward expansion and the Civil War. None of these nations or their members considered themselves as Americans nor did they strive to become Americans. They were Cherokee, Chickasaw, Choctaw, Creek, or Seminole, and sought to maintain their sovereignty up through the Civil War. Within each group, they differed over how to maintain their sovereignty and cultural identity, often walking a tightrope between the two tensions. These tensions led to splits within the nations, as some groups sought to adopt political methodologies from the Americans in order to secure their sovereignty, and others within each nation saw that as disruptive to the traditional cultural. The Cherokee provide one of the clearest and best-studied cases of these conflicts and struggles.[6]

Beginning with the French and Indian War (1756–1763), the Cherokee struggled to maintain their sovereignty in the face of a changing international landscape. Though they initially sided with the British, they changed their allegiance to the French in response to increased British settler encroachment during the war. Thus began what would become a familiar process of white squatters and the Euro-American inability to stop them. The British attempted to limit white encroachment after the French and Indian War with the Proclamation Line of 1763. This act prohibited British settlement west of the Appalachian Mountains, but it too failed to stem the tide. The Cherokee made an interesting choice at this juncture: they saw the colonists, not Britain, as their greatest enemy. Consequently, the Cherokee sided with the British during the American Revolution. They paid dearly for this allegiance as Americans "destroyed more than fifty towns, laid waste to fields, and killed livestock."[7] Once again, the Cherokee had to rebuild and regroup, both culturally and politically.

When the British defeated the French in the French and Indian War, England received France's right of discovery over the territories. This right meant "the British government recognized and accepted the rights of colonists and Indians to own and use their lands, govern themselves, shape their societies, and develop local economies." But the sovereign authority of England trumped all local efforts. For the Cherokee, this right meant they could continue to govern themselves through councils, set up their own economies and trading systems but remain under the oversight of the British. The British creation of the Proclamation Line demonstrated this belief. The Peace of Paris, signed in 1783 between the British and the Americans, "recognized the independence of the United States and conveyed to the new nation all of England's rights and claims to the land within its boundaries." Now, the United States became the sovereign authority, but the Cherokee assumed they would still maintain self-government and their own economies as they had before.[8]

The new Congress did not interpret it this way. It saw the Cherokee, as they did all Indian groups, as a defeated enemy, who should be dealt with as such. And, then, things got more complicated. In the early days of the Republic, when the government operated under the Articles of Confederation, Congress dealt with the Indians in the Northern colonies. South of the Ohio River, including Cherokee territory, the new Southern states treated the Indians as conquered nations. In other words, during the 1780s, the Cherokee found themselves under the thumb of individual states, like North Carolina and Georgia, who saw it as their right to deal with the Indians as they saw fit.[9] This pattern of states dealing with individual Indian nations would influence Cherokee–white relations well into the 19th century.

In 1785, the Cherokee signed the Treaty of Hopewell with the U.S. government, not the surrounding states. The treaty granted them the right to expel unwanted intruders and maintain their boundaries. It also signaled the beginning of their relationship with the relatively new federal government. The treaty failed as North Carolinians and Georgians continued to flood into Cherokee territory. Yet, the 1780s brought a change in relations between the Cherokee and the U.S. government. First, the United States stopped treating them as conquered enemies because the Indians, including the Cherokee, proved to be formidable in their military resistance to illegal settlement. In order to secure the frontier, the government sought to establish treaties with the Indian nations. This change in policy came just as the U.S. government reorganized under the Constitution, which placed "sole authority over Indian affairs in the hands of Congress and the president."[10] This reorganization cut the states out of the negotiation process. And it suggested to the Indians that the U.S. government treated them as almost equal nations, not as subordinate populations. The states disagreed with this interpretation because it limited their authority to grab more land. The Cherokee embraced this interpretation but not without internal conflicts and hesitation. In 1790, the first Indian Trade and Intercourse Act authorized the federal government to make treaties with the Indians and prohibited the states from doing so. Eventually, the Cherokee and the other Five Civilized Tribes would test this idea in court and in practice.

After struggling to maintain their territory throughout the American Revolution, the Cherokee began a rise to prominence in the Southeast at the end of the 18th century. Occupying land in western North Carolina, northern Georgia, eastern Tennessee, and southern West Virginia, the Cherokee had already transitioned to a more agricultural, staple crop society. The U.S. government supported and facilitated this change with the Treaty of Holston, which offered "plow, hoes, axes, spinning wheels, looms, and other equipment" for civilizing the Cherokee.[11] They traded with their white neighbors and hired some of them as blacksmiths, millers, and other skilled works. This interaction led to white intermarriages with the Cherokee.[12]

As more trade and intermarriage occurred, gender roles began to change. Prior to the American Revolution, women farmed and men hunted. As the Cherokee economy shifted more toward staple crops and mercantilism, social attitudes changed as well. Outsiders expected men to farm, but "most men flatly refused to engage in farming between spring tilling with horse and plow and harvest." They "engaged in commerce, herded livestock, and bought others to do their farming for them."[13] Following the law of unintended consequences, the new diversification of the economy led to the rise of bonded or slave labor.

Politically and socially, though, all was not well. In the 1790s, one group of Cherokee moved west attempting to avoid the cultural changes being brought by the mixed-race leaders. As the mixed-blood Cherokee became more like their Southern planter neighbors, this group rejected this transition.[14] They sought to remain traditional Cherokee, which meant hunting, farming, and tribal councils as opposed to Christianity, larger farms with bonded labor, new laws banning traditional forms of justice, the creation of a national government, and the adoption of American values.[15] In 1809, President Thomas Jefferson offered an exchange of land in the West for Cherokee land in the East. A group of Cherokee, under the assistance of Return Meigs, their Indian Agent, moved to Arkansas but soon discovered they did not possess clear title to the new land.[16] Two waves of settlers set out West: one settling first on the Mississippi and then the Texas frontiers; the other in Illinois and Arkansas. These two groups became known as the Old Settlers, eventually forming the Western Cherokee government in the early 19th century.

These moves west by small groups of Cherokee caused consternation within the nation. Though welcoming economic changes from the United States, the Cherokee maintained traditional ideas of "common title to land and resisted any attempt to allot the Cherokee domain to individuals. They also began to take steps to preserve their land base from sale by self-interested individuals."[17] Cherokee trading land in the West for that in the East appeared to violate these ideas, and the new National Council moved to ban such moves in 1809. While economically the Cherokee saw a diversification of their society, with some leaders and members becoming merchants and others focusing on becoming farmers, they still saw themselves as part of an interconnected nation where one's decisions impacted the lives of others.

In 1803, the Eastern Cherokee, referring to those who remained in the Southeast, sped up the process of acculturation and changed the structure and makeup of the nation. They invited white Protestant missionaries to come to their territory and start schools and churches.[18] American leaders interpreted this request as the Cherokee understanding white Protestant superiority, and they put out calls to raise money to support these efforts.[19] For the Cherokee, the request represented an understanding of how the region around them was changing and an attempt to stay on top of that change. "Comfortable with their own cultural orientation, Cherokees took full advantage of the lessons they found useful and ignored those they did not."[20] The request to the American Board of Commissioners for Foreign Missionaries extended this practice. The Cherokee sought to build schools that would teach their children

English and help acculturate them to American ways, while at the same time they retained their Cherokee ways at home. Eventually, this shift enabled the rise of a mixed-blood and bicultural population to secure their power within the nation.

By the early 19th century, the Cherokee nation exuded success in American terms, with farms, both large and small, a tradition of sending their top young men to seminary in the Northeast, and a burgeoning slave economy.[21] In many ways, the Cherokee had far more in common with the planter and yeoman class of farmers in the Southeast than they did with Indians in the Northeast and the West: a rising property class, the increased use of bonded labor, and a growing market economy. But not everyone embraced these changes. More Cherokee settlers moved west to join the groups there, as the process of state formation within the Cherokee nation gained momentum between 1810 and the late 1820s. A majority of these Cherokee settlers came from North Carolina and Tennessee, whereas the growing elite within the Eastern Cherokee came from Alabama and Georgia.[22] Those that moved west during this second period owned less property, few slaves, and tended to speak only Cherokee. These differences would become important in later Cherokee politics and in the Civil War.

Often forgotten, the Old Settlers represent typical settlers during this time period. Like the settlers in Illinois or other states in the Old Northwest, they moved for economic and political reasons.[23] Other groups, like the Chickasaw and Creek, also saw people move west into the unclaimed land that would become the territories of Mississippi, Arkansas, and Illinois. And like other settlers, these Indian settlers tried to take advantage of structures already in place: requesting land from the Spanish and Mexican governments, trying to solidify land claims through the U.S. federal government. They arrived in the new lands, established homes and farms, and started businesses.

The Cherokee, both those in Illinois and Arkansas, and those in Mississippi and Texas, encountered hostility from Americans in the West, who entered the same frontier. The Cherokee in Arkansas struggled with the Osage, who resented the appearance of the Cherokee in their territory.[24] These tensions increased when a second group of 1,100 Cherokee moved to Arkansas in 1811.[25] By 1817, an additional 7,000 Cherokee had joined these settlements.[26] Throughout the 1820s, war ensued when the Cherokee and Choctaw joined with "roving bands of Shawnees, Delawares, and Kickapoo" against the Osage.[27] These conflicts continued for the next 10 years and forced some Cherokee settlers into Texas from the north.

Soon, American settlers followed and demanded the land on which the Cherokee lived. As states rose up around them, Illinois in 1818 and Arkansas later in 1836, the pressure to move farther west rose, as well. Though the white settlers liked to trade with the Cherokee, they coveted Cherokee land. In 1819, the Cherokee traded land in the East for land in the West, in the newly established Indian Territory.[28] Known as the Old Settlers, in 1828, the Western Cherokee signed a treaty with the federal government, taking land in present-day Oklahoma.[29] At this point, one quarter of the Cherokee nation lived west of the Mississippi, including those in Mississippi and Texas who faced land competition, as well.[30]

When the Cherokee, Chickasaw, and Creek moved into Mississippi, it was unsettled territory and they had the same right to it as American squatters. Eventually, American settlers and Mississippi statehood in 1817 forced the Cherokee and the others into Texas, still under Spanish control. There, they sought an official grant from the Spanish, and eventually the Mexican government.[31] Instead, they signed a treaty that granted them the right "to select land and plant crops." The agreement did not give the Cherokee title. They ran into two roadblocks: Texas Indians who did not want more settlers in their territories, be they Americans or Indians, and Americans moving into Texas who did not come to Texas to be surrounded by Indians. Even as the Cherokee sought title, a group of Shawnee gained land and title, an upsetting development for the Americans in Texas.[32]

For political survival, the Cherokee formed two alliances. First, they joined with smaller Texas tribes who struggled, like everyone else, with the Comanche and their constant raids. Various groups, like the Alabama, Coushatta, and Tonkawa, fought to maintain their land, not just from American squatters but also from constant incursions by the Comanche. The Comanche controlled much of the Texas frontier in the early 19th century. Tonkawa and other small Indian groups, as well as the small Spanish population, found themselves under attack and sought help from the new Cherokee settlers. So, the Cherokee built a tenuous alliance with the Spanish. This alliance built relationships and established that the Cherokee were more interested in settlement than in raiding, like the Comanche.[33]

American settlers represented a bigger threat than the Comanche. They came into Texas in the 1820s and applied for *colonias*, or land grants, from the Mexican government, just as the Cherokee had. Unlike the Cherokee, who found their requests ignored or delayed, the government granted most of the Americans' requests. The new colonists agreed to abide by Mexican law and raise their children as Catholics, though many ignored this last stipulation.[34] Stephen Austin, leader of one of the fastest growing *colonias*, saw the Indians as troubling.[35] He complained that the leader of the Cherokee "is secretly making great efforts to unite all the Indian tribes of Texas in a confederation to destroy the new settlements."[36] Though the Comanche rarely raided as far south as Austin's colony, Stephen Austin argued they posed a threat to his settlements. He eventually succeeded in removing the Tonkawa and Karankawa Indians as a preemptive strike. Portraying the Cherokee as a threat, including accusing them of cannibalism, the Americans lumped them with the Comanche. The Spanish acquiesced to the Americans demands. By 1825, the Cherokee found themselves disenfranchised again, as the Mexican government granted the land on which they lived to American settlers. Despite their need to settle East Texas and secure it from the French, the American government, and the Comanche, the Spanish government still balked at granting land to a an Indian group, like the Cherokee or the Alabama. They thought the American settlers would be easier to control. Eventually, the Mexican government saw the rising American population as a threat because they bristled under Mexican control.

Austin, though, did see some use in having Cherokees in Texas. Though he feared they would create an alliance with the Wichita, Comanche, and other immigrant Indians against the Americans, he hoped to use the Cherokee as a bulwark against the same alliance.[37] In many ways, the American settlers and the immigrant Cherokee shared similar goals and desires. Despite seeming conflicts between the Cherokee and the new American settlers, in 1826, the Cherokee allied with some of those American settlers during the Fredonian Rebellion, a precursor to the Texas Revolution. The Fredonians tried to split from the Mexican territory and establish themselves as Americans or Cherokee. "By resorting to force the former [Americans] hoped to protect their rights and liberties; the latter [the Cherokee] saw in it the last hope of realizing their cherished plans for forming an Indian country."[38] Both the Americans and the Cherokee wanted to control their land. The Fredonians even designed a flag with two bars, one red and one white, to symbolize the alliance between the Americans and the Cherokee. Although the Americans and the Cherokee appeared to be united in their desire for control of land as Fredonians, the Mexican government realized this weakness in the alliance. It offered the Cherokee land farther west, if they would not aid the Fredonians and help hold the line against the Comanche in the West.[39] When the rebellion collapsed, the Cherokee executed the Cherokee participants "in a fit of unnecessary retribution."[40] The Cherokee took the deal only to be forced out of Texas in the 1830s by Americans who saw them as a threat. They joined their brethren in Arkansas.

The Cherokee's experiences in Arkansas and Texas demonstrate the complexity of life on the frontier. Opportunities for alliances appeared, either with other Indian groups or with the Americans or the Spanish. But these alliances came with a price: warfare, loss of sovereignty, removal. Additionally, the events in Texas show how the Cherokee had learned to play by the rules of the Americans and the Mexicans, seeking alliances, land grants, and support. They still maintained a healthy distrust of non-Cherokee, and the Americans and Spanish still viewed the Cherokee as savage and unpredictable.

At the beginning of the 19th century, the Cherokee made a choice: to adapt and adopt language, economic structure, and education from the Americans who began to surround their nation. The printing press provides a good example of these adaptations. "The Cherokee Council provided the funds" and the missionaries "made arrangements for the purchase of the press and types in both English and the syllabary invented by Sequoyah." Additionally, the Cherokee Nation "used the press to print the newspaper, and the missionaries used it to print" religious documents, like translations of the Bible.[41] These sorts of decisions led to one of the first political and cultural splits within the Cherokee. Those that went west over the first 25 years of the 19th century encountered problems similar to those encountered by white American settlers in Illinois, Arkansas, Texas, and Mississippi, including tensions with other Indian nations. Despite common challenges, the white American settlers saw the Cherokee as a threat. As the Old Settlers sought to secure a western homeland, they crossed international boundaries and made alliances and choices, which shaped their response to the arrival of the Eastern Cherokee after the U.S. government forced them west.

The process of the removal and the ensuing fight increased the political divisions within the Cherokee that resonated through the Civil War. The Cherokee and other Southeastern Indians that moved west, by choice and by force, maintained cultural ties within their nations and outside their nations with Southern whites. They shared slavery and certain cultural and political ideas, such as ideas about class structure and the importance of religion within society, with their white Southern neighbors. Their experience on the frontier, including conflicts with Western, more nomadic Indians, provided a commonality with other frontier pioneers. They viewed themselves as the forefront of Indian and American societies. As John Rollin Ridge, son of the Cherokee leader John Ridge, wrote in 1850, the Indians east of the Mississippi "have manifested the traits upon which the immemorial ideas of Indian heroism, nobility of character and dignity of thought are founded."[42] On the other hand, they saw the Plains Indians as savage and backward, just as whites viewed both Cherokee and Plains Indians. And, like other immigrants into new territories, they relied on the federal government to help police their borders, pay annuities, and at times settle internal tribal disputes. The Cherokee represent an important test case of removal and its consequences for burgeoning attempts at nationhood. All these shaped their responses to the Civil War and the tensions that resonated throughout the Indian Territory.

EASTERN CHEROKEE

Meanwhile, the Eastern Cherokee continued to move toward nationhood as defined by the Americans. With this pursuit came the rise of class divisions and the adoption of slavery. The Eastern Cherokee, though they called themselves just Cherokee, underwent a rapid period of cultural and political change between 1800 and 1828. These changes created tensions and disruptions within the tribe or nation that would resonate throughout the Civil War period.[43]

Prior to the 1820s, the Cherokee defined tribal membership strictly through one's mother. Clan and citizenship came through the maternal line. This practice allowed for intermarriage with both whites and black, as long as the woman was Cherokee. A black father and a Cherokee mother begat a Cherokee child. This structure allowed for the growing number of mixed-blood members who emerged from these marriages. The matrilineal structure remained despite changing gender roles within the nation, as the Cherokee adapted their gender roles to the acceptable ones of the British, and then the Americans.

Even as the Cherokee adopted cultural attitudes from their neighbors and attempted to accrue political power through nationhood, they suffered land losses. By 1800, they ceded land in Kentucky, Tennessee, and North Carolina. These land cessions consolidated the territory and forced factions into the center of the nation. They also led to a transition from subsistence farming to market farming for many. This transition required more land and more labor, helping aid in the expansion and justification for slavery within the Cherokee nation.[44] By the 1820s, slavery began to take hold within the Cherokee, or at least within the leadership of the Cherokee.[45] By 1835, enslaved Africans represented 9 percent of the Eastern Cherokee population.[46] The rise of a planter class, many of whom were mixed-blood, led to political and cultural changes to help them maintain and expand their power.

As slavery developed and expanded as an institution, racial ideas followed.[47] Though less mob violence emerged toward slaves, slavery in the Cherokee resembled slavery in the rest of the U.S. South.[48] Slavery grew slowly, both in the East and the West of the Cherokee Nation.[49] Though slaves remained less than 10 percent of the population, their existence challenged traditional Cherokee ideas about race and membership. In the Cherokee nation, the slave-owning class represented a mixed group of intermarried whites and half-bloods. As these groups rose into leadership, they sought to solidify their power through new definitions of Cherokee citizenship and maintain their own economic dominance.[50]

In the late 1700s, law enforcement consisted of the law of revenge, leaving the decision for punishment to the clans.[51] This form of justice focused on the restoration of the community rather than on the economic value of the crime. Beginning in 1808, when the Cherokee established a police force, the leading elites began to make the Cherokee tribe into a nation that the Americans and Europeans would recognize.[52] As they shifted toward a police force, the Council developed a more centralized government which supplanted town authority and clan powers. They banned clan revenge and shifted away from granting citizenship through matrilineal descent.[53] These changes, which appeared to result from white political pressure, continued to drive Cherokee west.[54] By leaving the eastern territory, those who joined the Old Settlers in the West, abdicated their power to the mixed-bloods that stayed behind.

Between 1810 and 1828, when the Cherokee wrote and passed a constitution, they began the transition to a government more like the U.S. federal one. They divided the Eastern Cherokee nation into eight electoral districts with a bicameral legislature. "The elected council made laws, established a treasury, and police force and "created a court system based on Anglo-Saxon procedures."[55] The move to a more formalized legal system emerged as the mixed-blood elite acquired more property, and "the vast majority of Cherokees followed the lines of descent and had little personal property for the Light Horse to guard."[56] The elites banned traditional forms of justice that did not take economic value into account. The shift to formal justice moved the Cherokee toward a more individualized society.

In particular, the Cherokee elite began to differentiate between clan and central government, and solidified power so that fewer people participated in the changes.[57] Most Cherokee embraced "the centralization of . . . government because it seemed the best way to protect the common title to their homeland and their integrity as a nation."[58] Leaders figured that looking and acting like a nation would only enhance their standing and negotiations with the United States. Realizing that the treaties they signed with the British and Americans granted them rights as a nation, they sought to legitimate these rights in ways recognized by those same nations.[59] They did not necessarily care or consider what the states growing around them believed about their status, focusing on federal recognition instead.

Leaders at the time saw the political shift toward a unified central government, and the cultural change toward a market economy and bilingualism as a solidification of Cherokee culture and a way to preserve it. The leaders believed such shifts would allow them sovereignty and control over their culture and society. Instead, these changes led to divisions. Education aggravated this split. In 1821, Sequoyah created a written syllabary for the Cherokee.[60] This accomplishment allowed the Cherokee to record business and life in their own language, rather than in English. Some remained Cherokee speakers only. Linguistically, divisions based on language emerged within the Eastern Cherokee. At the same time, more students attended English-speaking schools, increasing the number of bilingual, and bicultural, members of the Cherokee. Bilingual students were most likely to leave the nation for further education, where they developed ties with powerful whites. These educated mixed-bloods were the most likely to become slave owners.

Literacy and education influenced the writing of the Constitution. The Cherokee believed that the treaties where they ceded land helped create their basis for nationhood, because by signing treaties with them, the United States treated them as a nation.[61] They understood that seeing themselves as a nation was not the same as the United States seeing themselves as a nation, an issue many Western tribes would struggle with during this period. The Cherokee needed to act like a nation and separate themselves from U.S. perceptions of Indians in general, if they were to enter nationhood. Simply calling themselves a "nation of Southern Indians," as they did in the *Phoenix* newspaper in 1828, did not make them one in the eyes of the United States.[62]

To enhance this argument, the Cherokee wrote a constitution based on the American one in 1828. The Cherokee Constitution reflected an attempt to define citizenship more like the U.S. government and more like their neighboring states. While excluding anyone of African descent, free or slave, it also gave power to its writers. It embraced Christianity and the beliefs about humans that went with it. Yet, to try and maintain balance between the factions, the Eastern Cherokee Constitution banned ministers from office and tried to keep traditional ideas about clans and citizenship. But it now focused on male leaders of Cherokee blood.[63] In the new Constitution, one's father defined one's membership in the nation, not one's mother. The Cherokee became patrilineal, like their neighbors.

Modeled on the U.S. Constitution, many Eastern Cherokee leaders saw the Constitution's passage as a solidification of their nationhood. The new rising leaders had learned their lessons well at missionary schools and from the surrounding neighbors. The Cherokee Constitution represented a desire to prove to the powers that be that the Cherokee were more white than black, more like the Southern planters around them than like the slaves owned by those planters. "Cherokees identified more closely with whites, not just because of physical appearance but also in a perceived appearance of power and success."[64] Thus, the Constitution of 1828 defined citizenship within the Cherokee nation (East) differently than it had been perceived before.

The Constitution defined citizenship through free Cherokee males. Children of Cherokee men and slave women could not be Cherokee citizens.[65] This codification signified two changes. First, if the Constitution recognized the marriage of slaves, it recognized their human status. Second, clans no longer controlled citizenship. The Constitution legitimated changes that had been coming since the establishment of the police force. By 1828, clans did not mete out punishments nor did they define who could be Cherokee. Now, the nation did.

Who represented the nation had narrowed by 1828, as educated, bicultural, and bilingual elites wrote the Constitution. Those elites felt paternalistic toward the less educated common Cherokee.[66] It also protected the rising middle class who owned the most property. The Constitution regulated interracial marriage, both for whites and blacks. While excluding people of African descent from being citizens, the Constitution also limited the rights and political participation of whites who intermarried with Cherokee women.[67] As power became solidified in the hands of a few mixed-bloods in the East, changes in the surrounding area heightened tensions within the Cherokee and forced a conflict with Georgia.

The Old Settlers and the Eastern Cherokee, from 1800 to 1830s, sought land and security, but they defined security differently. Both wanted to protect their culture and society. The Old Settlers pursued this protection by moving west to avoid American influence. The Eastern Cherokee embraced American influence, hoping it would help define their sovereignty and their race in a way recognizable to their white neighbors. This division grew into other divisions over slavery and the future of the Cherokee, once the Eastern Cherokee rejoined the Old Settlers in the West.

CONFLICT AND REMOVAL

Not all who disagreed with changes within the Cherokee Nation went west. During 1826 and 1827, White Path's rebellion swelled against missionaries to the Cherokee nation and the nationalists, who proposed a constitution, which would fundamentally change the definition of Cherokee and shape a government to look more like the United States. Lasting only a year, it exemplified the recurring tensions over acculturation and political change. White Path and his followers did not reject all acculturation, but they wanted the Cherokee to remain as a distinct people, not a version of the Americans.[68] Though he called for the rejection of the Constitution, White Path eventually served in the Cherokee legislature. The rebellion, while short lived, illustrates the continuing debate about the direction of the Cherokee nation. Outside threats against sovereignty did more to quell the rebellion (and other dissenting movements) than compromise and concession.[69]

Even as the Cherokee sought to solidify their position as a sovereign nation, those actions appeared threatening to the populations around them. The Cherokee Constitution irritated Georgia, bordered by the large Cherokee nation to the north and the Creek to the south. Georgians saw it as a way for the Cherokee to deny them access to Cherokee lands, which in the eyes of Georgia fell within their territory. In 1828, the Cherokee discovered gold on their land. For the Georgians, this discovery represented yet another resource on Cherokee land that belonged to the Americans. Georgia promptly encouraged white intrusion onto Cherokee land to mine gold. The Cherokee expelled many of these illegal miners, demonstrating their sovereignty.

The Georgia legislature responded to this perceived threat and the new resources by passing anti-Cherokee laws in 1829, an attempt to prove to the Cherokee that the land belonged to Georgia and not the Cherokee nation. Georgia intended these laws to challenge Cherokee nationhood. The laws required that all Cherokee living within Georgia's territory become subject to Georgia's laws, as of June 1, 1830. Because of the large-scale agriculture in the Cherokee nation, their lands were productive and developed, making them particularly attractive to white settlers and the states. Having just removed the Creek through similar methods, the Georgians saw no reason not to remove the Cherokee.[70] With their Constitution and treaties with the federal government in hand, the Cherokee ignored these laws and sought help from the federal government, whom they considered their equal. The Cherokee were not the Creek. They had a constitution, a market economy, and laws and law enforcement.

They did not see themselves as Indians living in Georgia but as Cherokee living in the Cherokee nation.[71]

By the 1830s, treaties and negotiations had shrunk Cherokee Territory to the borderlands of North Carolina, Tennessee, Georgia, and Alabama.[72] As the Cherokee nation underwent cultural and political changes between 1800 and the 1830s, some Cherokee moved west to remain traditional. As they left, tensions still remained with the nation, tensions that the situation with Georgia and the federal government exacerbated. In 1830, Congress passed the Federal Indian Removal Act, stipulating that the Cherokee should move west of the Mississippi into what had been deemed Indian Territory, essentially rejoining the Old Settlers. The Cherokee immediately lobbied their allies in Congress expecting a stay, at minimum if not an outright appeal. At the same time, the Cherokee sued Georgia over the state's Indian Removal Act in 1831. The Supreme Court sided with Georgia, deeming the Cherokee a domestic dependent nation. This ruling meant the Cherokee had to abide by the laws of the United States, and by extension, Georgia.

Emboldened by this decision, in 1831, Georgia began to survey Cherokee territory for a land lottery to distribute gold mine claims. Georgia banned the Cherokee from participating in these lotteries because they lacked U.S. citizenship.[73] Ignoring the treaties between the Cherokee and the U.S. federal government, and ignoring the Cherokee Constitution, Georgia began to give away Cherokee land, opening it to miners and development, though much of it was already under production by the Cherokee. Essentially, Georgia granted land in another nation to its own citizens, while denying the owners their rights because they lacked U.S. citizenship. Even though many Cherokee had economic and familial ties to Georgia, the state's actions soured these relationships.

A year later, another case came before the Supreme Court, *Worcester v. Georgia*. Samuel Worcester, a Presbyterian missionary captured and tortured by the Georgia militia, argued that his rights had been violated when Georgia essentially left the United States and Georgia territory to enforce Georgian laws. The Supreme Court agreed with him, to a point. It deemed the Cherokee a "distinct community in which the laws of Georgia can have no force."[74] The court vacated Georgia's conviction of Worcester. More importantly, for the Cherokee and for the conflicts that lay ahead, the Supreme Court made it clear that only the federal government could deal with the Indians, including the Cherokee. Though they were not equals under the law, the United States inherited the responsibilities of Britain in dealing with the Indians. In other words, states' rights had no place in Indian relations. Though it might appear that the Cherokee had won their right to stay, they did not. The Federal Indian Removal Act now took precedence and the Cherokee faced being forced west. Though all Cherokee east of the Mississippi disagreed with these decisions, they did not agree on how to respond. The Cherokee did not accept this state of affairs passively. Instead, the leaders of the Eastern Cherokee responded through the proper channels for a nation: lawsuits, meetings with U.S. senators and lobbyists, letters to the President.[75] Through economic and social connections, several Cherokee leaders had attended schools with the current Congressmen where they found some sympathetic ears. But Georgia found help in Congressmen from Tennessee and North Carolina, who also saw a chance to gain valuable developed territory for their states.

Two important leaders emerged during this period: John Ross and Elias Boudinot. Ross served as Principal Chief of the Cherokee Nation from 1828 to 1866, covering removal, reorganization, and the Civil War.[76] Boudinot represented the rising new mercantile and educated class. Educated at a missionary boarding school, he married the daughter of one of the missionaries and became the influential editor of the *Cherokee Phoenix*.[77] Initially, Ross and Boudinot approached allies in Washington to help. When both groups went to Washington in 1834, President Jackson and his allies embraced the Treaty Party, led by Boudinot, snubbing Ross and his party.[78] Though the majority of Cherokee resisted removal, Boudinot and the Treaty Party negotiated a treaty to try and preserve their resources.[79] The Treaty Party was not the elite class, nor the traditionals, nor the common Indians. They owned slaves, like the elites, but owned a smaller number per owner than the elites. Unlike the elites, who made their money through commerce, they grew corn for the market economy. Additionally, they remained on the periphery politically. None of the signers of the Treaty of New Echota had participated in the creation of the Cherokee Constitution and only two had held elective offices.[80] Though the leaders of the Treaty Party originally supported tribal unity against Georgia and the federal government, by 1833 they saw the futility of this position.[81] Eventually, this small minority of Cherokee, led by Boudinot, feared forced removal and its consequences for the unity of the nation. Thus, signing the Treaty of New Echota allowed them to preserve their assets (slaves) and negotiate a land swap to allow them to continue cultivation.[82] But self-removal was a middle-class choice. Poorer Cherokee stayed behind between 1828 and 1838.[83] The signing of the treaty, the relinquishing of land, and the treaty's stipulation that slavery could not be abolished in the Cherokee Nation all set the stage for future conflicts.[84]

The Treaty Party exchanged land in the Eastern Cherokee nation for land in Indian Territory in December 1835. Slavery moved west with the Treaty Party.[85] Though they had little support within the Eastern Cherokee Nation, the federal government welcomed the Treaty Party with open arms.[86] Other Eastern Cherokee saw the Treaty Party as traitors—acting as individuals and not as a nation. A new crack emerged within the Cherokee over the removal. By 1838, the Cherokee existed as three factions: "the western Cherokees (later called the Old Settlers), the Removal (or Treaty) party, and the Patriot (or Ross) party." These divisions did not represent mild political differences. "In 1819, the eastern Cherokees had formally disowned as expatriates those Cherokees who moved west and refused to recognize them as a separate Cherokee Nation." The signing of the Treaty of New Echota completed a breach that had been coming for a while. After the removal, the two different parties' relationships with the federal government would continue to play out. And both the Union and the Confederacy did not understand how deep the fissures ran within the Cherokee Nation.[87]

The Treaty Party moved west in 1838, bearing with them the Cherokee Constitution. When they arrived in Indian Territory, they needed to work out power sharing with the Old Settlers already there. The Old Settlers governed in a more traditional manner with the clans still maintaining more power. The Treaty Party had embraced a more patrilineal model. The Old Settlers moved west to preserve their culture and not be forced to assimilate. That assimilation found them, now. The old tension over what it meant to be Cherokee reemerged on the Western frontier and under the worst circumstances. Now, the question became: How were the Eastern and Western Cherokee going to coexist after the final emigration?[88]

In June 1838, the federal government sent federal troops and state militias to remove the remaining Cherokee, known to other Cherokees as the National Party or Patriot Party, from their lands. The U.S. military corralled those that they caught in stockades, like cattle, and executed those who resisted. Some, as they were forced from their homes with wagons full of their possessions, watched whites move into their homes directly. The long march, which became known as the Trail of Tears, headed westward. Through poor planning and bad timing, the army that escorted them on the 1,500-mile march ran out of supplies and had to constantly buy or scrounge food from local communities. These same communities came out to attack the Cherokee, throwing stones, mud, and insults. Even the commander of the removal complained about the inhumane treatment. Disease, starvation, and hardship left 30 percent of the Cherokee on the Trail of Tears dead. They arrived in the Indian Territory with few resources, in a land unlike theirs, prairie with less water, few trees, and no housing. Ross had stood for Cherokee sovereignty, resisted removal, and refused to sell or settle under the belief that the Cherokee Nation would withstand the outside threats. He now arrived in the Indian Territory as a weakened principal chief of a divided people, split over what it meant to be Cherokee or a nation. By the time the National Party arrived in the Indian Territory, at least three political groups existed, complicating the future of the nation.

FIVE CIVILIZED TRIBES AS SETTLERS

The year 1839 opened with increased conflict within the Cherokee Nation, including guerrilla warfare and assassinations.[89] Ross and his followers expected to dominate the government in the West. They had the numbers to do it, with 14,000 members versus with roughly 5,000 Cherokee in the West.[90] But the Old Settlers and the Treaty

Party had time and local connections on their side. The Western Cherokee invited the new arrivals to a conference in 1839 at Takatoka. John Brown, principal chief of the Western Cherokee, stated, "We joyfully welcome you to our country."[91] Yet he made it clear that while the new emigrants could participate in the Western Cherokee nation, they could not import their own government and structures.[92] The federal government froze the annuity and removal payments during the controversy between the Old Settlers, the Treaty Party, and the National Party; the Cherokee nation had borrowed significant amounts of money, incurring severe debt.[93] By November 1839, dueling Cherokee delegations arrived in Washington. The Old Settlers/Treaty Party proposed splitting the territory into two, because the Treaty Party feared revenge from Ross's faction and the Old Settlers suspected they might be disenfranchised by them.[94] The Old Settlers and the Treaty Party initially united against Ross's party to resist the growth and power of the government.[95] Having worked out their differences, they did not look forward to reviving conflict.

The Old Settlers, the Treaty Party, and the National Party differed on several issues, besides their responses to removal. The National Party, which passed the 1819 law against individual land cessions, viewed the Old Settlers and Treaty Party as traitors deserving of death for signing treaties giving up land. Relations between the groups descended into chaos, when in 1839, less than a year after removal and several months after the conference at Takatoka, assassins killed Boudinot and John Ridge, both of the Treaty Party.[96] The assassination "proved disastrous for Ross's effort to attain tribal unity and stability."[97] Boudinot and Ridge became martyrs for those who felt the Treaty Party tried to remain true Cherokees. The assassinations became another sign of Ross's grasp for control, even though he did not order or participate in them.

The Western Cherokee had set up a very different type of government from the one imported from the East. Though the Western Cherokee wrote a constitution in the 1820s, they still relied on a clan system and more traditional means of power.[98] The Eastern Cherokee had adopted a more western style of government, with districts and a judicial system which meted out punishment. In other words, one government relied on community policing and the other relied on the rule of law. Yet, members of the National Party assassinated political enemies.

The Western Cherokee, or Old Settlers, had lived a simpler and more isolated life with less pressure from whites.[99] They maintained small farms without bonded labor. The leaders of the National Party owned the most slaves within the nation. Though the Treaty Party brought slaves with them, the National Party brought many more slaves to the West, creating an additional political and economic wedge between the groups. The number of slaves, though, still remained low. Nonetheless, slavery became another sore point between the three groups. Clashes occurred over abolition, seeing missionaries as the primary targets of this conflict. The Christian Cherokee, which included the Treaty Party and National Party members, split along different lines just as national Protestant denominations did at this time.[100] The government in the West feared abolitionists would come into the nation and add to the troubles. All Protestant missionaries became suspect in the eyes of the Cherokee government, which told them explicitly not to preach about abolition.

Christianity, in general, created tensions within the new western nation. Not all the Cherokee were Christians. And even within the Christian Cherokee community, divisions existed between denominations. These divisions created more tensions and conflict. Temperance emerged as one of those flash points. In much of the Christian Cherokee, temperance took root. The National Party embraced temperance, seeing it as a way to reject outside influence and reunite the community. Old Settlers rejected temperance seeing it as a cultural form of outside influence.[101] Economics complicated the moral debate. An active liquor trade from Arkansas increased tensions over temperance as alcohol became an important piece of commerce in a struggling economy.[102] Banning liquor endangered the fragile economy.

The power struggle did not remain an internal one. The Old Settlers/Treaty Party appealed to the local federal commander across the border in Arkansas for support and protection.[103] They asked the federal agent at Fort Gibson if they could receive all the annuities due to the Cherokee Nation. Previously, the U.S. government split the payments between the Eastern and Western governments. By claiming all the annuities, the Western Cherokee asserted themselves as the only legal government. Ross immediately went to Washington to gather support. "Ross did not want the Old Settlers in charge of the funds due the emigrants under the treaty, which were supposed to go for the cost of removal, claims for property destroyed or left in the East and per capita payments."[104] Both groups sought federal help in defining the Cherokee nation in the West, as federal funds hung in the balance. Ross wanted a unified nation to help garner more funds.[105] The Western Cherokee wanted to be reimbursed for their costs of moving West. The fact that both sides had connections into the federal government signified the complex relationships between the Cherokee and the U.S. government. Yet, "most Old Settlers continued to resist the act of union, and the Treaty Party bitterly opposed" the National Party.[106] As Ross pushed for stability yet continued to demonize the opposition, some in the Old Settlers and Treaty Party chose to become "marauders, horse thieves, robbers, barn burners, and murderers, bent on creating terrorism in the nation."[107] They found support among the Old Settlers and Treaty Party, who hid them, and whites in Arkansas, who viewed the assassination with disgust. Like any other frontier community, violence existed.[108] Yet, outsiders saw these interactions as the inherent savagery of the Indian, not the intertribal and internecine warfare of political and economic rivals.[109] For the Cherokee and white alike, "political violence and common crime" became indistinguishable.[110] The assassination not only damaged internal politics, but also played into stereotypes about Indians outside the nation. To whites in Arkansas and Texas, the Cherokee seemed no less civilized than the Comanche or the Osage.

The lines between the political groups were not as clear as outsiders wanted to believe they were. Not all Old Settlers supported the marauders and not all of the National Party approved of the assassination or Ross's negotiations. The intertwined relationships made the choices in the Civil War more difficult for both sides. The Western Cherokee had learned to rely on the federal government for trade and protection against other Indians and white squatters. The Eastern Cherokee saw the federal government in Washington as both the engineer of their removal and the institution that owed them money and political clout for that intervention. Finally, financial differences existed, as well. The Eastern Cherokee arrived destitute from removal, in debt from paying for resettlement, and anxious for a fiscal settlement from the U.S. government.[111] Though the leaders of Ross's party tended to be well-off, many of the other supporters had been small farmers who bore the brunt of removal. The Old Settlers occupied the best land already, making it hard for the new farmers to get established. Already established by the time the National Party arrived, the Treaty Party had been able to move slaves and resources and rebounded the fastest economically of all the removed groups, adding to the tensions between the parties.[112]

Yet, in other ways, the most recent emigrants into the Western Cherokee territory found a situation similar to what emigrants into other new communities would. Like other emigrants, Cherokee families tried to clear land, build log cabins, and obtain plows to sustain daily life. Described as "pioneers with no resources except their own hands, their traditional craftsmanship, their native ingenuity," the Cherokee struggled to build a new community in the West from a new environment.[113] Many arrived without farm tools and few livestock, and entered an environment unlike the one with which they were familiar.[114] Additionally, though the Treaty of New Echota required the U.S. government to supply rations, corruption and price gouging reduced these supplies. This problem led to widespread food shortages for poor and recently arrived Cherokee.[115] Based on tribal tradition, the Old Settlers and Treaty Party provided food and supplies to the new arrivals.[116] Even as political turmoil swirled the nation, individuals sought reconciliation to try and create a unified community. Like other emigrant groups to the West, including the Old Settlers in their initial move to the west, the National Party struggled with unfamiliar soil, climate, drought, and disease. Arriving with few resources, the National Party "had more in common with poor white and European immigrants to new territories than the Old Settlers and the Treaty Party."[117] These economic stresses increased the tensions and mayhem that ruled between 1839 and 1846.[118]

In 1846, the federal government forced Ross's hand and he signed the Treaty of 1846. By signing this treaty, Ross accepted $5 million for the Cherokee and formally recognized the Old Settlers, the Treaty Party, and the Cherokee who remained in the

East as legitimate Cherokee. The settlement greatly reduced the per capita payment to Ross's group "who had borne the brunt of the removal process." Yet, he gained political control as the Old Settlers "gave up their claim as sole owner" of the western territory. Besides other financial stipulations, the treaty also dissolved the lighthorse police, installed civil law, and granted amnesty for all crimes committed in the previous seven years, including the assassins of the Ridges and Boudinot.[119] Politically, the treaty granted Ross a lot of power, both political and economic.

By the 1850s, the political controversy had settled down, yet remained simmering under the surface. The Cherokee focused on establishing their frontier communities, like the other groups did. Like other frontiersmen, Ross realized the need for capital to jump start development in the new Western Cherokee nation. He hoped to use some of the settlement funds to establish a Cherokee National bank. Though, by 1851, money flowed into the Cherokee Nation through restitution payments, little remained to fund Ross's proposed bank. The lack of their own bank hampered economic development, making the Cherokee reliant on whites for loans and economic stimulus.

As the political turmoil calmed down, the average Cherokee settled into building and rebuilding their farms. Though many Cherokee farmers dealt with drought throughout the 1850s, the Cherokee also owned extensive saltworks, lead, coal, and timber resources. Thus, the Cherokee developed their roads and bridges to aid in the development of these resources. William McLoughlin credits the Cherokee's economic successes during this period to lessons learned between 1794 and 1840.[120] Like the Mormons, their hardships taught them valuable economic and political lessons which they applied to the new frontier.

The next priority for the Cherokee became the establishment of schools. In 1841, the Cherokee council created a public school system.[121] Previously, the Old Settlers had relied on missionary schools to educate their children, opening them up, ironically, to assimilation.[122] In the new territory, they created independent schools, run by the Cherokee, to educate Cherokee students. Though missionary schools did exist, and the tribal government regulated them, the nation wanted to create a school system more like those found in the East than what the missionaries offered.[123] Yet, the school system ended up exacerbating divisions within the nation rather than healing them.

In 1851, the Cherokee built the women's and men's seminaries to help produce Cherokee teachers and reduced the number of white missionary educators in the nation. Based on Mount Holyoke College in the Northeast, the Cherokee hired teachers from the Northeast to best replicate the curriculum and interests of the programs. With a required entrance exam, the seminaries only accepted less than half of 1 percent of the students in the nation. They tended to be mixed-blood and bilingual, thereby replicating the ruling class and excluding poorer and more traditional

Cherokee.[124] The entrance exam excluded the poorer, rural, more traditional population.[125] Thus, the schools aggravated the tensions between rich and poor, slave owners and yeoman farmers, mixed- and full-blood.

Teachers arriving from the East commented on the prosperity of the Cherokee nation. In addition to the large and impressive buildings of the seminaries, teachers and other visitors to the Cherokee nation in the West saw large farms and growing commercial ventures.[126] The Cherokee, economically and socially, had more in common with settlers in Kansas and Arkansas than with Western Indian groups or other removed groups. Their first priorities on the frontier became recreating important institutions on the frontier.

The economics and politics of the frontier, though, interrupted that plan. By 1856, an economic crisis forced the two seminaries to close and fall into disrepair.[127] Political pressures increased as Kansas exploded into political warfare. Additionally, it raised tensions between the various political factions within the Cherokee, helping to set the stage for the violence and political rupture brought on by the Civil War.

Perhaps, one of the most important lessons the Cherokee learned during the removal was that the United States would never accept their nation as equals. Though, after the Treaty of 1846, tensions declined between the Old Settlers, Treaty Party, and Ross faction, they never fully went away. And new tensions between mixed-bloods and full-bloods appeared. Ross and others hoped education would remove this problem, but it only aggravated it. The differences went far beyond complexion. About 300 mixed-blood families made up the Cherokee planter class with large farms (600–1,000 acres), growing staple and cash crops, owning 25–50 slaves, and investing in farm and other equipments. Some of their relatives were bankers, merchants, and traders, as well. The Cherokee sought to prove to the white population that they deserved sovereignty, but divisions emerged with their fellow Cherokees. "The two groups were working cross-purposes that would eventually stir up a far-reaching and bitter confrontation over slavery and secession."[128] The struggle within the Cherokee swirled around who was Cherokee and the future of the nation.

Both the Confederacy and the Union courted the Five Civilized Tribes to fight for them. To be more accurate, the Confederacy wooed their former Southern brothers. The North, in the form of the federal government, did everything they could to alienate the Five Civilized Tribes. Yet, it expected them to stay out of the fight or fight for the Union. Just before the outbreak of the Civil War, the federal government made several paternalistic moves that threatened the sovereignty of the Cherokee. The federal government-appointed Indian agents "granted licenses to white traders" and maintained a military post—Fort Gibson—on Cherokee land. This move made the Cherokee nation feel as if it were occupied by federal troops. In 1857, the Cherokee finally succeeded in getting Fort Gibson closed, though a recession and a need for more military on the Great Plains also influenced the federal decision. Additionally, Congress claimed it could turn Indian Territory into a U.S. territory at any time, suggesting that the Cherokee did not control their own territory. These two federal actions presented open challenges to Cherokee sovereignty. "Territorialization meant forced assimilation and the abolition of all tribal government, laws, and treaty rights."[129] And the federal government did not offer citizenship or rights to the Cherokee. The federal government cut rations, annuities, and stopped shipping into the Indian Territories just as the war began, depriving the Five Civilized Tribes of important economic resources at a time when many were just reestablishing their wealth. While some portray Abraham Lincoln as sympathetic to the Indians, the actions of the Bureau of Indian Affairs at the time belie this interpretation.[130]

The Five Civilized Tribes resided in Indian Territory in 1860, but in their territories. The Cherokee saw themselves as a constitutional democracy, not unlike the United States. Having passed a Constitution in 1828 and revised it in 1848, it shared much in common with the North and the South. Like the Union, it established the Cherokee as a governing body with rights and responsibilities. Like the South, the Cherokee authors incorporated race into their Constitution. Simply put, "whereas Southerners used definitions of race to establish how blacks differed from whites, the Cherokee used definitions of race to establish how much they resembled whites rather than blacks."[131] Their constitution codified these roles and further divided the tribe. Yet, the Constitution in the eyes of the Cherokee also codified the Cherokee as a nation. Though the Supreme Court defined them as a distinct community in *Worcester v. Georgia*, they still acted as a nation, albeit one with great divides.

The tensions within the Cherokee nation affected its responses to the Civil War. Their complicated relationship with the federal government affected their choice of with whom to ally. The three main factions of the Cherokee (the Old Settlers, the Treaty Party, and the National Party) pursued interactions with the federal government. The Old Settlers had relied on the government to help them gain solid territory in the Indian Territory after being forced out of Arkansas, Illinois, and Texas. Once it secured the land, it expected the United States to stay away. The Treaty Party felt the same way, but it expected annuities and reimbursements to help aid the economics of the nation. The National Party had the most complicated relationship. Ross thought his relationship with Congressmen would save his nation. After Removal, he spent months in Washington, lobbying for restitution. Yet, all the groups saw the western land as neutral land. The U.S. government saw it as U.S. territorial land occupied by the Cherokee.

Four

STATEHOOD AND CRISIS

The Cherokee moved west in waves. The first few waves from 1790 to the 1830s consisted of people who wanted to preserve their way of life and start anew somewhere. Those settlers often encountered hostile populations west of the Mississippi and found themselves moving a second and third time until the federal government granted the Old Settlers land in the Indian Territory. The last two waves crashed west with momentum behind them from the East. In 1838, the Treaty Party, in an effort to save the Cherokee nation as they knew it and conserve resources moved west. Like emigrants to other parts of the West, they relied on the previous migrants to help them survive and formed an alliance and government with them. The final wave, the National Party, came west expecting to reinvent Western Cherokee society as they saw it. Principal Chief John Ross thought he would maintain his position and recreate the Cherokee Nation as it was for him. Economic and political struggles tried the patience of the Cherokee settlers. And, as did all settlers in the West, the divisions of the East arrived fully formed in the West.

Like the Cherokee, other immigrants and settlers flooded into the West, motivated by economics, politics, and opportunity. This movement included the gold and silver miners, lumbermen and farmers drawn west by opportunity and the Mormons driven west by conflict. All these groups brought with them political and social ideas from their homes in the East, which in turn shaped their ideas about their new communities in the West. As diverse groups settled in the new territories, like California or Kansas, conflicts ensued over the direction of those territories. While many historians have studied these conflicts from the East, looking at how Congress and Eastern states debated Western states' future, this chapter examines how the actual settlers engaged in and resolved these conflicts over statehood.

WESTWARD MIGRATION

The end of the Mexican-American War, the addition of the Oregon territory, and the California gold rush created the perfect storm of immigration to the West. People from New England, the Old Northwest, the South, and the Old Southwest flooded into the new territories, whether they were organized or not. The flood of settlers did not abate until well after the Civil War. Many came not only for economic opportunity, but they also bore with them ideas and perceptions about what makes a territory American: small farms versus large farms, free labor versus bonded, white settlers versus brown, black, or red.[1] Who migrated and from where shaped the debates that swirled in the new western territories before the Civil War. Unlike settlement east of the Mississippi, large populations existed in the new territories with certain expectations. Eighty-five thousand Hispanics, 75,000 Great Plains Indians, and 84,000 removed Eastern Indians already resided west of the Mississippi in 1847.[2] These populations already had societies, systems of government, economies, and social ties that did not need to be challenged.

This chapter focuses on five specific territories or states: California, Oregon, Utah, Kansas, and Texas. California attracted immigrants through the gold rush, initially, and then the ensuing trade and resources continued to draw migrants from around the world. Oregon appealed to the farmer, lumberman, and fisherman. Utah became the focus and home of the Church of the Latter-day Saints. Like Utah, Kansas, finally being declared fertile after years of being categorized as a desert, drew in farmers and townspeople. And Texas drew in immigrant farmers, slaveholders, and others who looked to the vast territory for opportunity. While most history textbooks at least imply that Americans settled the United States from east to west, in reality settlers turned the West Coast from territories into states much earlier than the center of the country.

Initially, California and Oregon enticed the most settlers to their territories. Though the migration patterns ebbed and flowed, the average was between 10,000 and 20,000 people per year to these two territories. The two territories could not have been more different. California attracted a more urban group of settlers, who often planned to be temporary settlers.[3] Oregon attracted more families who came to stay. Both territories desired more migrants. In 1856, California petitioned Congress for help in attracting and protecting overland migrants. In it, Californians claimed they got their best portion of population from overland migration. This statement subtly damns those that came by boat from Asia and Latin America as not the same quality, extending the debate of the Mexican-American War about degraded populations. Additionally, the petition complained that the Indian threat limited migration to the great state and that the federal government needed to build more forts, since the Indian attacks made the migration "nearly impracticable."[4] Migrants to Oregon suffered some of the same challenges, but they remained a different breed. Risk takers went to California, while farmers and families went to Oregon. In either case, between 1840 and 1860, fewer than 300,000 people migrated to California, Oregon, and Utah.[5]

Oregon grew differently than California. Until the gold rush, California's American population remained small. But during the gold rush it exploded, quickly surpassing the 60,000 residents needed for statehood. Oregon, with the arrival of whalers and missionaries, had seen a steady increase until the settlement of the controversy. By 1845, 6,000 Americans had migrated toward Oregon. This movement created new problems for the federal government. As early as 1847, military volunteers who came to serve in the garrisons (established to help settle tensions in Oregon) staked claims to the territory.[6] Their wooden curtain of forts, meant to keep settlers and Indians at bay, now suffered a large hole, leaving room for conflict.[7] The Oregon Trail became the nexus of conflict between Indians and travelers, and the military, which had to deal with both.

The settlement of the trans-Mississippi West differed from the settlement of the previous states in the East and the land between the Appalachians and the Mississippi river. The settlement of Kentucky, Tennessee, Illinois, and other regions immediately west of the Appalachian Mountains often jumped out ahead of governmental structures. Settlers flooded into new lands before the U.S. government signed treaties with the Indians, built forts, established roads. This pattern changed in the trans-Mississippi West. While many Plains Indians had not signed treaties by the 1840s and 1850s, treaties did exist for those on the West Coast. Additionally, garrisons and the wooden curtain did exist. Though Congress clamored to build more forts to protect migrants, more forts existed in the trans-Mississippi West ahead of settlement than there were in the East.[8] Settlers expected safety and security from the government as they plodded west to Oregon or California, something they had not expected in previous migrations. These expectations shaped the development of the trans-Mississippi West as the federal presence led the way.

CALIFORNIA

Though California entered the union as a free state in 1850, "the nature and scope of freedom and equality continued to be hotly contested."[9] Two debates framed the entrance: whether to exclude blacks and other non-whites from settling in California, and proslavery versus antislavery. The territory and then the state fought internally over whether blacks or other non-white groups could settle in California. "By 1850, California was both an extraordinarily diverse society and a violent one."[10] This sentiment shaped the slavery debate within the state. These arguments combined with the unusually large and divided non-white population, some of which predated the arrival of the Americans, made California different from other states entering the Union at this time and shaped their response to the Civil War.

Before the Mexican-American War, Indians and Mexicans dominated the population. Yet, American immigrants began to move into California in search of better fortunes. Some Euro-American immigrants began to arrive in the 1840s to find established *rancherias*, peonage, and Indian missions. The *Californio* population found itself under attack. As landowners, both large and small, they encountered stiff competition and pressure from the incoming Americans, both miners and settlers. As early as 1842, *Californios* developed a "heightened sense of caution against an American government and American immigrants who proved capable of, if not intent upon, defying the political sovereignty of their territory."[11] By the time of the Mexican-American War, those same Americans classified the *Californio* landowners with "mestizos, who were racially denigrated by U.S. troops as a 'mongrel', largely Indian race."[12] The Mexican-American War changed the population as "settlers and soldiers meant that their [Indians] conditions of life grew worse, their autonomy was sharply reduced, and their interactions with settler society became ever more heavily policed."[13] Despite remaining as the majority of the population, the Indians throughout California found themselves reduced to reservations and under threats of violence within 10 years of the end of the war.[14] Such attitudes set the stage for the coming debates about who should settle California and whether slavery should be allowed.

Before the new immigrants could exclude the *Californios* and blacks, they needed to deal with the Indian population. The majority of the Indians at this time lived in missions or on former Spanish land grants called *rancherias*, pursued farming and, in the earliest stage of the gold rush, worked as miners alongside the other miners. The Treaty of Guadalupe-Hidalgo set the stage, designating Indians as savage tribes and guaranteeing protection from them to the Hispanic population.[15] The designation came naturally as many of the new American immigrants crossed the Great Plains and Southwest and had "come to regard Indians as threats to their physical safety or as obstacles in the path of their economic success."[16] These beliefs justified "Yankee settlers" and their use of Mexicans as "virtual slaves," much in the same way that genetic and social arguments justified black slavery in the East.[17] Labeling them as savage excluded them from the general diverse population and opened the door for their removal and extermination.

Though the *Californio* and Indian populations made up the bulk of the California native population, black migration, whether as free men or as slaves, became the focus of much debate within California both before and after statehood. Like other migrants, blacks came for the gold rush, though the majority settled in other areas.[18] By 1850, California had outlawed intermarriage between blacks and whites.[19] Soon, the territory tried to ban blacks from settlement, from juries, and from civic life.[20] These restrictions mirrored those that existed in the eastern United States at the time, in both the Old Northwest and the South.[21] Even as the territory began the discussion about statehood, the issue of racial settlement emerged, often as a justification for banning the institution of slavery. Much of the opposition to slavery in California centered on the importation of blacks and unfair economic competition, not around states' rights or the immorality of the system.[22]

The fault lines over slavery and black settlement appeared during the Constitutional Convention in 1849. "Whiteness became the new criterion upon which citizenship in California now resided." The delegates spent time establishing who was white and who was not, including "white male citizens of Mexico" but excluding Indians and African Americans. The members of the convention banned slavery to help limit the lure of blacks to the state. They considered banning blacks "regardless of status" but feared that such a ban would violate the U.S. Constitution.[23] While politicians in Washington debated whether California could come in as a free state without disrupting the delicate balance of free and slave states, Californians debated who should be counted as a legitimate citizen of the state.

The conflict over the settlement of blacks ran deep within the state. Northern California, around San Francisco, threatened to break off over slavery because it would bring blacks into the state.[24] Southerners, ironically in Southern California, also opposed slavery, which they feared would give slave owners an advantage in the gold fields, but feared an outright ban on black settlement would delay Congress's passage of the California state constitution.[25] So, Northern California threatened to secede, while Southern California played politics to garner statehood. These fault lines remained active as the Civil War began.

By 1860, California had passed "an 'appallingly extensive body of discriminatory laws' that marked people of color as inferior outsiders."[26] The Civil War only increased divisions and tensions within the state, as Texans and other Southerners moved into the state to escape the war.[27] Jefferson Davis, who would become president of the Confederate States of America, predicted that Southern California would want to take advantage of the southern railroad plan in 1853, when he served as secretary of war and oversaw the mapping of that route.[28] The passage of the Kansas-Nebraska Act resolved that issue. Once the Confederacy captured Arizona, which would connect California to Texas, some Californians and the federal government feared that Southern California would secede.[29] The federal government sent in additional troops to prevent a break away. Additionally, federal authorities attempted to draw in other stable white populations, touting California to Mormon volunteers "as yet only sparsely settled and therefore not hostile to their conventional beliefs, offered them a rich new land in which to build their communities."[30] During the Civil War, California provided the most Union volunteers of any area of the West, which might suggest strong support for the Union.[31] And, in 1862, the California Column helped push the Confederates out of Arizona.[32] Though this appears to support the federal position on slavery, California still remained restrictive to non-whites.

California began its life as a state born out of the hurly-burly of war and the gold rush. The invading army and the flood of miners from throughout the world shaped the debates within California about citizenship and statehood. From the Foreign Miners' Tax through the removal of California Indians to the exclusion of African Americans from civic life, California sought to create a white paradise that restricted the rights of those races considered degraded. Their constitutional convention and state laws enshrined the beliefs of the Mexican-American War and Manifest Destiny.

OREGON

Oregon faced many of the same debates as California did over the settlement of blacks and the institution of slavery, but with its own unique twists. Both territories grew out of international conflicts: California out of the Spanish empire and Oregon out of the British one. Oregon, though, lacked a large Mexican population. Instead, it had a small French and British population mixed with several large Indian populations. As American settlers began moving into the Willamette Valley with the Whitmans, tensions increased between the Indians, the British, and the new settlers. The Oregon Controversy with Britain in 1844 inspired Stephen Douglas to propose that Congress look into expanding garrisons and extending the railroad.[33] By 1846, the suggestion of a northern route for the railroad to Oregon erupted into a conflict as the South wanted a southern route.[34] Despite the conflict, these changes remained a pipedream until 1854.[35] Through all the debates in Washington, settlers continued to plod westward toward Oregon, 5,000 in 1847 alone.[36]

The Whitman Massacre in November 1847 helped speed up the settlement of the territory and split it. Congress sent a garrison of soldiers to Oregon to protect the settlers after the massacre, but tensions remained high until 1859 which hampered the settlement of the interior, though settlers continued to move to Oregon.[37] Whereas the bulk of non-Indians before the 1840s worked on the coasts, trapping and trading, after the Whitman period and massacre, settlers focused on farming, which demanded land from the Indians and isolated them from trade.[38] The rise of agrarianism produced several important changes for the territory. First, it created conflict with the Indian population as whites demanded more land from the late 1840s through to the 1850s.[39] Second, as these wars and conflicts progressed, the Indian population declined, freeing more land for white settlers but also reducing the availability of Indian labor. As white farms grew, the need for labor grew as well, opening the door for slavery in some people's eyes.[40]

Migration patterns into Oregon also changed in the 1850s, affecting the debate about settlement. Whereas Whitman recruited from the Northeast, the next wave came from the Border States, "notorious for turbulence and readiness to self-help" and "Southern uplanders, contentious, ignorant and suspicious."[41] While this implies a preference for Northern settlers, they began the conflicts with the Indians over land. The new migrants from the Border States, including a greater number from the Mississippi Valley and the upland South, moved in looking for the same opportunities with specific expectations for their own freedoms and rights.[42] Additionally, these new immigrants brought with them specific attitudes about Indians and blacks.

Those coming from the upland South had witnessed, in their minds, the successful removal of the Southeastern Indians. They understood the government's ability to open up new land through removal and the opportunities that lay within that. Those from the Mississippi Valley had witnessed Indian wars, the migration of the Southeastern Indians, and the closure of the Indian frontier through the building of forts. As they now moved into Oregon, they expected a similar pattern and solution to the Indian problem there, including the establishment of forts for protection of the new agricultural frontier. They expected a strong federal presence for security.

Oregon attracted settlers through generous territorial land grants. In 1843, the provisional government offered 320 acres to white males and another 320 to their wives, thereby granting 640 acres to married couples, more than double the size of a farm in the South at this time. The Oregon Donation Land Act of 1850 legitimated those claims filed before 1850 but halved the acreage to 160 per married person. It also included dispossessed Indians, allowing them to gain land, but excluded other non-whites, like African Americans or kanakas, meaning Hawaiians.[43] Many in Oregon and Washington viewed Oregon as a place for the individual white man to make his place in a paradise of other white men.

The same provisional government that generously gave away land passed the first resolution for all free blacks to leave the area.[44] By the time the territory became established in 1849, Oregon passed laws banning all blacks and requiring slave owners to remove slaves within three years, similar to an Illinois territorial law of 1813.[45] The white settlers of Oregon wanted a territory free of Indians, blacks, and kanakas, not just of slavery. Much of the historical evidence points to two separate debates within Oregon just as there were within California. On the one hand, the white men of Oregon did not want black settlement, because they did not view blacks as equals and saw them as competition for their own labor. On the other hand, many, but not all, resented slavery and saw it as giving an economic advantage to the slave owners over the yeoman farmer. While Congressional debates echoed the second part of the argument, histories that focus on those debates miss the crucial first stage.

From the beginning, Oregon sought to regulate who would settle the new territory. The first session of the legislature of the provisional government prohibited the presence of blacks. The territorial legislature echoed this sentiment a few years later: "the people of Oregon repudiated most emphatically all relations with the Negro, free or bond."[46] Some feared an alliance between blacks and Indians, leading to the downfall of the territory.[47] These concerns echo those fears about Mexicans after the Mexican-American War that those races needed to be cared for and could not actively participate in democracy.

The debate about slavery providing an economic advantage did not just extend to black slavery imported from the East. As Oregon argonauts, or gold miners, flooded into California, they displayed an intense dislike and anger toward Indian miners there. This conflict between Oregon Argonauts and Indian miners could be attributed to the aftermath of the Whitman massacre and the ensuing decade of the Cayuse War, as those two events shaped attitudes against Indians. But Oregon miners protested the "economically advantageous relationship" with Indian miners that Californians and others held.[48] By using Indian laborers, either as peons or as cheap labor, they produced more gold than the Oregonians who labored for themselves. As far as many Oregonians were concerned, such advantages flew in the face of the American ideal of Manifest Destiny and individualism. White settlers divided over slavery and blacks. "Some wished that slavery would be forever prohibited, others desired to align with the South."[49] Few, though, supported the settlement of blacks in the territory.

Many Oregonians, while conflicted about slavery, proudly expressed nativist ideals.[50] During the debates about black exclusion in the late 1850s, representatives stated that "the United States is a government of white men" and "the declaration of independence [is] a declaration of the equality of free citizenship for white men."[51] Whereas nativist ideas expressed in the East often focused on anti-immigration, in Oregon it revolved around banning blacks, Hawaiians, and Indians from citizenship and settlement. The free land in Oregon, wrested from the British, deserved a proper settlement, like the Southwest did after the Mexican-American War—white yeoman farmers. As R. R. Russell points out, "The process of acquisition was accompanied by interesting debates in Congress and out as to the ability of the United States to colonize, assimilate, and retain such distant possession with such a vast mountain barrier separating them from the settled eastern states."[52] Could the United States maintain an American colony so far away from the soul of the democracy? For many Westerners, as demonstrated by Oregon and California, it meant attracting a certain type of settler with certain values. After the Mexican-American War, "the entire configuration of the nation had changed both on maps and in the minds of its citizens. No longer was the Mississippi River some sort of ultimate boundary."[53] The new boundary appeared to be either the Rocky Mountains or the Pacific Ocean, but the extension of American society and democracy depended on the extension of Americans, meaning white property-owning males. In Oregon, settlers "far separated from the arena of sectional strife had no thought of interfering with the Negro question or of allowing it to interfere with them."[54]

Some Oregonians embraced slavery and sought to make it part of the Pacific West. The Knights of the Golden Circle was formed in Oregon in the 1850s. Dedicated to resisting the conscription of men into Union forces during the Civil War, the branch in Oregon also proposed creating a "Pacific republic of Western states." These states would "discard universal suffrage and to establish a servile cast of South Sea Islander and Negro immigrants with a virtual feudal organization controlling them and their labors."[55] The republic would provide labor and stability for expansion into the Pacific.

For many of the settlers of Oregon, the land represented a place for new beginnings and a reimagination and revitalization of American democracy. "Westerners looked West, not East, toward the opportunities of the frontier, not back towards the slavery of the East."[56] Although the East had failed to maintain the equality of opportunities by allowing slavery, Oregon would correct this mistake. Banning non-white settlement limited the competition of cheap labor. Excluding slavery as an institution leveled the playing field for all white settlers. While some settlers did bring in slaves, for most, "far out on the North pacific, with conditions and interests wholly foreign to those within the arena of conflict," Oregon sought to chart its own course on black settlement and slavery.

As the nation began to debate the issue of popular sovereignty, or the right for the residents of the territory to choose slave or free state, just after the Mexican-American War, Oregonians embraced the debate. They did not want to be a colony of the United States but an equal partner. Oregonians "expressed the hope that the time had fully arrived when the citizens of a territory were no longer to be considered the property of the United States."[57] Popular sovereignty would free Oregon from the pressures and requirements of a government who did not understand the territory or its needs. It did not need free blacks or bondsmen to compete with the white men who flooded the territory. It did not need Indians as laborers when there were white laborers to be had. And it did not need a federal government telling the people of Oregon that they needed to include these elements.

In the summer of 1857, George H. Williams, chief justice of Oregon Territory and a Democrat, published a letter, eventually known as the Free State Letter, explaining exactly why slavery would not work in Oregon. He ignored the moral aspect, focusing only on its incompatibility with Oregon. He begins with a strong nativist point, typical of both Republicans and Democrats in Oregon: "One white man is worth more than two Negro slaves." Then, he zeroed in on why slavery would not work in Oregon specifically. The long rainy winters would make the slaves perfect leeches on the farmers, the distance and cost of transportation would price them beyond most people's finances, the vastness of the territory encouraged escape and the Indians would aid in that, and an Indian-black alliance would prove a serious menace.[58] While he made other political points, about maintaining a friendship with the North for example, the bulk of the letter focused on why slavery wouldn't work in Oregon specifically. These types of beliefs married the Manifest Destiny ideals that sought to exclude blacks with the practical territorial reasons why the institution of slavery would not work. At the same time, Republicans accused Democrats of only wanting to extend slavery "out of love for the poor Nigger," whereas Republicans sought to protect "free labor" and "making Oregon a free State, as the best and only means for securing it for the white race."[59] Leander Holmes, a Republican who argued against slavery, stated, "We prefer the society of white people."[60] For Oregonians, the West was different and deserved to make their laws based on that difference.

When Oregon voted for statehood, they resoundingly rejected free blacks and slavery with the constitutional vote. Only a 10th of the voters supported the settlement of free blacks in the territory.[61] In other words, 9 out of 10 voters supported "Black Exclusion," as "the electorate wanted none of the Negro race." Oregon became "the only free state with a Negro exclusion provision in its original constitution that Congress ever admitted."[62] Only a quarter of the voters chose slavery. Slavery was an economic institution that threatened the yeoman farmer. Free blacks were a people who threatened the American nature of the territory. They would drive away whites from northern states and Europe depriving Oregon of the "habits and industry [and] thrift."[63] In the end, the small plots, the fear of economic competition from both black laborers and slave owners, led to the rejection of both blacks and slavery.[64]

UTAH

Although California and Oregon already had European and Indian populations when the American population started moving in to the territory, Utah did not. The territory had Shoshone, Ute, Paiute, and Bannock Indians but few Europeans or Americans. Utah attracted a specific group of settlers, those who belonged to the Church of Jesus Christ of Latter-day Saints. Called Mormons today, during the 19th century they referred to themselves as Saints and to outsiders as Gentiles. The Saints and their settlement of Utah demonstrate different tensions over slavery and states' rights compared to California and Oregon, yet they also demonstrate familiar conflicts over the role of African Americans and slavery for the West in the lead-up to the Civil War. Unlike settlers to Oregon and California, the Saints drew more exclusively from the North and, more interestingly, from Western Europe.

The 1850s saw tensions between the federal government and the territorial government of Deseret/Utah. The federal government appointed Brigham Young as the territorial governor. This position made him both head of state and head of the Church of Latter-day Saints. Not everyone in the new territory belonged to the Church and Gentiles "recoiled at the Church's theocracy, resented the enormous power held by local probate courts and ridiculed the practice of polygamy."[65] Saints, on the other hand, saw this appointment as a way to protect their position and religious freedom. By 1857, President Buchanan became disturbed enough by complaints—that the Church built a theocracy west of the Rockies—that he fired Young as the territorial governor and ordered the army into the territory. From then until the start of the Civil War, when the federal government needed to withdraw the troops back east, Utah remained an occupied territory. Known as the Mormon War, it increased the rising pressure between the federal government and the Mormons, especially since the Mormons believed they had proved their loyalty by supplying men to fight the Mexican-American War.

The tensions between the Church and the federal government frustrated Saints in Deseret. They believed they embodied what John C. Calhoun had meant when he said that a regional majority must be able to veto the action of the national government when the actions were objectionable. To the Mormons, "The simultaneous existence of the government regimes, one called 'Utah' and appointed by the Federal authority, the other called 'Deseret' and elected by the settlers was exactly what Calhoun meant."[66] The Saints wanted the territorial right to govern themselves in a manner acceptable to the majority who lived in that region. In many ways, the Mormons shared much in common with the Cherokee. Like the Cherokee, they lived on land granted to them by the federal government, who also granted them the right to a territorial government. The Mormons hoped to live their lives as they chose, religiously, culturally, economically, and politically, not unlike the Cherokee. And like the Cherokee, the Mormons found the federal government willing to assert its power over them when necessary.

This argument mirrored the one made by politicians about popular sovereignty and slavery. "By the early 1850s, both the Saints and slaveholding southerners looked upon popular sovereignty and states' rights as the best means to protect their respective 'peculiar institutions' from outside attack."[67] Just as Congress passed the Kansas-Nebraska Act in 1854, the Saints in Utah created theocracy through popular vote. It demonstrated, for better or worse, the uses of popular sovereignty that Congress had not imagined. At the same time, it presented a serious challenge to the idea of federal union. If Utah could become a theocracy named Deseret, what would prevent other territories from creating other states that challenged some aspect of the status quo? An Indian-run state? "To the Mormons, Stephen Douglas's 'popular sovereignty' justified polygamy, just as Republicans saw his 'squatter sovereignty' as a way to expand slavery."[68] The circumstances of the West challenged the political ideas of the East.

Mormons did not see themselves as political radicals. On hearing the Dred
Scott decision in 1857, Mormons declared, "Congress has no power over the
question of slavery in the Territories and of course none over the question of polygamy." The statement continued pointing out that slavery and polygamy "can
now flourish wherever the people will it in any of the Territories," and "Uncle
Sam can attend to his own business without troubling himself any further about
them."[69] They felt they upheld the Constitution through their practice of freedom of religion and helped develop the territory in way in keeping with the
ideals of Manifest Destiny: small family owned farms run by white men. While
they tacitly approved of slavery, they also sought to ban African Americans from
the territory. Like others during this time, the Mormons looked to the Bible
for guidance and viewed "blacks as inherently inferior and therefore fit subjects
for involuntary servitude." Previously, they had limited the role of blacks in the
Church of Latter-day Saints. Banning them from the territory resolved several
issues at once, including participation in the church. Though the territory allowed slavery, the restrictions on it sought to keep as many blacks out of the
territory as possible, and certainly sought to discourage free blacks as Young,
like other biblical literalists at the time, associated blacks with "Cain and the
Devil." Consequently, they wrote "antiblack proscriptions into the constitutions
for their proposed state of Deseret in 1856, 1860, and 1862."[70] Like other western territories, slavery and black rights remained two distinctly different issues
politically and socially. Young envisioned Deseret as an active part of the Union,
writing as late as 1861, when the telegraph first reached Salt Lake City, "Utah
has not seceded, but is firm for the Constitution and the laws of our once happy
country."[71]

The national political parties did not appreciate this loyalty. The Republican Party
convention of 1856 designated polygamy as one of the "twin relics of barbarism"
along with slavery.[72] Such a designation effectively demonized polygamy in the eyes
of many in the United States. Like slavery, polygamy enslaved someone (women),
provided an economic disadvantage (through larger families), and belonged not to
the general population but to an elite few. Many pointed to the fact that only leaders of the Latter-day Saints practiced polygamy, shutting out average men from the
possibility. Like slavery, polygamy privileged the elite while holding down the small
yeoman farmer, whom many believed should be settling the western territories. Ironically, in an effort to pacify critics, in 1852 Utah "became the only territory west of the
Missouri River and north of the Missouri Compromise line . . . to legalize slavery."
Since most of their converts came from the Northeast and Europe, this position
"seems baffling."[73]

In addition to the national political problem, the territorial government of
Utah also struggled to control its Indian population. Young instituted his "open

hand, mailed fist" policy: "Feed the Indians when possible (to make them dependent), but attack them whenever necessary."[74] Between the constant expansion of Mormon settlements in the territory, as more and more settlers came for sanctuary in Deseret and the constant flow of overland travelers who chose a route through Utah because of the ease of gaining supplies, the Indians in Utah felt under attack. In the 1850s, they began attacking the mail routes and other supply routes.[75] By the time of the Civil War, the federal government had sent troops into Utah twice. Utah could have been expected to be pro-secession, as "Federal authority had been exerted over the Mormons only by military force and much of the misfortune which had accompanied their migrations to Utah was laid to the inhabitants of the Northern communities."[76] Despite being Northerners and wanting to enter the nation as a free state, like other western states, Utah bore remarkable similarities to the South: desire for popular sovereignty, proponent of states' rights, and resentment of persecution by Northerners.

KANSAS

Unlike Utah, Kansas appeared to bear few similarities to the South. "Bleeding Kansas," as many historians refer the territory in the 1850s, exploded as a contest between abolitionists and slave owners, Free Soilers, and popular sovereignty proponents. Two violent episodes roiled the West in the 1850s. "Both arose from the prospect of white settlement, and both concerned the role of race in the controlling of natural resources."[77] One of these was California; the other one was Kansas. But Kansas actually entered the fray over the same issues of black settlement, frontier security, and slavery that other territories did. Its location, near the slave states of Nebraska, Missouri, and Arkansas, and just above the Indian Territory where many Cherokees and others owned slaves, did not help resolve the issue.

Throughout the 1820s and the 1830s, Americans saw Kansas as a territory one must pass through to get to the riches of the Far West. In the late 1830s, it became part of Indian Territory and the U.S. government moved Eastern Indian groups, like the Shawnee, into Kansas. Two reasons drove this decision. First, the U.S. government considered it too arid to farm, so it made sense to place Eastern Indians on the land since whites would not want it. Second, Kansas fell beyond the wooden curtain of forts, originally designed by Lewis Cass. By the 1840s, several problems arose. As Oregon Territory drew settlers west, they left Missouri and cut through Kansas. The U.S. government thus extended forts into the Indian Territory/Kansas to protect those settlers from the Indians the government had placed there. "Rather than concentrating its scattered garrisons, the army built new ones, providing business for local contractors and invaluable way stations for travelers."[78] The extension of the forts drew settlers into the territory as they gave the impression of security and law. With the invention of the steel sodbusting plow, the land suddenly became desirable for agriculture.

Kansas attracted settlers mainly from New England and the Midwest, at least until the controversy over its status. Though often portrayed by early historians as being settled by those of Puritan stock, in reality a wide variety of settlers flocked to Kansas for the treeless prairie with the rich soil, with 83 percent from the Old Northwest.[79] Yet, the land was not open. In addition to Plains Indians, the federal government gave groups, like the Shawnee, the Delaware, and the Sac and Fox, reservations in Kansas and did not expect settlers to flood their land.[80] When the Kansas-Nebraska Act was passed in 1854, "Not a single acre of land had been ceded by the Indians."[81] The tension between these groups and the rising number of immigrants to Colorado and other places farther west prompted the government to build more forts in the territory. In the 1840s and 1850s, these forts helped extend white settlement and small farms into Kansas. These same forts, in particular Fort Leavenworth, would then serve as the staging ground as the U.S. government withdrew federal troops from the West at the beginning of the Civil War.[82]

The passage of the Kansas-Nebraska Act in 1854 split Kansas apart. It repealed the Missouri Compromise, which banned slavery from the Louisiana Purchase territory and allowed slave owners to take their property into the territory north of 36° 31'.[83] Introduced by Douglas, a proponent of a transnational railway, the act made two territories out of Nebraska territory: Nebraska and Kansas.[84] With the use of popular sovereignty, the supporters of the bill hoped that one state would be slave and one would be free. For Douglas, this act made a northern and a southern route for the railroad possible. But the political explosion in Kansas over the act made either route hard to build, as all political debates focused on Kansas and not on plotting out routes.[85] Many in the region feared the passage of the bill because they thought it would draw populations from Arkansas and Missouri to shape the outcome of the state.[86] As land became tighter in the territories, people feared that the open land in Kansas would draw people in for settlement, regardless of political issues. The Arkansas paper, *True Democrat*, wrote: "With Kansas a slave state, all will be well. With it as a free state, our property [meaning slaves] will be rendered insecure and annoyances unnumbered will be the lot of our people."[87] Slave owners in Missouri and Arkansas feared an increase in escaped slaves and creeping abolitionism if Kansas became a free state.[88]

Immediately upon the passage of the Kansas-Nebraska Act, Northern groups began to mobilize to save Kansas from slavery. Northeast abolitionists organized "emigrant aid societies" to encourage "free-soilers to move west." These societies helped put together communities and buy plots of land together to form towns. The societies bore the names of eastern towns like Manhattan, Boston, and Pittsburgh. With capital and organization behind them, the first emigrant aid society entered Kansas in 1854 on the heels of the act. Despite the publicity and historical focus on these groups, "the majority of northern migrants to Kansas were unaided."[89] And though thousands of Missourians flooded into the state, most came for land, although Easterners "presumed they were attempting to secure the territory for slavery."[90]

Immigrants rushed in from all over the continental United States and from outside as well, with the bulk coming from the Midwest.[91] Like Texas and Minnesota, a sizeable number of Germans headed to the open lands in Kansas.[92] They felt torn during the conflict between "their desire to see their personal liberties and political rights safeguarded and their hope to carve free homesteads out of the public lands of the western territories."[93] Many immigrants felt the same way: they simply wanted to build their new life without the conflict that swirled in the territory. They objected to slavery because they "feared the social and economic effect on the small white farmer."[94] As in Oregon, California, Utah, and most of the West, the eastern debates mattered little to the settlers who wanted land.

Though the South believed that the majority of settlers in Kansas were abolitionists, they were wrong. The majority of Kansas settlers who opposed slavery in the territory did, but not for abolitionists' reasons. Like other western territories, Kansans held certain attitudes about blacks, separate from their ideas about slavery. Many thought blacks to be inferior to whites and that they should be subordinated to whites. While abolitionist leaders, like the Topeka Movement or Free State party, embraced equal rights for all, the majority of settlers from the Midwest and Northeast saw excluding slavery from Kansas as equal to excluding blacks.[95] This group included Free Soilers, who opposed black migration and settlement west. "A large group of settlers was more anti-Negro than antislavery."[96] This issue became apparent during the Topeka Constitutional Convention of 1855. They considered the rights of blacks in five areas: "suffrage, office holding, militia service, slavery, and exclusion." The convention delegates excluded blacks from the first three giving them to white men and "Indian males who would give up their tribal membership."[97] Like California designating Californians as citizens if they were white, Kansas considered enfranchising Indians if they would cease being Indian. These restrictions mirror what other territories did at this time, though Kansas is only one of a handful to grant Indians such rights. The other rights became contentious issues. One member explained why he approved of Negro exclusion: he had "a holy horror of 'niggers' and abolitionists."[98] In the end, 72 percent voted in favor of black exclusion. Only Lawrence, Manhattan, and Wabaunsee rejected the provision, all hotbeds of abolition. But this constitution and provision were not the final ones. As the few slaveholders in Kansas removed their slaves, the issue seemed to fade, not because people wanted to grant blacks rights but because they ceased to be a threat. Slavery faded as an issue in Kansas and the final constitution did not contain a black exclusion provision, unlike Oregon and California.[99]

The tensions among settlers in Kansas affected the army and the rest of the West. Essentially a civil war, the Kansas troubles required the army to act as a constabulary between the various groups. This role raised internal conflicts within the army as they were not trained to act as such. They could not use lethal force in their intervention as they did in the Indian Wars. As more immigrants flooded into Kansas, including those simply looking to homestead and stay out of politics, the army began to resent both sides of the conflict and felt the government and the public would blame them for any adverse outcome. Many officers participated in land speculation which "further tested the uncertain alliance between the military and the civilians."[100] By 1856, resignations among army officers reached new heights. These resignations created a crisis as already one-seventh of the Army in the West patrolled polling stations and the Missouri border. To compensate for these losses and to beef up the presence of the military, in 1856 the army suspended an offensive against the Cheyenne so they could concentrate on Kansas.[101] The peaceful settlement of Kansas outstripped the security of the Oregon Trail, originally one of the main responsibilities of the army.

The Kansas troubles also spilled into Indian Territory. Unlike Missouri, the troubles did not consist of border skirmishes because southern Kansas was not very densely settled.[102] Instead, it focused around Kansas politicians looking covetously at Indian lands and the Cherokee fear of an influx of abolitionists which would add to a conflict already present in their territory. Cherokee law barred any teacher or missionary "suspected of harboring abolitionist sentiments." Passed to keep the conflict over slavery quiet, especially because wealthy half-bloods owned most of the slaves, this law created a different conflict. Northern Protestant churches "demanded dismissal of slaveholding members from the congregation." The conflict between the Northern church boards and the Cherokee law generated two problems. Ministers who expelled slaveholders "might find themselves preaching to an impoverished, politically powerless congregation of traditionalists and slaves." Additionally, they could then be expelled.[103] The Cherokee did not agree with the issues in Kansas and they didn't need or want more settlers either.

Kansas did not have to bleed. "It took a world of mismanagement, to turn poor houseless squatters who have fences to make and corn to raise, and wives and children to feed into rebels to be kept down with balls and bayonets."[104] And the issues that shaped Kansas went beyond just slavery. "Writing on this period of Kansas history, eastern historians stressed the importance of the slavery question while ignoring the issue of the place of the Negro in the territorial society."[105] Many settlers flew north to Nebraska territory or west to Colorado, to escape the tensions in Kansas.[106] By 1860, Kansas represented a free state, built on small family farms and a white population.

TEXAS

Unlike the other states and territories, which saw American immigrants flood into their territories after the Mexican-American War, Texas had a history of American immigration. Spanish and Mexican governments had sought American immigrants to help stabilize their frontier, beginning in the early 19th century. In addition to failing to follow the rules of the *colonia*, including practicing Catholicism, these American immigrants created tensions with the Indians of Texas, including those, like the Cherokee and other Indian groups, who also arrived in the territory in the early 19th century. Eventually, the American immigrants joined with *Tejanos* in the Texas Rebellion. The original American immigrants to Texas shaped Indian and land policies, which caused problems for the newer immigrants who arrived after the Mexican-American War.

Before and after independence and statehood, Texas pursued its own Indian policies, from which settlers in later years would reap the benefits. In 1835, Governor Mirabeau Lamar, originally from Georgia, helped expel the Cherokee who had tried to gain official land grants from the Mexican government.[107] This move left only the Alabama-Coushatta in East Texas, thereby opening land for settlement. The Alabama-Coushatta gained a state reservation in 1854 and remained in East Texas.[108] By 1856, Texas pursued a policy of assuming Indians off-reservation were hostile and should be treated as such, ahead of when federal policy made such an assumption. But reservations within Texas did not last, as the Texans drove Indians off the Brazos reservation into Oklahoma in 1859. These actions, mainly by the Texas Rangers, set up future conflicts with the federal government, as Texas believed that the federal government should pay for the cost of driving Indians off their reservations and out of the state.[109] While chafing at the federal presence, Texas still expected it to pay for its frontier security.

Unlike other states at this time, Texas pursued an expansionist and individualistic Manifest Destiny, and tried to push as far west as possible. "Prior to the sectional conflict, Texas's westward line of settlement kept advancing, not retreating."[110] As they pushed westward, conflicts between Texas settlers increased with the Comanche who did not want the new settlers in their territory. Between 1844 and 1860, Texas developed a double line of federal forts with the outer forts to ward off the Indians, and the interior posts garrisoned mounted troops. This system mirrored the one proposed by Charles Gratiot in the 1830s, using the outer forts for security and inner ones for domestic conflict. These forts helped protect the southern route to the gold fields and allowed settlers to move farther west. And they added millions of federal dollars to the Texas economy.[111] The establishment of federal forts helped expand Texas's boundaries as far west as the Rio Grande. These actions helped fuel Texans' belief in perpetual expansion, and made its expansion into California and Mexico avid dreams for many Texans and eventually the Confederacy.[112] Yet, that expansion relied on federal forts and enforcement to protect their frontier, something the Confederacy struggled to do when it took over.

As Texas pushed Indians out and expanded the territory to be settled, after independence and statehood they attracted more settlers and industries. By 1846, northeastern Texas was filled with cotton farmers and cattle ranchers.[113] Texas and the rest of the South attracted a sizeable German immigrant population. Most people think of the German population at this time in Minnesota and the Dakotas, and a sizeable one emerged there as well. Like American immigrants, Germans in the northern territories and those in Texas came for trade and farming. They also bore with them a belief in the sanctity of hard work and the power of labor. This belief often saw slavery as a threat to individual labor and, therefore, a problem. And like American immigrants, both groups bore racial ideas about Indians and African Americans with them to the Texas frontier.

The German immigrants to Texas settled in two areas: Southwest Texas and East Texas.[114] These areas differed both in climate and population. The Germans in East Texas tended to be older, more acculturated, more economically suited to having large farms or plantations. Those in the West consisted of more recent immigrants, few slaveholders, and were more exposed to Indian attacks.[115] Those Germans and Anglos in East Texas reaped the benefits of policies and pushes just before the Mexican-American War.

East Texas lent itself to larger scale farming and slavery. Southwest Texas did not. Small holdings worked best in the climate and environment. Additionally, the proximity to Mexico made life difficult for immigrants to the area. Indian raiders crossed the border regularly to steal from farmers in the region.[116] Mexico outlawed slavery in its Constitution of 1824, though Anglos in Texas, then part of Mexico, still retained their slaves. Mexico, though, remained a haven for escaped slaves because of different racial attitudes and the offer of freedom. Even before the Mexican-American War, Texas and the Spanish West became a safety valve for African Americans seeking freedom.[117] As the border between Mexico and Texas became more delineated, more African Americans, both free and slave, fled to Mexico, especially after Texas became a state.[118] Between the climate, the type of farming, and the proximity to Mexico, owning slaves in Southwest Texas did not make sense for the German immigrants there. Overall, less than 5 percent of Germans owned slaves in Texas.[119] These factors shaped the German attitudes toward slavery and Texas's response to the Civil War, and created a debate among historians over the reaction and stability of Texas.

Just as Texans who immigrated from within the United States carried racial attitudes about African Americans with them, so did German settlers. The majority of American settlers to Texas came from the upland South, thereby bearing conflicting ideas about slavery and African Americans.[120] Many German settlers worried that

African American free labor would crowd out their efforts. And although Germans "advocated the free distribution of public lands, they had no objection to the introduction of slavery into those lands."[121]

In general, they did not care for African Americans, seeing them as degraded peoples. By the late 1850s, Texas found itself in a unique position. It had freed itself of Indians internally, but still had an active Indian frontier, particularly to the west and north. The state sought to expand west into New Mexico and Arizona, and had eyes on becoming the terminus for a southern railroad route to the California goldfields. Its proximity to an active international boundary with Mexico represented both a positive and a negative influence. It not only opened opportunities for trade and possible expansion, but it also created a vacuum for escaped slaves and home for Indian raiders who plundered South Texas. A burgeoning immigrant population not only aided the economy, but also pushed the boundaries westward, increasing conflict with Indian nations. And though it perceived itself as independent and successful, the frontier populations in Texas knew it relied on federal support in the form of the military to continue on its expansionist path. Right before secession, "Texas was on the point of being the scene of railway struggles and land speculation and settlement, the likes of which the South had not yet seen."[122]

FIVE

THE REGION RESPONDS

When the Civil War began in 1861, much of the West remained in flux, and not just over the issues of slavery and states' rights. California, Oregon, and Washington had gained statehood, while excluding African Americans from settlement and barring them from participating as active citizens within the state. Yet, these states remained split over the issues of slavery and its effects on their territories. Utah struggled with its own battle with the federal government and the Mormons quickly found themselves and polygamy equated with the evils of slavery by Northern reformers. Texas appeared to be the gateway to a western and southern empire, meaning Mexico, for the Confederacy. Yet the West faced outward migration, international conflicts, and challenges from the active Indian frontier to the north and west.

For many of the territories in the West, the conflict over slavery remained a debate within the federal capital in Washington. They struggled with their own challenges. Minnesota, Kansas, and Colorado faced Indian nations as eager as the Confederacy to throw off federal shackles and reshape the frontier in their favor. Westward migration continued at a steady pace throughout the Civil War and western territories absorbed those settlers and pursued their own interests, worrying more about federal withdrawal than the success or failure of the Confederacy.

TEXAS

While much of the population and culture of Texas might appear to be Southern, at the beginning of the Civil War, Texas possessed Western concerns.[1] It became the only Confederate state with an active Indian frontier, which created tensions within Texas between those residents on the Indian frontier and those in the interior.[2] And it became the only Confederate state with an active international border.[3] Texans claimed they seceded because of these contentious frontiers, stating that the federal government lacked the will and resources to adequately protect Texans from both Mexico and Indians.[4] Despite employing the Texas Rangers, Texas quickly discovered that securing their Indian and international borders would not be an easy task.

Texans listed frontier protections as second only to the protection of slavery as a major reason for secession.[5] Despite a double line of forts protecting the western and southern frontiers of Texas, the U.S. Army failed to prevent raids by the Apache, Kiowa, and Comanche.[6] To stop some of these raids and violence, Texas removed the reserve Indians just before the Civil War.[7] Even as newspapers proclaimed the dangers of the western frontier of Texas, the frontier continued to march west, with Texans eyeing New Mexico territory as an extension of their state. Even as they bemoaned the lack of protection on their western and southern frontiers, they sought to expand the western one. Secession simply complicated this expansion. Soon after the beginning of the Civil War, federal troops withdrew from Texas, leaving its southern and western frontiers unguarded and causing other complications.[8]

Nature complicated the situation further. The years 1860 and 1861 saw severe drought plague Texas and the Indian Territory. Comanche, Kiowa, and other Indians found themselves on the brink of starvation, complicated by the withdrawal of the federal troops who had provided rations and trade. Consequently, the Indians were too starved to raid while newspapers at the time firmly blamed the Indians for frontier violence. Whoever did it, the Texas frontier roiled with it. The outbreak of the Civil War drove all sorts of men into West Texas to avoid the war, and eventually conscription. As Gary Clayton Anderson points out, "West Texas became a hotbed of discontented people, some trying without much luck to protect their property, others defending either the Union or the Confederacy, and finally others simply using the chaos to steal and plunder."[9] As German immigrants, Indians, and disenfranchised settlers struggled on the western frontier of Texas, the government of Texas chose sides in the war.

Settlers on the western frontier of Texas "cared less about the war effort and more about their own welfare."[10] Though the Lone Star flag quickly replaced the U.S. flag after the declaration of war, the bulk of the population remained between the two sides.[11] The War seemed like an abstraction when Comanches or Apaches might attack one's farm at any moment.[12] Yet, Texas remained staunchly Confederate, passing a law that made it illegal to support the Union. For those settlers on the western edge of Texas, particularly the German settlers, physical and political survival clashed. Even before secession, German settlers worried about the consequences of federal troops withdrawing. This fear led to pro-Union sentiments amongst many Germans in West Texas. But political survival dictated that these same Germans at least feign support for the Confederacy, as the new law required Unionists to leave Texas within 40 days. This move would mean that German and other settlers lost everything they had built. So they stayed and tried to survive the shifts of the political winds.[13] Others did not wait. Texas saw out-migration increase beginning in 1860, as settlers moved on to California and other states to avoid the conflict altogether.[14]

In February 1861, Texans plotted to gain control of the federal arsenal in San Antonio. Commanded by Brevet Major General David E. Twiggs, it became a target of John Baylor, "a hotheaded frontier Indian fighter." Twiggs came from Georgia and seemed conflicted over the recent turn of events. On February 16, after negotiations and correspondence with his superiors, Twiggs surrendered to the Texas secessionists. The Union not only lost San Antonio, but also access to the Texas Gulf Coast, where ships came to remove western troops and return them to the East for the Civil War. The surrender also hurt the Union as Texas comprised an entire military department, including 15 percent of the total Union army.[15] Twiggs empowered the Texans and the Confederacy just two months before Fort Sumter, also punching a hole in the Union's western defenses and holdings. The Union lost access to the West through Texas ports, access to Mexico, and access to the resources of Texas.

As soon as the federal government withdrew Union troops, Texas asked for Confederate troops to replace them. This demand created a conundrum as the Texas governor, Edward Clark, "believed Texas had no obligation to fight in the East."[16] When the Confederacy failed to act, he created reserve units for protecting Texas, essentially undercutting the population which might serve the Confederacy. Governor Francis Lubbock, Clark's replacement, created Frontier Regiments, designed to protect Texas and not the Confederacy. The 1st Regiment Texas Mounted Rifles protected the northwest frontier; the 2nd protected the border with Mexico.[17] Though they saw little combat in Texas, the governor refused to let them fight in the East, though they did fight in Arkansas and the Indian Territory. Texas Rangers replaced them in these forts to protect Texas from both Indians and Unionists.[18]

Texas played an important role for the Confederacy, which had designs on the Pacific Coast. Initially, the Confederacy saw itself extending west into Arizona, New Mexico, and California, south into Mexico, and north into Colorado.[19] California would provide an outlet to the Pacific Asian markets and gold. Arizona, New Mexico, Mexico, and Colorado all provided mining. These resources would help shore up the Confederacy's economy. The Confederacy hoped that Texas and Texans would play an important role in this expansion. Texans quickly proved their mettle in the spring of 1861.

In May 1861, Mexico warned the Lincoln administration of Confederate ambitions in New Mexico. Mexico already suffered from internal strife and upheaval, and feared that the British, French, and Spanish were simply waiting for the nation to collapse so they could claim the spoils. They didn't need problems to their north. Nor did they want the Confederacy contemplating an expansion in to Mexican territory. Yet, the federal government still withdrew troops from New Mexican territory, leaving the residents open to attacks by the Apache and weakening the border. By 1862, Texans began marching toward New Mexico. They had received communications that parts of the Mesilla Valley, in what was to become Arizona, favored the Confederacy. The Convention of the People of Arizona sent a delegation to Richmond, seeking support.[20] Texans occupied Tucson, one of the few cities to repel the Apache. The local Confederate commander, Brigadier General Henry Hopkins Sibley, believed that Arizona would allow communications with California, which Baylor claimed teetered "on the eve of a revolution."[21]

Though much of the Union force had been withdrawn, Union troops still held on to a few forts. Forces from Colorado and California soon joined them to help repel the Confederates, making this frontier unique as Westerners fought Westerners for the Union and the Confederacy. Slavery and states' rights were not the issues; access to the Pacific and the mining resources of the West made it a western battle of conquest. The army instructed the Union troops to pursue the Confederates into Mexico if necessary, but to route them from New Mexico.[22] By March 1862, it appeared the Texans and the Confederacy would take New Mexico and Arizona and move onto California. Colonel G. R. Paul in command of Fort Union, which protected the eastern approach to New Mexico, bemoaned, "Should this expedition [the arrival of the units from Colorado] prove successful the Territory will be saved to the United States, but should it fail the country will be lost."[23] Paul spoke the truth. Had the Confederates held these western territories, the Confederacy would have claimed vast mining resources and an outlet to one of the most active international markets at the time, China. But by April 1862, the Confederates, including the Texans, had been pushed back into Texas, holding California, Colorado, Arizona, and New Mexico for the Union. Texas claimed a need for support from the Confederacy for its northern frontier against the Comanche, its forces pushed west on behalf of the Confederacy.

INDIAN TERRITORY

As the Civil War broke out, the Indian nations in the Indian Territory faced several challenges. To their north, Kansas continued to churn and roil with dissent and conflict. Though little of it had spilled into their territories, it became clear that Kansas would be a Union state and the large number of federal troops massed along the border with Indian Territory and at Fort Leavenworth became cause for concern.[24] To their south, Texas became part of the Confederacy and immediately embarked on expansionist moves into New Mexico. Many feared Texas might expand north as well or cross through the territories to get to Kansas. Most of the Indians in Indian Territory never had good relations with Texas or Texans. To the east, Arkansas also joined the Confederacy, effectively pinning the Indian Territory between both sides.

Within the nations, turmoil swirled over which side to join. For those nations forcibly removed by the federal government in the 1830s, the outbreak of the Civil War created a dilemma. Should they join the Union, which guaranteed their annuities, provided forts for protection against criminals from Arkansas and Texas, yet had removed them and violated the rule of law? Or should they join the Confederacy, to which individuals had family ties, supported states' rights, a concept that might eventually aid Indian nations in their attempts at self-determination or rule, yet Southerners had used these same states' rights to remove the Indians? Complicating their position, internal politics erupted between mixed-blood slaveholders and the majority of the nations who did not own slaves. Though they all had factions who sought to reject the United States, they also had large groups who wanted neutrality or to remain with the United States.[25] Few sought to join the Confederacy because they wanted to be just like them or preserve slavery forever. Even those that became pro-Confederate did so for specifically Cherokee, Creek, Seminole, Chickasaw, and Choctaw self-interest.

The Union seemed to do everything in its power to drive the Indians away. First, many of the Indian agents hailed from the South and expressed sympathies or outright support for the Confederacy.[26] The Union did little to discourage this practice because if the Indians joined the Confederacy, it freed the government from the payment and administration of annuities. Additionally, from a fiscal point of view, the Indians faced a conundrum. The federal government had invested their annuity money heavily in southern bonds which would be forfeited if the Union won.[27] If the Confederacy won and the Indians had joined it, they still lost those annuities. Financially, no matter which side they joined, their annuities would be reduced or stopped. Adding insult to injury, in 1861 the federal government stopped annuity payments to the Indians in Indian Territory, citing security issues.[28] This move devastated the economies of the tribes, including the Cherokee, who used these funds, as deemed by the treaties, to support schools and the police force.[29] The federal government also withdrew troops from frontier posts. Settlers protested these withdrawals, fearing Indian reprisals and violence. But the withdrawals also exposed the Indians to conflict and economic hardship. Farther west, military forts often doubled as trading posts. Their closing ended the needed economic influx, as forts provided trade and jobs for the Indians. In Texas and the Indian Territory, Texans, acting on behalf of the Confederacy, quickly took the posts. And, during 1861, as the Cherokee debated whether to stay or go, Washington offered Ross little or no official support.[30] The Union could do little more to force the Indians to choose the Confederates.

The Confederacy saw great potential in the Indian Territory, as "the South seems from the first to have appreciated the importance of the Indian Territory as a possible storehouse for provisions, as a highway to and from Texas and in some slight degree, no doubt, as a base for securing Colorado Territory and the new state of Kansas."[31] Texans and Arkansans traveled throughout the Indian Territory early in 1861, attending councils and making the case for secession and joining the Confederacy. President of the Confederacy Jefferson Davis saw great potential in the Indian Territory. Having served as Secretary of War for the United States, Davis had more interactions and experience with the Indians than most Southerners by this time period. He must have realized they could potentially share similar desires: self-rule, slavery, freedom from a central government. Within months of secession, Davis organized a Bureau of Indian Affairs and appointed a commissioner and negotiators to deal with Indians. Representatives quickly headed toward Texas and Indian country to sign treaties with the Five Civilized Tribes and western nations.

The Confederacy made an enticing proposal to the Indians in Indian Territory. It offered money, political participation, and sovereignty in hopes of securing the western border. All of these solved problems facing the Indians in the Territory. The Confederate money replaced what the Union withheld. More importantly, though, offering sovereignty, while seemingly a reversal from southern policies of the 1830s, fulfilled a desire of the nations to be recognized as self-determined. "Sovereignty included the right to determine citizenship, restrict residence within the nations, reject allotment and statehood, and control trade."[32] These rights represented what the Cherokee had sought to do with their Constitution, which led to the violent response from Georgia in 1827. Now, the Confederacy offered those same rights. Additionally, without the nations becoming Confederate states, the Confederacy offered them participation in the legislature, something never offered by the U.S. government. So, by joining the Confederacy, they would have self-determination and a voice in the Confederacy. Initially, the Five Nations (or Five Civilized Tribes) attempted to present a united front to the Confederacy and the Union. In January 1861, the Chickasaw called for a meeting of the Five Nations. But by the time it was organized in February, the Chickasaw did not bother to send delegates. The Creek, Chickasaw, Seminole, and Choctaw had joined the Confederacy.

Internal tribal politics affected the choices as well. Within the Cherokee, rising tensions between the mixed-blood slave owners, a minority of most nations in numbers but who were disproportionately politically powerful, and the full-blood yeoman farmers mirrored tensions in other western states. In 1861, "less than one out of ten Cherokee families" used slave labor. Small farmers felt disenfranchised and economically oppressed by the larger landowners, who were more likely to own slaves and have political power. "The nonslaveholding majority began to doubt the loyalty of this faction [slaveholders] because it placed its special interest before that of national unity and independence." Unlike in the South, in the Cherokee nation small farmers did not side with the planter class but saw them as bad Cherokees. "Nonslaveholding Cherokees, having a nonacquisitive tradition, did not cherish" the hope of eventually owning slaves. They eventually came "to regard the elite as no longer truly Cherokee."[33] So, there it was. The 50-year fight over what made the Cherokee the Cherokee, which had driven the Old Settlers and Treaty Party move west, now came down to slavery.

Remember, 1861 came barely a decade after political turmoil within the Cherokee Nation. John Ross, principal chief of the Cherokee, who initially preached neutrality, still bore the scars of that turmoil as did Stand Watie, who saw his brother Elias Boudinot of the Treaty Party assassinated.[34] Both men served on the Cherokee National Council in 1861 but shared few political views.[35] Because of these tensions, by the start of the Civil War, the Treaty Party, which had signed the treaty for removal in hopes of preserving Cherokee resources, soon to be called the Southern Rights Party, already had an "armed company" for their own protection.[36] Watie strongly urged going to the Confederacy. His new Southern Rights Party believed that alliance with the South would be "more profitable and wiser for the nation."[37] This platform became "a convenient way to undermine Ross's support among the elite," many of whom owned slaves. But Watie's new party also drove many nonslaveholders into Ross's party because neutrality seemed to not promote slavery. Ross, fearful of the consequences of loss with either alliance, wrote, "We do not wish our soil to become the battleground between the states and our homes to be rendered desolate and miserable by the horrors of war."[38] Eventually, though, Ross's desire to hold the Cherokee nation together led him to urge that they join their brothers in the Five Nations and side with the Confederacy. He wrote, "The state on our border [that is Arkansas] and the Indian Nations about us have severed their connection with the United States. Our general interest is inseparable from theirs, and it is not desirable we should stand alone."[39] Despite Ross's reversal deciding to join the Confederacy, Watie saw the decision as a loss for his Southern Rights Party since Ross remained in power.[40] This stance did not hold for long. Yet again, Cherokee politics revolved around the future of the nation, not individual choices.

The Confederacy offered a treaty that not only gave the Cherokee much of what they wanted, but also helped legitimate and support their constitution. The treaty "agreed to the important principles that the Cherokee people had the right to decide who was or was not a citizen." It also allowed them to extradite criminals from the surrounding states and hold their own courts, again supporting what the Cherokee already considered their right. It "guaranteed the payment of all Cherokee annuities," a direct slap at the United States' failure to do so during the crisis. And the Confederacy agreed to pay any outstanding claims for losses sustained during removal in 1839.

This part of the agreement went to the heart of the conflict within the Cherokee over who could be reimbursed after removal. Additionally, unlike federal treaties, the Confederate treaty did not grant the Confederacy the right to intervene in Cherokee "domestic strife."[41] On paper, at least, the Confederacy seemed comfortable with the Cherokee self-governing, or "a free people, independent of the Northern States of America."[42] Finally, it promised that Cherokee troops would not be used against other Indians. The Confederacy would violate this clause first.

Conflict ensued within the Cherokee over the decision to join the Confederacy. While it may seem simple, the first struggle erupted over who could call themselves Cherokee Mounted Rifles. Watie, who had already been commissioned by the Confederacy and had formed his unit first, claimed the name. But John Drew, nephew of Ross and a former slave trader in the Indian Territory, demanded the name for his unit. Both units consisted of blood relatives of the commanders, recreating the two sides of the intratribal conflict, something of which the Confederacy seemed unaware.[43] Drew's unit pledged their loyalties to Ross and his position, not to the Confederacy. On the other side, Watie's nephew, Elias C. Boudinot, son of the assassinated leader of the Treaty Party, Elias Boudinot, served as the representative to Richmond and the Confederacy. Watie saw this position as a way for the Treaty Party to regain the upper hand.[44] In June, Watie's forces engaged in battle in Missouri and won high praise from Confederate forces. This event garnered him more support within the Cherokee.[45]

In November 1861, a civil war came to the Indian Territory, but not the American Civil War. Despite the fact that the Five Nations signed treaties with the Confederacy, none of the nations were unanimous in that decision. Like the Cherokee, other nations split between the powerful, often slave owning, and the more traditional small farmers. The Creek leader Opothleyahola gathered up pro-Union women and children and called themselves the "loyal Creeks."[46] They headed toward the Union lines in Kansas for their protection.[47] Confederate Indian forces aided by Texans tried to stop them. In the battles of Round Mountain, Chusto-Talash, and Chustenahla, Confederate Indians produced an internal civil war and highlighted differences between the Civil War in the Indian Territory and the Civil War in the United States.[48] The battles consisted of Indian-to-Indian fighting, something not seen elsewhere in the Civil War.[49] During the battle at Bird Creek, the specter of Indian-to-Indian fighting led to the desertion of many of Drew's men. It also involved civilians who chose to exit the battlefield, but were chased. Opothleyahola's attempt to take his people to safety led to splits within the Cherokee and other groups who had not expected to be pitted against their own people.[50] After the battles, Cherokees and Creeks fled to Kansas for protection.

The conflict with Opothleyahola pointed out problems of the alliance with the Confederacy. The Confederates, as did the Union, assumed that the Indians joined them in mutual defense of the Confederacy and agreement. In reality, the Indians joined the side they thought would best allow them to protect their own land.[51] While they may have joined as the Five Nations, they acted autonomously for their own best defense and interests.[52] Also, pairing them with Confederate Texans did not work. Texans held strong prejudices against the Indians, in general. They had raided Indian Territory in the past. And they had expelled the Cherokee from Texas. Texan commanders ordering attacks on fellow Creeks or Cherokees created an internal conflict for most Indian Confederates. They often sided with their blood, not with the Confederacy.

Ironically, the Cherokee and their response to the Confederacy and the Civil War shared much in common with the Texans. Neither group wanted their troops sent east to defend the Confederacy. Both saw the protection of their territory and sovereignty as tantamount to any other force. Both joined the Confederacy out of spite against Union policies and frustration with the Union rather than in outright support of the Confederacy. And both continued to act autonomously through the Civil War. And, unlike other parts of the Confederacy, both the Cherokee and the Texans struggled with international and Indian border issues.

On the other side, by the end of the war, Confederate Indians and their families escaped to Texas where they found little sympathy or protection.[53] Watie sent his family south to Texas, but they received little in aid or protection. Texas and Texans represented another problem for the Cherokee. Many of the Old Settlers remember being driven out of Texas. The Cherokee felt that Confederate Texans wanted Cherokee help. But they also recognized that those same Texans would willingly violate those terms as they had with the Cherokee and other Indian groups in Texas. For the Treaty Party members, Texas seemed to represent a powerful ally, but one that could not be trusted either. Texans' willingness to drive Indians out of their own territory bothered even their Indian allies.

The Cherokee, the Creek, and the other Five Nations did not split over free or slave. They split along previous political fractures. In the Cherokee case, it became a continuation of the power struggle over the future of the nation and its sovereignty and self-rule. The issue of slavery would be decided by the Cherokee when they had secured their sovereignty. Those that chose the Confederacy did so against their own individual interests. Ross and Drew had more to lose from the demise of slavery than Watie and Boudinot. Yet, Ross and his allies went for neutrality, supported the Confederacy only to support Cherokee unity and, eventually, switched to the Union for protection from Confederate forces and allies.

In March 1862, the Confederacy lost the battle of Pea Ridge. For the Cherokee, it represented a different sort of loss. Much to Ross's horror, both Drew's and Watie's units served at Pea Ridge, outside the Cherokee Nation. Ross and others had thought that the treaty with the Confederacy prevented the Confederacy from using

Cherokee troops outside of the Nation. They believed that the Cherokee units would be used for home defense, not to invade Union territory or protect Confederate Territory. Pea Ridge proved them wrong and widened the split within the Cherokee between the Union, the neutrals, and the Confederates.[54]

When the Confederacy came calling, they came not to an immigrant population, nor to sons of the South but to a foreign power that would choose to join the fight for the Confederacy for its own reasons and on its own terms. Seeing the Cherokee, the Creek, the Seminole, the Choctaw, and the Chickasaw in that context reshapes the understanding of the battle and struggles that followed as the Civil War progressed. The Five Civilized Tribes had more in common with France or England and their role in the Civil War than they did with either the North or the South. They might not have been a critical strategic area for the North or the South and their military, but they did play an important part in the struggle over Confederate territory.[55] And, in many ways, the Confederacy treated them as nations, united nations. The Confederacy sent envoys to negotiate with the people they perceived as being in power, missing the internal and external struggles and conflicts that hampered each nation from making just one choice. And the Confederacy offered up terms that suggested nationhood: sovereignty and representation.

The Confederacy assumed that the Five Civilized Tribes agreed to join the Confederacy for the same reasons the Texans and Arkansans did. Yet, the Texans and Arkansans joined for different reasons themselves. And the members of the Five Civilized Tribes who joined the Confederacy, in some cases temporarily, did so for their own individual reasons. By assuming the same motivations, the Confederacy and the Texas and Arkansas commanders by default often found themselves perplexed by the actions of the Five Civilized Tribesmen. When members of the Five Civilized Tribes at Chustenahlah faded into the night rather than fight kinsmen, even kinsmen who had joined the other side, the Confederate commanders could not fathom why. Like other Westerners, the fight during the Civil War revolved around old familiar questions for the Cherokee: sovereignty and the future of the nation.

UTAH

Secession and the beginning of the Civil War immediately affected Utah. After 10 years of tension between the federal government and the Church of Latter-day Saints, an active U.S. military resided in Utah. In 1860, less than 7 percent of federal soldiers were stationed in the East, the majority in areas like Utah in the West trying to quell problems.[56] This de facto occupation coupled with the Mormon belief in their right to practice their religion and run the state as they chose led the Confederacy to believe that they would "readily accept allegiance to almost any other government other than that in Washington."[57] But initially, Utah remained loyal to the Union.

Despite their conflict with the federal government, they also relied on the U.S. Army to help with the Indians, as did many other western states. But the Confederacy remained interested in Western states, especially Utah where mining strikes had just occurred, possibly providing resources to help pay for the war. Even as the Confederacy eyed the West, the federal government removed troops from Utah, New Mexico, and Colorado, making these territories more vulnerable to Indian attacks and Confederate overtures.[58]

By 1862, new problems erupted between the Mormons and the federal government. Indians continued to disrupt the mail and gold routes that ran through Utah. The Mormons failed to stop their raids.[59] The federal government sent in soldiers from California, under the command of Colonel Patrick Edward Connor, to stop these raids.[60] Connor appeared to be hostile to the Mormons, describing them as "a community of traitors, murderers, fanatics and whores."[61] While many Americans might have agreed with his assessment of the Mormons, his open hostility did nothing to squash tensions between federal troops and the Mormons. Only four years before, federal troops had marched into Salt Lake City as part of the Mormon War, and many Mormons did not look kindly on the return of those troops. Some interpreted this invasion as a sign that the federal government did not trust the Mormons.[62] Connor promptly made it his mission to weaken the Mormons' hold over the territory. In December 1862, Connor claimed that "Brigham Young was organizing military resistance against the U.S., a heady charge in the middle of the Civil War."[63] Such accusations did little to smooth tensions between Utah and the Union.

Brigham Young found himself in an unusual position. He not only wanted Utah to be a free state, but also recognized that many of the others who felt that way demonized his church. Few of his followers sympathized with the South but felt invaded by the Union.[64] He neither actively sought to support either side nor to break with either side. He simply, like many of the Indian groups, hoped that the conflict would deflect attention from his people and their way of life. In a sermon in 1863, Young reminded his followers "that the Church had long forseen the present civil war and he then wished the Mormon prophecy that the North and South would destroy each other 'Godspeed.' "[65] Most Mormon men apparently felt the same way; less than 1 percent of the Westerners who participated in Union troops came from Utah.[66] "Mormon leaders recognized that Abolitionists of the North and slaveholders of the South had interests which did not directly concern the inhabitants of Utah."[67] They, therefore, hoped to lay low.

In addition to the federal troops now stationed in Utah, Congress did not help matters by passing the Morrill Anti-Bigamy Act in 1862. This act not only banned plural marriages, but also limited how much property churches and nonprofit organizations could own in any U.S. territory, a direct strike at the Mormons in Utah. President Lincoln did not enforce the act in exchange for the Mormons not choosing sides in the Civil War. Or as Lincoln viewed it, "Utah could be plowed around while the timber of the southern rebellion was being cleared away. If the Church would leave the Union alone, Lincoln would leave the Church alone."[68] The Democrats did not protest the lack of enforcement because it created a conundrum for them: it "usurped legislation passed by the territories and states." In other words, the Morrill Act violated states' rights, setting the stage for other federal acts. Lincoln accused the Democrats of not allowing polygamy but would happily let the Mormons use "squatter sovereignty" as "a mere deceitful pretense for the benefit of slavery."[69] The "twin relics of barbarism" remained intertwined within the concept of states' rights no matter how much others might want to separate them. The same states' rights that covered slave or free also covered polygamy or monogamy. Utah, then, resided in the same no-man's land as the Cherokee: mixed messages from the federal government and weak offers of support from the Confederacy. Statehood, for Utah, remained on hold throughout the Civil War.

SIOUX UPRISING

Just as Lincoln dealt with the Mormons and their tensions, he faced an uprising in Minnesota that stirred fear in the halls of Washington. The Dakota War of 1862, previously called the Sioux Uprising, raised multiple questions about the frontier, the relationship of the Confederacy to Western Indians, and the loyalty of western territories and states to the Union. The Dakota faced the same problems that the Indians in California, Texas, Oregon, Washington, and other territories did: increased immigration.[70] Between 1850 and 1860, tens of thousands of immigrants flooded into Sioux territory in southern Minnesota. Promoters touted Minnesota as an alternative to California and the gold rush and sought to attract New England settlers to the area.[71] Competing with Oregon and Kansas as well, promoters played up the "territory's potential for agriculture," playing on the popular American metaphor for "the frontier as a future garden, a paradise created without travail by yeoman farmers." Whereas the promoters positively compared Minnesota to California, they denigrated Midwestern and Southern states and territories, calling the southern slave states "enervating, sickly, and unproductive."[72] By 1856, Bleeding Kansas and Indian troubles in Washington and Oregon made Minnesota a prime destination for settlers.

After land cessions with the Dakota in 1851, promoters focused on southern Minnesota as "the garden spot." The Dakota felt squeezed off their land as the federal government, with the help of missionaries, signed several treaties with them, forcing them onto a small strip of land near present-day New Ulm.[73] To aid in their relocation, the federal government granted them annuity payments. But third parties, such as traders and local merchants, complained that the Dakota owed them money and the U.S. government paid these third parties first, limiting the actual payments that the Dakota received. By 1862, tensions between the Dakota, the surrounding communities, several of which were German, and the local traders and Indian agents reached a head.

In the summer of 1862, the local Indian agent, Thomas Galbraith, called the Dakota to the agency to await annuity payments, which did not come. During the wait, the Dakota missed the buffalo hunt and the planting season, both of which supplied them with food for the winter. Their leader, Little Crow, asked that trader Andrew Myrick to open the warehouse so that the Dakota could obtain food on credit. Myrick refused, though another agent relented. Meanwhile, rumors swirled around the encampment that the U.S. government had spent the annuity payments on the Civil War, which did nothing to soothe the anxiety in the encampment.[74] And considering the federal government had stopped annuity payments into Indian Territory, these rumors did not seem completely baseless.

The large numbers of Dakota living around the agency for the summer did not endear the Dakota to the local German settlers. These settlers came from many of the same regions and for the same reasons as the German settlers in Texas. They wanted to farm, build businesses, and families. The clash between North and South meant little to them as they focused on their daily life. Many did not see themselves as Americans but rather as Germans living in the United States, so felt little loyalty to either side. They considered both African Americans and Indians less than human, not unlike many of their American neighbors.

Minnesota already had one long simmering crisis over who belonged in the territory. As soon as Minnesota became a territory in 1849, it moved to deny black men the vote, the right to be elected in village elections, and to serve on juries. But in 1850, only 39 blacks lived in Minnesota territory.[75] Yet Minnesota, like Oregon, Washington, and other western states, sought to regulate their settlement while limiting their rights. In the West, blacks represented "walking paradoxes": they could "associate with white people . . . even gain respect, but they could never expect to share in the decision-making process of their community, in the brokerage of power." As the Civil War approached, the constitutional congress of Minnesota focused on the abolition of slavery, temperance, and "the commitment to stand up to southern hegemony." And, though it proposed preventing "civil disabilities on account of color or religious opinion," tensions over the Civil War led Democrats to label Republicans as nigger worshippers, as they had in Oregon and Kansas. Many feared that any rights granted to blacks would lead to a flood of black settlement, which would threaten labor stability and act as a "voting bloc to counterbalance the votes of immigrants." Minnesota, though, stood out on this issue as its constitutional congress debated granting rights to Indians as well as immigrants, but not to blacks.[76]

A long summer of the Dakota squatting near their land raised fears of attack and did little to dispel the Germans' belief that Indians were lazy. By the end of summer, some of the younger Dakota became restless and raided a farm for food. This act split the Dakota. Some saw the theft as payment for the land the settlers now possessed. Others saw it as an act of theft beneath the Dakota. The settlers saw it as theft and challenged the Dakota, who fired at them. "Though the historical record differs, in the end five whites lay dead."[77] The Dakota struggled with how to react. Some wanted war. Some wanted peace. After a council with Little Crow, they attacked the agency, and the war spread to the surrounding communities. The governor of Minnesota dispatched the state militia. It initially failed to quell the uprising. Almost a month later, after the Sixth Minnesota Regiment arrived, close to 500 whites and 60 Indians were dead. It ended on September 26, 1862, and the trials for the Dakota began two days later.

When word of the uprising reached Washington, the initial assumption was that Confederates had spurred the Indians to revolt. While this assumption might appear like a conspiracy theory, Washington knew that the Confederacy had signed treaties with Indians in Texas and Oklahoma and had approached the Five Civilized Tribes about siding with them.[78] It also demonstrates the federal government's misunderstanding of how angry Western Indians were at the government and a lack of understanding of how effective Indian revolts might be. The Dakota War sent shivers through Washington as the federal government continued to withdraw troops from the West to fight the Civil War. What if other Indian groups chose this moment to push back? Who would protect the settlers in the West and the newly gained territories?

The Dakota War presented Lincoln with another challenge as well. "After hundreds of Dakota surrendered, [head of the Sixth Minnesota Regiment Henry] Sibley, promptly broke his promise and convened a military court."[79] This court sentenced 303 Dakota to death. After calling for such a resolution, Governor Ramsey lost his resolve to sign them and sent the death sentences to Washington to let the Justice Department review them. President Lincoln faced a dilemma. The speed of the trials, the translation, and types of evidence raised problems with almost all the convictions. But failing to convict anyone sent the wrong message to the settlers of Minnesota, who needed to feel that the federal government protected them from the Indian threat, just as the Texans and Mormons demanded as well. President Lincoln signed an order for 39 of the convicted to hang. Within hours of the execution, the government of Minnesota admitted having hung at least two innocent Indians by mistake. The message, though, had been sent: the federal government would punish Indians and continue to protect settlers on the western frontier. Between Utah and Minnesota, Lincoln faced not just the Confederacy but western problems as well. Utah showed an American population ready to break off if pushed. The Dakota War sent the warning that Indian nations might push back and reclaim territory during the Civil War. Lincoln and the Union faced the possibility of western dissolution.

OREGON

Despite being on the opposite coast from the Confederacy, Oregon and California both harbored Confederate sympathizers who agreed with the positions of the new Confederacy.[80] In the lead-up to the passage of each of their constitutions, both states struggled with the issues of black settlement, black rights, and whether or not to allow slavery. In the end, Oregon banned black and mulatto settlement as well as slavery, but for different reasons. They excluded blacks because they saw them as labor competition and a racial threat. They voted down slavery because it created an unfair advantage for slave owners over the yeoman farmers.[81] California also excluded blacks, but only from civic life. The constitution allowed them to settle but did not allow them to vote, serve on juries, or run for office. Californians also disenfranchised Mexicans and Indians as well, preserving the Bear Flag state for white development.

Despite these seemingly Republican and Unionist decisions, both states had strong Confederate loyalties based on other issues. While Oregon voted to prohibit slavery, some still wished to own slaves and aligned with the South over this issue. And the law prohibiting slavery did not mean Oregonians wanted to free the slaves. The provision in the constitution required all blacks, free or slave, to leave the state within two years.[82] But Oregonians, especially those in the southern Oregon, also adhered "to long-held political beliefs that emphasized small government and states' rights." Additionally, many Oregonians "agreed that the South had a clear constitutional right to maintain its 'peculiar institution' of slavery," just not in their territory.[83]

In the late 1850s, Oregon's population underwent a significant change. Whereas previous immigrants often hailed from New England and the Ohio Valley, the discovery of gold changed this pattern. As in other parts of the West, gold mining drew in populations from the South with experience in southern gold mines of the 1820s through to the 1840s. The California gold rush attracted Southern miners as did the much later Colorado strikes. Like every group of immigrants, these Southerners bore with them political and social ideas about slavery and states' rights. As they settled in southern Oregon and the Civil War broke out, they expressed these ideas.

Additionally, southern Oregon experienced the Rogue River Indian War in 1855–1856, when conflict broke out between the Rogue River Indians led by Tecumtum and white settlers. After nine months of constant warfare, the settlers defeated the Rogue River Indians and removed them to the Coast Reservation. During the war, federal troops failed to aid the settlers. The settlers felt abandoned by the government in the face of Indian attacks. But the troops failed to arrive because there were too few of them to dispatch.[84] Southern Oregonians formed their own militia to resolve the war, seething at the lack of federal support. Like the Texans, the people of southern Oregon expected the federal government to protect them from the Indians even as they squatted on Indian land.

Southern sympathies also appeared in organizations that became established in Oregon. In the 1850s, a chapter of the Knights of the Golden Circle started in Oregon.[85] Founded to resist conscription into the Union army, historians most often associate the organization with the South and filibusters, people who sought to invade Mexico and Central America and take the territory for the United States, or later, the Confederacy. In Oregon, it focused on resisting the Union by force if necessary and developing a Pacific republic of Western States. This republic would create servants of South Sea Islanders and blacks allowing the state to control them and their labor.[86] Oregonians did not envision themselves joining the Confederacy, but rather creating their own version of it. Oregonians might have rejected plantation slavery, but they certainly accepted the tenet of Manifest Destiny that other races needed supervision and labor to keep them in place.

Once the Confederacy fired on Fort Sumter, "Southern Oregon's Civil War—albeit a war of words—had begun."[87] The lines, though, were not as clearly drawn as in the East. While many southern Oregonians supported the Union, they thought "the South has been imposed upon."[88] Oregon had a sizeable population of Southerners, many of whom had risen to hold political office.[89] Yet, this sympathy did not mean they wanted to "see the stars and stripes exchanged for a palmetto tree?"[90] Settlers of southern Oregon struggled with their yeoman farmer instincts versus the overreach of the federal government. The withdrawal of federal troops from Oregon created a conundrum similar to that in Texas and Oklahoma. While complaining about the Union's imposition on the South, southern Oregonians still did not want to see the federal troops leave, opening them to Indian attacks.[91] Memories of the Rogue River Indian War remained in the forefront of people's minds. To stop that withdrawal, some argued that Confederates posed a threat to the government of Oregon, as R. A. Stratton did when writing to General Bull Sumner, "A few men of desperate fortunes with arms in their hands might give us infinite trouble."[92] Like those who thought the Sioux Uprising stemmed from Confederate sources, settlers in southern Oregon hoped that the Confederate threat would keep federal troops close. To solve this problem, they created their own volunteer force which guarded emigrant trails, mining camps, and watched for the imminent Confederate threat.[93] This fear of Confederate takeover and invasions did not seem as far-fetched as the Confederates' attempt to march toward Southern California to claim the goldfields for themselves.

ARIZONA, NEW MEXICO, AND GLORIETA PASS

At the beginning of the Civil War, New Mexico territory, which included present-day Arizona, straddled the line between Union and Confederate. Freed from Mexico a little over 10 years before the Civil War, many of the residents remained ambivalent, if not hostile, to the U.S. government. Like Texas, they struggled with constant Indian raids, which they felt the U.S. government had done little to stop.[94] The Apache, in particular, treated the few settlements as resources for food and goods without the benefit of trade. On the other hand, a growing number of forts dotted the countryside, though few represented substantial installations.

Adding to these tensions, the Hispanic population felt as if they neither belonged to Mexico, which suffered from its own internal turmoil, nor to the United States. The Hispanic population resented the U.S. forts, because they felt the army failed to provide protection from raiding Indians and Mexican bandits while demanding precious resources. Racial tensions also hindered interactions between the Mexican population and the army. Just 13 years after the Mexican-American War, members of the army still viewed the local population as, Horace Greeley once wrote, "ignorant and degraded and demoralized and priest-ridden."[95] Additionally, the 1840s and 1850s saw forays by Texans into the territory to claim it as their own. Nuevomexicanos did not really want to be Texans either.[96]

From the east, Arizona and New Mexico simply looked like a link to the goldfields of California. As the railroad debate swirled from the 1840s until the Civil War, Eastern senators and promoters argued for the southern route through these territories to better access the gold fields. They seemed oblivious to the terrain and climate and convinced of the efficacy of the route. Once the Civil War erupted, the Confederacy quickly saw the value of these territories. They provided an opening not only to the gold fields, but also to the rest of the western territories and states, providing room for the expansion of slavery and political alliances. The Confederacy believed "they could count on help from the sympathizers in most of the territories" and California and Oregon.[97]

Remember that 85 percent of the U.S. Army in 1861 patrolled the West. The majority of the officers came from the South, and many immediately resigned their commissions and headed East after Fort Sumter. The U.S. military frantically began to pull back troops to the East, ordering men into Texas, to Indianola on the Gulf Coast, and Fort Leavenworth in Kansas, to begin moving East. Though Western volunteers and recruits took over some of the forts, the U.S. government abandoned many that they deemed too difficult to maintain during the war. These forts they had burned to the ground, including Fort Breckinridge and Buchanan in New Mexico.[98] Such decisions by the military did not help endear the local population, who now felt exposed to Indian attacks, to the Union. Additionally, many of these forts served

as trading posts and provided an economic boost to the local populace. Their disap-
pearance hurt local economies, as well.

The Confederates moved with lightning speed to claim the abandoned forts for
the Confederacy, utilizing a force that already had experience in trying to take the territory: Texans. The Confederacy's desire to expand westward to access the goldfields
and provide a link to a potential foray into Mexico, coupled with the Union's desire
to hold onto New Mexico and Arizona, led to Glorieta Pass, the only Civil War battle
in the Far West in the early part of the War. It could be argued that it is also the only
Western battle because it pitted exclusively western forces, Texas for the Confederacy
and Coloradans for the Union, against each other, rather than Union and Confederate troops from outside the region.

In late July 1861, the Confederate Texans captured Fort Fillmore in Mesilla, New
Mexico. Texas Confederate John Baylor, the Indian fighter, drove the Union troops
from the fort and across the desert.[99] He hoped, then, to catch Union troops coming
through the fort from others on their way east. Instead, they first encountered the
California Confederates led by Albert Sidney Johnston, a brigadier general in the
Union army. He had resigned his position and led other Southern sympathizers from
California toward Texas. California also had Confederate sympathizers, like Oregon,
including politicians. They saw an alliance with the Confederacy as a way to create a
cross-country southern nation and build a railroad from the goldfields east. This last
issue represented an internal conflict in California, as Northern California wanted
the railroad to connect to them as well. Allying with the Confederacy allowed Southern California to circumvent this argument.

While the Texans cheered their success in routing the Union from Mesilla and
greeted the California Confederates, they received word of federal troops landing
in Guaymas, Mexico. This news reminded the Confederacy of the international
connections which the Union could exploit. Suddenly, New Mexico became the
center of the western front. On August 1, 1861, Baylor declared the creation of
Arizona territory within the Confederacy and made himself governor of the new
territory. It appeared a gateway to the riches of the Pacific Coast would soon be
open to the Confederacy.

Not everyone applauded the creation of this new territory under the new
government. The Chiricahua and Mimbrenos Apaches quickly struck the new Confederate territory, seeking to "drive every white man out of their country."[100] Despite
Baylor's best efforts, the attacks continued throughout the fall. He angrily wrote to
the commander of the newly formed Arizona Guards that "The Congress of the
Confederate States has passed a law declaring extermination of all hostile Indians."
He, then, proposed that the commander bring the Indians in for a peace treaty and
"kill all the grown Indians and take the children prisoners and sell them to defray the
expense of killing" them.[101] Such approaches did little to resolve the Indian attacks

and illustrated, yet again, why Indian nations from the Apache to the Cherokee disliked and distrusted the Texans.

Another western problem cropped up in the summer and spring of 1861: tensions with Mexico. The rumors turned out to be true. At the same time, the U.S. government requested permission to land troops in Mexico and march them into New Mexico territory through Mexico, the troops Baylor feared would soon be arriving from California. The Confederacy sent an emissary to Mexico to ask them not to let Union troops cross their territory to get to Arizona territory. The Confederacy's support for filibusters and designs on expanding into Mexico for silver weakened the request.[102] Yet again, territory in the West became part of an international intrigue and a tug of war between outside forces seeking to conquer and control the region.

Though the Confederacy occupied southern New Mexico territory, calling it Arizona, the Union continued to hold, however tenuously, the rest of New Mexico's territory. The Confederacy eyed the Santa Fe Trail, hoping that by taking control of it they would force the Union out, as supplies and travelers came down it and through Glorieta Pass. In March 1862, Confederate forces from Texas, led by Major Charles Pyron, marched on Glorieta Pass. From the north, Major John Chivington, later of the Sand Creek Massacre, led Union forces from Colorado down to the Pass. As a Methodist minister, Chivington had turned down a chaplaincy to be able to lead a fighting force against the Confederacy. On March 26, Chivington moved into the pass. Over the course of the day, they pushed the Confederates back, and they retreated to a ranch at the south end. The next day, Confederate reinforcements, led by Lieutenant William Scurry, arrived as did more Union troops led by Colonel John Slough.[103]

On March 28, the battle ensued with the Confederates pushing the Union back up the pass. By the end of the day, Scurry and the Confederates left the battle thinking they had won as the Union retreated back to Kozlowski's Ranch to lick their wound. But while the battle progressed, Chivington and his men had orchestrated a nasty surprise for the Confederates. In a move worthy of Hollywood, they flanked Scurry and destroyed all his supplies and animals. Chivington's men rappelled down a cliff using their belts and ropes. They burned or destroyed all the supplies and bayoneted several hundred horses. "With barely enough food, low on ammunition and lacking blankets, tents and medical supplies, the dismayed Texans . . . mostly afoot, in torn, disheveled uniforms and shoes that were wearing out, retreated to Santa Fe."[104] By the end of April, Confederate forces began marching down the Rio Grande back toward Texas, followed by Brigadier General Edward Canby, head of the Union's New Mexico department. Much to the dismay of the Confederates, they learned the California Union reinforcements were finally arriving, signaling the end of the Confederate dreams. By June, the Texans began to cross the desert back to El Paso, abandoning the territory to the Union.[105]

The Union victory at Glorieta Pass ended Confederate dreams of a western empire. Once the Texans retreated, the Union regained the territories. But the battle remains significant for Westerners beyond the Union's victory. While not the only battle fought west of the Mississippi, it represents the only one fought between Westerners during the Civil War. Scurry and Pyron's men hailed from Texas and came not only for the Confederacy, but also for Texas, which had hankered after New Mexico territory for 20 years. Chivington's forces came down from Colorado, a state split over the war but nevertheless able to produce Union troops. And they fought a western-style battle, stashing supplies and camp where water existed. Unlike many eastern battles of the Civil War, it was not fought on a field or in the woods but in a mountain pass, flanked by steep sides, with only one entrance and exit. It also marked a turning point in the war for the West. As Glorieta Pass erupted, settlers swarmed across the West, away from the conflict in the East, to take advantage of the Homestead Act, which changed the settlement patterns in the West immediately.

THE FINAL ACT

In 1862, as the Dakota War erupted and tensions rose with the Mormons, Congress passed the Homestead Act, an idea that had been part of Lincoln's 1860 platform. This act opened federal land to homesteaders in 160 acre parcels. Settlers had to pledge they intended to become citizens and improve on the land within five to seven years. They could also buy the land outright at $1.25 an acre. The Homestead Act changed the game. It opened vast amounts of federal land to development and settlement. But it did so in a way that solidified the yeoman farmer model over that of the plantation owner. The 160 acres represented a small family farm, not a large one with paid or bonded workers. Though fraud allowed some to gain extra acreage and speculators also grabbed land, the overall effect was to preserve the single-family farm for the West.[106] After Oregon's experiment with larger land grants, Congress settled on one that preserved individual labor. The Homestead Act did not make an equal playing field, though. Immigrants and settlers still needed a sizeable amount of cash to be able to buy seeds and supplies to develop the land.[107]

The Homestead Act, though, failed as an unmitigated success. It did not take into account the various landscapes and ecosystems of the West and needed to be revised several times as the Desert Land Act, the Timber Culture Act, and the Timber and Stone Act. Corruption ran rampant with "making use of dummy-entry men and false swearing, and sometimes conniving with officers of government land offices, the speculators skimmed the cream off the top."[108] Groups, other than individuals, benefited from the act: land companies and the railroads. Land companies sought to bring in groups of settlers to predetermined plots. The federal government helped the railroads move west by granting them large land parcels from the public domain.

The railroads then sold this land to immigrants and settlers at 6 percent interest, locking many into debt and thwarting the intent of the Act. For many Westerners, the Homestead Act became the most important moment of the 1860s. As Daniel Freeman, one of the disputed first homesteaders under the act, wrote, "The Civil War was on and I was a soldier and had to go to the front on New Year's Day, and I wanted to take a homestead before I went to the front."[109] Before aiding in the Civil War, he wanted to secure land and his future in the West.

The Homestead Act also added a new layer of federal oversight and power to the West. The government controlled vast amount of lands in all the western states and territories, except Texas. The federal government, thus, oversaw the distribution of these lands as well as their protection. This type of oversight was unprecedented on other frontiers within American history. The Homestead Act incorporated squatter sovereignty, making squatting legal, valid, and required. Though the government insisted that Indian lands and those not yet covered by treaties would be exempt, with few accurate maps or landmarks, many Indian acres became legal property of settlers through the Homestead Act. The numbers were startling. Between 1862 and 1866, the Pacific Territories welcomed more than 85,000 families from east of the Mississippi.[110] Between 1862 and 1900, 1.4 million people moved into the trans-Mississippi West, dwarfing the Indian population and flooding into lands previously considered uninhabitable. Slave or free, virtually free land trumped all. The conversation about free or slave in the West ended with a whimper as the government changed the subject.

In a 60-year period, the trans-Mississippi West went from being an underpopulated area of international tensions to a fast growing region of the United States. Spain, England, and France had faded away, leaving a vacuum filled slowly at first, and more quickly after the Mexican-American War, by Americans. Hundreds of Indian nations found themselves inundated by American settlers and their conflicts. Seven western states came into the Union between the Mexican-American War and the end of the Civil War. Territories like Utah, Arizona, Washington, and Oregon also became an active part of the United States.

Even though the Americans who settled these territories came mainly from the East, the debates in which they engaged in the West were not eastern ones. More states and territories argued about African American settlement than about slavery. Though Congress waffled and worried about how to resolve which states would be free and which would be slave, the actual territories worried more about African American settlement and its effects on preserving the West for white yeoman farmers. Consequently, debates about slavery focused around whether it granted an unfair advantage to slave owners over yeoman farmers. Many Westerners supported states' rights so they could choose who lived in their state and how their state might be organized, such as the Mormons. They wanted the same rights the Old Northwest and Old Southwest had when they became states: the right to choose.

While western states and territories argued that they wanted the federal government to let them govern themselves, they still relied heavily on that same government
for security and economic support. Without the military, who led the way west in
many cases, western states and territories could not have withstood the onslaught of
Indian Wars, as the Indians sought to push the settlers back. Settlers also needed the
military to help establish U.S. boundaries against European empires, fading or not.
Westerners expected the military to map the territories, build the roads, and provide economic stimulus through forts and the needs of the soldiers. While pushing
the federal government away with one hand, Westerners held tight with the other.
The eruption of the Civil War threatened western communities in a way it did not
threaten those in the East. The withdrawal of regular troops left many communities
in the West vulnerable, both physically and economically.

CONCLUSION

Between 1800 and 1848, the Spanish North, the British Pacific Coast, and the smattering of French settlements coalesced into a region, on paper at least, for the United States. But while the political borders changed, the population remained as Indian nations still controlled the Great Plains, most of the Great Basin, and much of the Southwest and Pacific Coast. Small but significant populations of Mexicans and *mestizos* remained in missions, in settlements, and on ranches. For these populations, conflicts remained local, over resources at hand and not national issues.

For the continental United States, which now included Texas, the newly formed trans-Mississippi West provided a canvas onto which Americans could project their dreams about expansion and their debates about slavery. Congress, at the end of the Mexican-American War, considered only Texas, Louisiana, Missouri, and Arkansas as western members. The vast territory between the Mississippi and the Pacific Coast lacked a voice in Washington and, therefore, a voice in policy. For Congress, Manifest Destiny meant the potential of the riches of Asia and the resources of the West. These prizes drove the plans for the transcontinental railroad and shaped the debates about slavery in the West, oblivious of the realities of the terrain and population, and how that would affect the extension of the institution. Though it seemed as if the international conflict had ended, in reality, the borders remained fluid. Over the course of the 10 years between 1848 and 1858, the U.S. military expanded westward, outpacing the reach of settlements in an effort to secure the new territories for the United States. The military found themselves fighting both traditional international conflicts against Europeans and the various Indian nations, and as a constabulary police on the frontier. Both these roles shaped the future of the West and the relationship of that region with the federal government.

The racial makeup of the West differed dramatically from the Northeast and Southeast. Whereas in parts of the South, blacks made up the majority of the population, as in Georgia and South Carolina, the black population and the white population remained low overall in the trans-Mississippi West. Instead, the biggest Western populations consisted of Indians and Mexicans/*Tejanos*. The biggest growth in the white and black population came right before and during the Civil War. These differences shaped racial tensions in the West, where residents often not only opposed slavery, but also the settlement of non-whites, including blacks, Mexicans, and Indians, within their territory. As the Civil War approached, western states, like Oregon and California, sided with the South over states' rights but not over slavery. They supported states' rights for the ability to limit or ban blacks and other non-white groups from settling in their states. But the blending of populations created regional versions of these debates. The West did not become a homogeneous region, because as it grew, the West morphed again and again as new populations interacted with previous ones, in many ways, following the prescription of Frederick Jackson Turner.

These blending populations required a force to help with the settlement and peace. This force became the U.S. military, which evolved over the 50 years before the Civil War. Emerging from a period of militias and a small standing army, the army grew into a major force in western development. The army became responsible for the security of western migrants as they leapfrogged the Great Plains to the West Coast. Additionally, the army mapped much of the West and its resources, provided stability and economic outlets to frontier communities and served as a frontier constabulary. One of the great ironies of the pre–Civil War period in the West is that as territories became states and demanded the right to govern themselves, they sought more and more protection and support from the army. Even states that broke off from the United States during the Civil War worried about the effect of the withdrawal of the military from their active frontiers. As thousands of soldiers withdrew to the East for the Civil War, the western communities faced economic collapse and exposure to Indian and international enemies.

Not all Indians sought to push the settlers out, though. The Cherokee became Western settlers, moving in waves over the course of the first half of the 19th century. Splitting into three political factions during this period, the Old Settlers, Treaty Party, and National Party went on to represent the conflicts within the Cherokee during the Civil War. These groups clashed over the cultural and political future of the Cherokee nation, separating into two nations during the first 25 years of the 19th century.

When Georgia and the federal government succeeded in removing the Cherokee west, the conflicts reemerged as the Old Settlers/Treaty Party attempted to reconcile, without losing power, with the National Party, who expected to assume power. Not as simple as who owned slaves or who owned land, the conflicts within the Cherokee rose and fell in the lead-up to the Civil War as they tussled for dominance. The outbreak of the Civil War simply reignited these conflicts as it did in other states and territories in the West.

While each state and territory in the West experienced its own unique development, they shared several traits and processes. The origins of migrants shaped debates within the states over rights and slavery. Many of the migrants came west to forge American communities of white citizens, without rights for blacks, Hispanics, Asians, or Indians. In the case of the Cherokee and other Eastern Indians, they wanted the right to create Cherokee communities of their citizens just as the Mormons wanted to make Utah in their image. Immigrants also sought to make the family farm the dominant economic system. They wanted a level playing field where hard work produced success, both economic and political. The debate about slavery divided up along several similar lines. In some places, new settlers feared the unfair advantage that slave labor would give to slave-owning settlers. In other places, small farmers feared that the importation of slaves would create a system that promoted large farms and plantations. At the least, one part of the population in all these territories resented the importation and settlement of blacks, whether free or slave.

Each state also made their own argument against slavery, whether it be about climate, types of industries, or patriotic beliefs. The simplified position that these states settled by Northerners rejected slavery appears false when looking at the facts. Oregon had its share of New Englanders who rejected black settlement. All these cases also demonstrate the complexity of the West. Blacks did not represent the only threat. California, Oregon, and others sought to disenfranchise Asians, Indians, half-breeds, and other non-white groups. The social side of Manifest Destiny that whites would be the only ones with the moral fiber to develop the new lands affected not just the Southwest and former Spanish/Mexican territories, but also the Northwest and the Great Plains as well.

Finally, westward migration did not slow before or during the Civil War. And the Confederacy wanted a part of this. While the territories and new states produced new resources, like lumber and gold, the migrants themselves also created new economies in the East. The jumping off points for westward migration saw economic booms as more and more people headed West. The Confederacy wanted in on this process and wanted to gain control of the western resources. This desire for westward growth also drove the railroad debate as the Confederacy sought to map out a southern railroad to better send migrants west and bring resources east, just as the federal government explored routes in the north.

Ironically, the growing areas of the West shared much in common with the North and South, yet these commonalities did not predict loyalty. Settlers in Oregon and Washington, while rejecting slavery, also rejected black settlement. They wanted their state to have the right to decide who settled there and how they settled, not just whether they would be slave or free. California not only had populations that sided with the South on attitudes toward a state's rights, but also sided with the North on ideas about settlement and the economic problems of slavery. Texas seemed the most ubiquitous Southern state, as Southerners settled it and wanted to continue slavery. Yet, they wanted the federal government to protect them from the Indians while wanting the right to produce their own militia, the Rangers, and follow their own ideas about Indian policy. And Utah shared the most with both sides. Utah, settled by Northerners, wanted their state to have the right to create a theocracy. Slavery could come or go but religious freedom, which they believed the Constitution guaranteed them, needed to be protected through state's rights. In all these cases, the independence of the state or territory relied on the idea of states' rights. Yet, the protection and support of the federal government, through the military and land policy, created and protected these emerging states. The western states and territories could not exist without the federal government and they looked to the federal government to grant them the right to exist as they wanted to.

By examining the trans-Mississippi West during the antebellum period and the very beginning of the Civil War, a different story of the period emerges. Groups that headed west for survival and independence, like the Mormons, the Cherokee, African Americans, and others, cared little for the conflict that erupted on the East Coast. What worried them became their day-to-day relationship with the federal government, with local populations, and with economic institutions. Their alliances and choices during the Civil War emerged from these positions, not from national ones over slavery and states' rights. The West moved from a diverse region compiled of different empires into a region dominated by the federal government and internal conflicts. The Civil War, while central to American history in general, remains background noise to the struggles to define each western territory and state in the same period. Many hoped the Civil War would remain in the East so they could pursue their dreams and ideas in the West.

When the Civil War began in 1861, the West acted like a conduit on the edge of the conflict. The majority of the Union army resided in the West, drawn to protect the rising number of immigrants and settle intertribal Indian disputes and conflicts between the settlers and Indians. Settlers flowed West at a steady rate, as people sought new opportunities there Gold and trade flowed east, funding the federal government and helping states on the eastern edge of the Mississippi River to grow. Less than 20 years before, much of the territory belonged or was claimed by Mexico and Britain. The end of the Mexican-American War and the establishment of the Oregon Territory in 1848 had extended the lands of the United States from the Atlantic to the Pacific and ended 50 years of international conflict between the English, the Russians, the Spanish, and the French. Within these territories, rose a region encompassing the Great Plains, the Southwest, the Rocky Mountains, the Pacific Northwest, and California to be transformed by the draw of the Civil War.

NOTES

PREFACE

1. Elliott West, "Reconstructing Race," *The Western Historical Quarterly*, Vol. 34, No. 1 (Spring 2003), 25.

2. Robert Athearn, "West of Appomattox: Civil War beyond the Great River: A Stage-Setting Interpretation," *Montana: The Magazine of Western History*, Vol. 12, No. 2, Civil War in the West (Spring 1962), 3, 4.

CHAPTER 1

1. David Weber, *The Spanish Frontier in North America* (New Haven, CT: Yale University Press, 1994), 285–287.

2. Weber, *The Spanish Frontier*, 133–141.

3. Andrew Knaut, *The Pueblo Revolt of 1680: Conquest and Resistance in Seventeenth-Century New Mexico* (Norman, OK: University of Oklahoma, 1994).

4. Weber, *The Spanish Frontier*, 92–121.

5. Elizabeth Fenn, *Pox Americana: The Great Smallpox Epidemic of 1775–1782* (New York: Hill and Wang, 2001), 226.

6. While some historians portray the Spanish as a dying empire grasping at far flung lands, others view these expeditions as a way to reinforce their control of territory they already considered theirs. Iris H. Wilson Engstrand, "Of Fish and Men: Spanish Marine Science during

the Late Eighteenth Century," *Pacific Historical Review*, Vol. 69, No. 1 (February 2000), 3–30; Kenneth L. Holmes, "Three Nootka Documents," *Oregon Historical Quarterly*, Vol. 9, No. 4 (Winter 1978), 397–402; Henry Wagner, "The Last Spanish Exploration of the Northwest Coast and the Attempt to Colonize Bodega Bay," *California Historical Society Quarterly*, Vol. 10, No. 4 (December 1931), 313–345.

7. Wagner, "The Last Spanish Exploration," 313; Holmes, "Three Nootka Documents," 400.

8. Hubert Howe Bancroft, *The Native Races of the Pacific States of North America*, Vol. 1 (New York, NY: D. Appleton and Company, 1875); Herbert Eugene Bolton, *The Colonization of North America, 1492–1783* (New York, NY: The MacMillan Company, 1920); William Ray Manning, "The Nootka Sound Controversy," *Annual Report of the American Historical Association, The Year 1904* (Washington, DC: Government Printing Office, 1905).

9. J. Holland Rose, "Captain Cook and the Founding of British Power in the Pacific," *The Geographical Journal*, Vol. 73, No. 2 (February 1929), 103.

10. J. M. Mancini, "Pedro Cambón's Asian Objects: A Transpacific Approach to Eighteenth-Century California," *American Art: Smithsonian American Art Museum* (Spring 2011), 28–52.

11. http://www.napoleon-series.org/research/government/diplomatic/c_ildefonso.html. Accessed January 24, 2013.

12. Wilfrid Schoenberg, "Frontier Catholics in the Pacific Northwest," *U.S. Catholic Historian*, Vol. 12, No. 4, Frontier Catholicism (Fall 1994), 70.

13. Manning, "The Nootka Sound Controversy," 286; Rose, "Captain Cook and the Founding of British Power in the Pacific," 103.

14. Fenn, *Pox Americana*, 229; Schoenberg, "Frontier Catholics," 69.

15. For contemporary accounts, see United States Bureau of Indian Affairs, *Letter from the Secretary of the Interior Communicating, in Compliance with the Resolution of the Senate of the 2nd Instant, Information in Relation to the Early Labors of the Missionaries of the American Board of Commissioners for Foreign Missions, Commencing in 1856* (Washington, DC: Government Printing Office, 1871). For a different perspective, see Jean Barman, *The West beyond the West: A History of British Columbia*, Rev. ed. (Toronto: University of Toronto Press, 1996), 48; Julie Roy Jeffrey, *Converting the West: A Biography of Narcissa Whitman* (Norman, OK: University of Oklahoma Press, 1994); Robert Burns, "Missionary Syndrome: Crusader and Pacific Northwest Religious Expansionism," *Comparative Studies in Society and History*, Vol. 30, No. 2 (April 1988), 273.

16. Clifford Drury, "Joe Meek Comments on Reasons for the Whitman Massacre," *Oregon Historical Quarterly*, Vol. 75, No. 1 (March 1974), 72.

17. Robert Boyd, "The Pacific Northwest Measles Epidemic of 1847–1848," *Oregon Historical Quarterly*, Vol. 95, No. 1, Early Contacts between Euro-Americans and Native Americans (Spring 1994), 8.

18. Burns, "Missionary Syndrome," 273.

19. Schoenberg, "Frontier Catholics," 73.

20. H. H. Spalding, "Narrative of an Overland Journey to Fort Vancouver and Lapwai in 1836 together with an Account of the Beginning of the American Protestant Missions beyond the Rockies," typescript copy, Western Americana Collection, Bienecke Rare Book Library, Yale University; Schoenberg, "Frontier Catholics," 74.

21. Thomas R. Garth, "Wailaptu after the Massacre," *The Pacific Northwest Quarterly*, Vol. 38, No. 4 (October 1947), 315; Drury, "Joe Meek Comments," 72.

22. Henry Commanger, "England and Oregon Treaty of 1846," *Oregon Historical Quarterly*, Vol. 28, No. 1 (March 1927), 18–38.

23. For contemporary accounts, see United States Bureau of Indian Affairs, *Letter from the Secretary of the Interior Communicating, in Compliance with the Resolution of the Senate of the 2nd Instant, Information in Relation to the Early Labors of the Missionaries of the American Board of Commissioners for Foreign Missions, Commencing in 1856* (Washington, DC: Government Printing Office, 1871); United States Bureau of Indian Affairs, *Letter from the Secretary of the Interior Transmitting, in Compliance with the Resolution of the House of the 15th Instant, the Report of J. Ross Browne, in the Subject of the Indian War in Oregon and Washington Territories* (Washington, DC: Government Printing Office, 1858).

24. Garth, "Wailaptu after the Massacre," 315.

25. Sean Kelley, "'Mexico in His Head': Slavery and the Texas-Mexico Border, 1810–1860," *Journal of Social History*, Vol. 37, No. 3 (Spring 2004), 711.

26. Weber, *The Spanish Frontier in North America*, 313–314.

27. Kelley, "'Mexico in His Head,'" 711.

28. Kelley, "'Mexico in His Head,'" 711, 714.

29. Shelley Streeby, "American Sensations: Empire, Amnesia, and the US-Mexican War," *American Literary History*, Vol. 13, No. 1 (Spring 2001), 30.

30. Andrés Resendez, "National Identity on a Shifting Border: Texas and New Mexico in the Age of Transition, 1821–1848," *The Journal of American History*, Vol. 86, No. 2, *Rethinking History and the Nation-State: Mexico and the United States as a Case Study: A Special Issue* (September 1999), 632.

31. Richard Nostrand, "The Borderlands in Perspective," *Conference of Latin Americanist Geographers*, International Aspects of Development in Latin America: Geographic Aspects, Vol. 6 (1977), 12.

32. Kelley, "'Mexico in His Head,'" 716–717.

33. Durwood Ball, *Army Regulars on the Western Frontier, 1848–1861* (Norman: University of Oklahoma Press, 2001), 13.

34. Roger Nichols, *Indians in the United States and Canada: A Comparative History* (Lincoln, NE: University of Nebraska Press, 1998), 147–150.

35. Captain R. C. Carter, *On the Border with Mackenzie, or Winning West Texas from the Comanches* (New York: Antiquarian Press, 1961), 367, as cited in Sherry Smith, *The View from Officers' Row: Army Perceptions of Western Indians* (Tucson: University of Arizona Press, 1990), 31.

36. Nichols, *Indians in the United States and Canada*, 151–173.

37. For the best brief history of the background of the Church of the Latter-day Saints, see Todd Kerstetter, *God's Country, Uncle Sam's Land: Faith and Conflict in the American West* (Urbana: University of Illinois Press, 2008).

38. Newell Bringhurst, "The Mormons and Slavery—A Closer Look," in *African Americans on the Western Frontier*, ed. Monroe Lee Billington and Roger D. Hardaway (Niwot: University of Colorado Press, 1998), 27.

39. *Book of Mormon*, 2 Nephi 26:33; Bringhurst, "The Mormons and Slavery," 33.

40. Bringhurst, "The Mormons and Slavery," 27.

41. *Doctrine and Covenant*, 134:12, first published in *Latter Day Saints Messenger and Advocate*, August 1835. Cited in Bringhurst, "The Mormons and Slavery," 28.

42. Frederick Merk, "The Oregon Pioneers and the Boundary," *Oregon Historical Quarterly*, Vol. 28, No. 4 (December 1927), 380.

43. Bringhurst, "The Mormons and Slavery," 24.

44. Carol Higham and William Katerberg, *Conquests and Consequences: The American West from Frontier to Region* (Wheeling, IL: Harlan Davidson, 2009), 136.

45. Bringhurst, "The Mormons and Slavery," 32.

46. Higham and Katerberg, *Conquests and Consequences*, 137.

47. James M. McCaffrey, *Army of Manifest Destiny: The American Soldier in the Mexican War, 1846–1848* (New York: New York University Press, 1992), 147–148.

48. McCaffrey, *Army of Manifest Destiny*, 208.

49. McCaffrey, *Army of Manifest Destiny*, 157.

50. Gary Vitale, "Abraham Lincoln and the Mormons: Another Legacy of Limited Freedom," *Journal of the Illinois State Historical Society*, Vol. 101, No. 3/4 (Fall-Winter 2008), 265.

51. Paul Foos, *A Short, Offhand, Killing Affair: Soldiers and Social Conflict during the Mexican-American War* (Chapel Hill: University of North Carolina Press, 2002), 6.

52. Kelley, " 'Mexico in His Head,' " 710.

53. Louis Bernard Schmidt, "Manifest Opportunity: The Borderlands in Perspective," *Conference of Latin Americanist Geographers, International Aspects of Development in Latin America: Geographic Aspects*, Vol. 6 (1977), 245.

54. Gertrude Cunningham, "The Significance of 1846 to the Pacific Coast," *The Washington Historical Quarterly*, Vol. 21, No. 1 (January 1930), 42.

55. Douglas Monroy, *Thrown among Strangers*, 173–180, cited in Shirley Ann Wilson Moore, " 'We Feel the Want of Protection': The Politics of Law and Race in California, 1848–1878," *California History*, Vol. 81, No. 3/4, Taming the Elephant: Politics, Government, and Law in Pioneer California (2003), 101.

56. Elizabeth Hass, "War in California, 1846–1848," *California History*, Vol. 76, No. 2/3, Contested Eden: California before the Gold Rush (Summer-Fall 1997), 334.

57. Haas, "War in California," 349; Moore, " 'We Feel the Want of Protection,' " 102.

58. Moore, " 'We Feel the Want of Protection,' " 102.

59. Reginald Horsman, *Race and Manifest Destiny: The Origins of American Anglo-Saxonism* (Cambridge, MA: Harvard University Press, 1981), 260, as cited in John Carlos Rowe, "Highway Robbery: 'Indian Removal,' the Mexican-American War, and American Identity in 'The Life and Adventures of Joaquín Murieta,' " *NOVEL: A Forum on Fiction*, Vol. 31, No. 2, 30th Anniversary Issue: II (Spring 1998), 152.

60. Moore, " 'We Feel the Want of Protection,' " 99.

61. *Daily National Intelligencer* (Washington, DC), 14 September 1847; Chancellor James Kent to Daniel Webster, in *The Papers of Daniel Webster, Series I: Correspondence,*

Vol. 6, ed. Charles M. Wiltse (Hanover, NH, 1974–1986), 242, as cited in Michael Morrison, "'New Territory versus No Territory': The Whig Party and the Politics of Western Expansion,1846–1848," *The Western Historical Quarterly*, Vol. 23, No. 1 (February 1992), 25.

62. Foos, *A Short, Offhand, Killing Affair*, 8.

63. *Daily National Intelligencer* as cited in Morrison, "'New Territory versus No Territory,'" 25.

64. Matthew Frye Jacobsen, *Whiteness of a Different Color: European Immigrants and the Alchemy of Race* (Cambridge: Harvard University Press, 1998).

65. Streeby, "American Sensations," 14; Morrison, "'New Territory versus No Territory,'" 39.

66. Schmidt, "Manifest Opportunity," 245.

67. Foos, *A Short, Offhand, Killing Affair*, 3.

68. Archer B. Hulbert, *The Paths of Inland Commerce* (New Haven: Yale University, 1921), 149, as cited in R. R. Russell, "A Revaluation of the Period before the Civil War: Railroads," *The Mississippi Valley Historical Review*, Vol. 15, No. 3 (December 1928), 341–354.

69. Streeby, "American Sensations," 14; Resendez, "National Identity on a Shifting Border," 677.

70. Foos, *A Short, Offhand, Killing Affair*, 96.

71. Rowe, "Highway Robbery," 156.

72. Foos, *A Short, Offhand, Killing Affair*, 151–152, 155.

73. Foos, *A Short, Offhand, Killing Affair*, 5.

74. Moore, "'We Feel the Want of Protection,'" 102.

75. Robert G. Athearn, "West of Appomattox: Civil War beyond the Great River: A Stage-Setting Interpretation," *Montana: The Magazine of Western History*, Vol. 12, No. 2, Civil War in the West (Spring 1962), 7; Eugene Berwanger, *The Frontier against Slavery: Western Anti-Negro Prejudice and the Slavery Extension Controversy* (Urbana: University of Illinois Press, 1967), 66–67.

76. Rowe, "Highway Robbery," 151, 155–156.

77. Foos, *A Short, Offhand, Killing Affair*, 25.

78. A. B. Bender, "The Soldier in the Far West, 1848–1860," *Pacific Historical Review*, Vol. 8, No. 2 (June 1939), 176.

79. Robert Wooster, *The American Military Frontiers: The United States Army in the West, 1783–1900* (Albuquerque: University of New Mexico Press, 2009), 119; A. B. Bender, "The Soldier in the Far West," 159.

80. Rowe, "Highway Robbery," 156.

81. Rowe, "Highway Robbery," 156; Moore, "'We Feel the Want of Protection,'" 108.

82. Moore, "'We Feel the Want of Protection,'" 108; Broussard, *Expectations of Equality*, 8–9.

83. Rowe, "Highway Robbery," 151.

84. Wooster, *The American Military Frontiers*, 128.

85. Cameron Addis, "The Whitman Massacre: Religion and Manifest Destiny on the Columbia Plateau, 1809–1858," *Journal of the Early Republic*, Vol. 25, No. 2 (Summer 2005), 249.

CHAPTER 2

1. Robert Wooster, *The American Military Frontiers: The United States Army in the West, 1783–1900* (Albuquerque: University of New Mexico Press, 2009), 119.

2. Durwood Ball, *Army Regulars on the Western Frontier, 1848–1861* (Norman, OK: University of Oklahoma Press, 2001), 24.

3. Wooster, *The American Military Frontiers*, 155; A. B. Bender, "The Soldier in the Far West, 1848–1860," *Pacific Historical Review*, Vol. 8, No. 2 (June 1939),178; Fairfax Downey, "From Plumes to Buckskin: High-Hatted Dragoons of the Revolution Became Our Hard-Bitten Indian Wars Cavalrymen," *Montana: The Magazine of Western History*, Vol. 13, No. 1 (Winter 1963), xxii.

4. Sherry Smith, *The View from Officer's Row: Army Perceptions of Western Indians* (Tucson: University of Arizona Press, 1990), 9; Ball, *Army Regulars*, xiii.

5. James M. McCaffrey, *Army of Manifest Destiny: The American Soldier in the Mexican War, 1846–1848* (New York: New York University Press, 1992), 16.

6. F. A. Mitchel, "How to Make West Point More Useful," *The North American Review*, Vol. 159, No. 452 (July 1894), 62.

7. Paul Foos, *A Short, Offhand, Killing Affair: Soldiers and Social Conflict during the Mexican-American War* (Chapel Hill: University of North Carolina Press, 2002), 9.

8. Foos, *A Short, Offhand, Killing Affair*, 31.

9. Foos, *A Short, Offhand, Killing Affair*, 86, 113; Wooster, *The American Military Frontiers*, 152.

10. Foos, *A Short, Offhand, Killing Affair*, 23.

11. Ball, *Army Regulars*, 57.

12. Foos, *A Short, Offhand, Killing Affair*, 23, 25.

13. Foos, *A Short, Offhand, Killing Affair*, 13, 33.

14. Ball, *Army Regulars*, 57.

15. McCaffrey, *Army of Manifest Destiny*, 15.

16. Wooster, *The American Military Frontiers*, 96.

17. Wooster, *The American Military Frontiers*, 80, 93; Downey, "From Plumes to Buckskin," 18.

18. Wooster, *The American Military Frontiers*, 80.

19. Wooster, *The American Military Frontiers*, 85.

20. Wooster, *The American Military Frontiers*, 89–93.

21. Downey, "From Plumes to Buckskin," 18; McCaffrey, *Army of Manifest Destiny*, 16.

22. Ball, *Army Regulars*, 73.

23. Foos, *A Short, Offhand, Killing Affair*, 21.

24. Ball, *Army Regulars*, 60.

25. McCaffrey, *Army of Manifest Destiny*, 110.

26. Wooster, *The American Military Frontiers*, 83, 103.

27. Foos, *A Short, Offhand, Killing Affair*, 31; McCaffrey, *Army of Manifest Destiny*, 16.

28. McCaffrey, *Army of Manifest Destiny*, 16, 17.

29. McCaffrey, *Army of Manifest Destiny*, 119.

30. McCaffrey, *Army of Manifest Destiny*, 99.

31. Foos, *A Short, Offhand, Killing Affair*, 32.

32. McCaffrey, *Army of Manifest Destiny*, 20.

33. McCaffrey, *Army of Manifest Destiny*, 13.

34. Foos, *A Short, Offhand, Killing Affair*, 87.

35. Ball, *Army Regulars*, xiii.

36. McCaffrey, *Army of Manifest Destiny*, 130.

37. Downey, "From Plumes to Buckskin," 22.

38. Ball, *Army Regulars*, 72.

39. Wooster, *The American Military Frontiers*, 94.

40. McCaffrey, *Army of Manifest Destiny*, 120.

41. Foos, *A Short, Offhand, Killing Affair*, 84.

42. McCaffrey, *Army of Manifest Destiny*, 111, 175; Foos, *A Short, Offhand, Killing Affair*, 21.

43. Wooster, *The American Military Frontiers*, 118.

44. Wooster, *The American Military Frontiers*, 103; Foos, *A Short, Offhand, Killing Affair*, 23.

45. Ball, *Army Regulars*, xi.

46. Wooster, *The American Military Frontiers*, 96.

47. Congressional Globe, February 18 and July 2, 1836; and U.S. Statutes at Large, Vol. 67, footnote 6, Milton E. Holtz, "Old Fort Kearny, 1846–1848: Symbol of a Changing Frontier," *Montana: The Magazine of Western History*, Vol. 22, No. 4 (Autumn 1972), 46.

48. Wooster, *The American Military Frontiers*, 83.

49. Holtz, "Old Fort Kearny," 48.

50. *American State Papers, Military Affairs*, Vol. 6, No. 659, 149, as found in Footnote 7, Holtz, "Old Fort Kearny," 48.

51. Holtz, "Old Fort Kearny," 48.

52. *American State Papers, Military Affairs*, Vol. 6, No. 659, 149, as found in Footnote 10, Holtz, "Old Fort Kearny," 49.

53. Holtz, "Old Fort Kearny," 48–49.

54. Wooster, *The American Military Frontiers*, 89.

55. Holtz, "Old Fort Kearny," 50.

56. Frank Heywood Hodder, "The Railroad Background of the Kansas-Nebraska Act," *The Mississippi Valley Historical Review*, Vol. 12, No. 1 (June 1925), 5.

57. Holtz, "Old Fort Kearny," 54.

58. Clifford Drury, "Joe Meek Comments on Reasons for the Whitman Massacre," *Oregon Historical Quarterly*, Vol. 75, No. 1 (March 1974), 72.

59. Holtz, "Old Fort Kearny," 54.

60. Richard Durbin and Elizabeth Durbin, "Wisconsin's Old Military Road: Its Genesis and Construction," *The Wisconsin Magazine of History*, Vol. 68, No. 1 (Autumn 1984), 8.

61. Leroy Hafen, "Thomas Fitzpatrick and the First Indian Agency of the Upper Platte and Arkansas," *The Mississippi Valley Historical Review*, Vol. 15, No. 3 (December 1928), 377.

62. Wooster, *The American Military Frontiers*, 108. "Fort Smith Historic Site," http://www.exploresouthernhistory.com/fortsmith.html.

63. Ball, *Army Regulars*, xxi.

64. B. Sacks, "The Origins of Fort Buchanan: Myth and Fact," *Arizona and the West*, Vol. 7, No. 3 (Autumn 1965), 211.

65. Bender, "The Soldier in the Far West," 162.

66. Bender, "The Soldier in the Far West," 163.

67. Sacks, "The Origins of Fort Buchanan," 215.

68. Bender, "The Soldier in the Far West," 162–163.

69. Wooster, *The American Military Frontiers*, 125.

70. Sacks, "The Origins of Fort Buchanan," 213–215.

71. Sacks, "The Origins of Fort Buchanan," 213–215, 218.

72. Bender, "The Soldiers in the Far West," 163; Wooster, *The American Military Frontiers*, 127.

73. Ball, *Army Regulars*, 28, 32.

74. Alison Hoagland, "Village Constructions: U.S. Army Forts on the Plains, 1848–1890," *Winterthur Portfolio*, Vol. 34, No. 4 (Winter 1999), 216.

75. Bender, "The Soldiers in the Far West," 178.

76. Foos, *A Short, Offhand, Killing Affair*, 37; McCaffrey, *Army of Manifest Destiny*, 35.

77. Bender, "The Soldiers in the Far West," 159.

78. Ball, *Army Regulars*, xxi.

79. Senate Documents, 24th Congress, 1st Session, Vol. 1, No. 1, 43, as cited in Holtz, "Old Fort Kearny," 46.

80. Wooster, *The American Military Frontiers*, 78.

81. Holtz, "Old Fort Kearny," 46.

82. Wooster, *The American Military Frontiers*, 83.

83. Foos, *A Short, Offhand, Killing Affair*, 21.

84. Wooster, *The American Military Frontiers*, 134.

85. Samuel Blessing, "Colorado Catastrophe," *Montana: The Magazine of Western History*, Vol. 11, No. 1 (Winter 1961), 13.

86. Blessing, "Colorado Catastrophe," 13; Bender, "Soldiers in the Far West," 159.

87. Wooster, *The American Military Frontiers*, 133.

88. Wooster, *The American Military Frontiers*, 142.

89. Bender, "Soldiers in the Far West," 178.

90. Wooster, *The American Military Frontiers*, 81.

91. Bender, "The Soldiers in the Far West," 168; Ball, *Army Regulars*, 89.

92. Wooster, *The American Military Frontiers*, 158.

93. W. H. Timmons, "American El Paso: The Formative Years, 1848–1854," *The Southwestern Historical Quarterly*, Vol. 87, No. 1 (July 1983), 3, 5.

94. Timmons, "American El Paso," 34.

95. Ball, *Army Regulars*, xxviii.

96. Article XI, Treaty of Guadalupe-Hidalgo.

97. Ball, *Army Regulars*, 89.

98. Timmons, "American El Paso," 18, 19.

99. Wooster, *The American Military Frontiers*, 110.

100. Hoagland, "Village Constructions," 218.

101. Ball, *Army Regulars*, xiii.

102. Wooster, *The American Military Frontiers*, 120, 121.

103. William McLoughlin, *After the Trail of Tears: The Cherokee Struggle for Sovereignty* (Chapel Hill, NC: The University of North Carolina Press, 1992), 52.

104. Wooster, *The American Military Frontiers*, 121.

105. Smith, *The View from Officers' Row*, 9.

106. Wooster, *The American Military Frontiers*, 113.

107. Wooster, *The American Military Frontiers*, 127.

108. McCaffrey, *Army of Manifest Destiny*, 147.

109. Ball, *Army Regulars*, 153–154.

110. Wooster, *The American Military Frontiers*, 145.

111. Wooster, *The American Military Frontiers*, 147.

112. Wooster, *The American Military Frontiers*, 144, 145.

113. Smith, *The View from Officers' Row*, 96.

114. Ball, *Army Regulars*, 171.

115. Wooster, *The American Military Frontiers*, 143.

116. See Smith, *The View from Officers' Row*; Ball, *Army Regulars*.

117. Hoagland, "Village Constructions," 218.

118. Holtz, "Old Fort Kearny," 53.

119. Ball, *Army Regular*, 15.

120. Wooster, *The American Military Frontiers*, 118.

121. Hafen, "Thomas Fitzpatrick," 380; Wooster, *The American Military Frontiers*, 136.

122. Ball, *Army Regulars*, 12.

123. Ball, *Army Regulars*, 13, 23.

124. Wooster, *The American Military Frontiers*, 106.

125. Holtz, "Old Fort Kearny," 53.

126. Wooster, *The American Military Frontiers*, 161.

127. Wooster, *The American Military Frontiers*, 161.

128. Mitchel, "How to Make West Point More Useful," 61.

129. Wooster, *The American Military Frontiers*, 158.

130. Sacks, "The Origins of Fort Buchanan," 211.

131. Timmons, "American El Paso," 3.

132. Hoagland, "Village Constructions," 217.

133. Hoagland, "Village Constructions," 215.

134. Bender, "The Soldiers in the Far West," 159.

135. Bender, "The Soldiers in the Far West," 159.

136. Hoagland, "Village Constructions," 237.

137. Hoagland, "Village Constructions," 218.

138. Bender, "The Soldiers in the Far West," 159.

139. Wooster, *The American Military Frontiers*, 159.

140. Ball, *Army Regulars*, 17.

141. Ball, *Army Regulars*, 85.

CHAPTER 3

1. Roger Nichols, *Indians in the United States and Canada* (Lincoln: University of Nebraska, 1998), 174–175, 178–179, 189–192.

2. Nichols, *Indians in the United States and Canada*, 184.

3. Nichols, *Indians in the United States and Canada*, 201–202.

4. Frederick Jackson Turner, "The Significance of the Frontier in American History," *Report of the American Historical Association* (Washington, DC: Government Printing Office, 1893), 199–227.

5. Nichols, *Indians in the United States and Canada*, 204–205.

6. For a comprehensive history of the Cherokee, see Theda Perdue, *The Cherokee Nation and the Trail of Tears* (New York: Penguin/Viking, 2007). For a quick history of the change, see Theda Perdue, *The Cherokee Removal: A Brief History with Documents* (New York: Bedford/ St. Martin's, 1995).

7. Perdue, *Cherokee Removal*, 6–7.

8. Perdue, *Cherokee Removal*, 7.

9. Perdue, *Cherokee Removal*, 8.

10. Perdue, *Cherokee Removal*, 9–10.

11. Perdue, *The Cherokee Nation and the Trail of Tears*, Kindle ed., location 424.

12. Perdue, *The Cherokee Nation and the Trail of Tears*, Kindle ed., location 433.

13. Perdue, *The Cherokee Nation and the Trail of Tears*, Kindle ed., location 401.

14. Russell Thornton, "Boundary Resolution and Revitalization Movements: The Case of the Nineteenth-Century Cherokees," *Ethnohistory*, Vol. 40, No. 3 (Summer 1993), 364.

15. Thornton, "Boundary Resolution and Revitalization Movements," 367–368.

16. Perdue, *The Cherokee Nation and the Trail of Tears*, Kindle ed., location 533.

17. Perdue, *The Cherokee Nation and the Trail of Tears*, Kindle ed., location 510.

18. Bob Blackburn, "From Blood Revenge to the Lighthorsemen: Evolution of Law Enforcement Institutions among the Five Civilized Tribes to 1861," *American Indian Law Review*, Vol. 8, No. 1 (1980), 52.

19. Perdue, *The Cherokee Nation and the Trail of Tears*, Kindle ed., location 462–467.

20. Perdue, *The Cherokee Nation and the Trail of Tears*, Kindle ed., location 486.

21. Blackburn, "From Blood Revenge to the Lighthorsemen," 50.

22. Thornton, "Boundary Resolution and Revitalization Movements," 364.

23. John Mack Faragher, *Sugar Creek: Life on the Illinois Prairie* (New Haven: Yale University Press, 1988).

24. Edward E. Dale, "Arkansas and the Cherokees," *The Arkansas Historical Quarterly*, Vol. 8, No. 2 (Summer 1949), 96.

25. Thornton, "Boundary Resolution and Revitalization Movements," 366.

26. Dale, "Arkansas and the Cherokees," 96.

27. Gary Clayton Anderson, *The Conquest of Texas: Ethnic Cleansing in the Promised Land, 1820–1875* (Norman: University of Oklahoma, 2005), 50.

28. Brad Agnew, "The Cherokee Struggle for Lovely's Purchase," *American Indian Quarterly*, Vol. 2, No. 4 (Winter 1975–1976), 348.

29. William McLoughlin, *After the Trail of Tears: The Cherokee Struggle for Sovereignty* (Chapel Hill: The University of North Carolina Press, 1993), 4.

30. Russell Thornton, "Nineteenth-Century Cherokee History," *American Sociological Review*, Vol. 50, No. 1 (February 1985), 125.

31. Ernest William Winkler, "The Cherokee in Texas," *The Quarterly of the Texas State Historical Association*, Vol. 7, No. 2 (October 1903), 103–105.

32. Anderson, *The Conquest of Texas*, 51–52.

33. Sheri Marie Shuck-Hall, "Borderland and Identities in Imperial Texas: The Alabamas and Coushattas in the Anti-Comanche Union, 1820–1840," *The International History Review*, Vol. 25, No. 2 (2003), 563–591.

34. Carol Higham and William Katerberg, *Conquests and Consequences: The American West from Frontier to Region* (Wheeling: Harlan Davidson, 2009), 138.

35. Anderson, *The Conquest of Texas*, 52.

36. Winkler, "The Cherokee in Texas," 117.

37. Anderson, *The Conquest of Texas*, 53–54.

38. Winkler, "The Cherokee in Texas," 143.

39. Winkler, "The Cherokee in Texas," 151.

40. Anderson, *The Conquest of Texas*, 63.

41. Perdue, *The Cherokee Nation and the Trail of Tears*, Kindle ed., location 491.

42. John Rollin Ridge, *A Trumpet of Our Own*, 69, as cited in John Carlos Rowe, "Highway Robbery: 'Indian Removal,' the Mexican-American War, and American Identity in 'The Life and Adventures of Joaquín Murieta,'" *NOVEL: A Forum on Fiction*, Vol. 31, No. 2, 30th Anniversary Issue: II (Spring 1998), 152.

43. Thornton, "Boundary Resolution and Revitalization Movements," 362.

44. Thornton, "Boundary Resolution and Revitalization Movements," 363.

45. Theda Perdue, "Clan and Court: Another Look at the Early Cherokee Republic," *American Indian Quarterly*, Vol. 24, No. 4 (Autumn 2000), 565.

46. Faye Yarbrough, *Race and the Cherokee Nation: Sovereignty and the Cherokee Nation* (Philadelphia: University of Pennsylvania Press, 2008), 42.

47. Clarissa Confer, *The Cherokee Nation in the Civil War* (Norman: University of Oklahoma, 2007), 25.

48. Circe Sturm, "Blood Politics, Racial Classification, and Cherokee National Identity: The Trials and Tribulations of the Cherokee Freedmen," *American Indian Quarterly*, Vol. 22, No. 1/2 (Winter-Spring 1998), 232.

49. Confer, *The Cherokee Nation in the Civil War*, 25.

50. Confer, *The Cherokee Nation in the Civil War*, 25.

51. Blackburn, "From Blood Revenge to the Lighthorsemen," 49.

52. Blackburn, "From Blood Revenge to the Lighthorsemen," 52; Perdue, "Clan and Court," 564.

53. Thornton, "Boundary Resolution and Revitalization Movements," 365; Perdue, "Clan and Court," 564.

54. Thornton, "Nineteenth-Century Cherokee History," 126.

55. McLoughlin, *After the Trail of Tears*, 7.

56. Blackburn, "From Blood Revenge to the Lighthorsemen," 50; Perdue, *The Cherokee Nation and the Trail of Tears*, Kindle ed., location 515.

57. Perdue, "Clan and Court," 564, 566; Theda Perdue, "The Conflict Within: The Cherokee Power Structure and Removal," *The Georgia Historical Quarterly*, Vol. 73, No. 3, Special Issue Commemorating the Sesquicentennial Of Cherokee Removal 1838–1839 (Fall 1989), 474.

58. Perdue, *The Cherokee Nation and the Trail of Tears*, Kindle ed., location 515.

59. Thornton, "Boundary Resolution and Revitalization Movements," 364.

60. McLoughlin, *After the Trail of Tears*, 7.

61. Thornton, "Boundary Resolution and Revitalization Movements," 363.

62. Henry T. Malone, "The Cherokee Phoenix: Supreme Expression of Cherokee Nationalism," *The Georgia Historical Quarterly*, Vol. 34, No. 3 (September 1950), 163.

63. Mary Young, "The Cherokee Nation: Mirror of the Republic," *American Quarterly*, Vol. 33, No. 5, Special Issue: American Culture and the American Frontier (Winter 1981), 511.

64. Yarborough, *Race and the Cherokee Nation*, 4.

65. Yarbrough, *Race and the Cherokee Nation*, 31, 33, 41.

66. Perdue, "The Conflict Within," 482.

67. Yarbrough, *Race and the Cherokee Nation*, 47–48.

68. Thornton, "Boundary Dissolution and Revitalization Movements," 367.

69. Young, "The Cherokee Nation," 524.

70. H. David Williams, "Gambling Away the Inheritance: The Cherokee Nation and Georgia's Gold and Land Lotteries of 1832–33," *The Georgia Historical Quarterly*, Vol. 73, No. 3, Special Issue Commemorating the Sesquicentennial Of Cherokee Removal 1838–1839 (Fall 1989), 520.

71. Young, "The Cherokee Nation," 507.

72. Agnew, "The Cherokee's Struggle for Lovely's Purchase," 348.

73. Williams, "Gambling Away the Inheritance," 524–525.

74. *Worcester v. Georgia* (1832).

75. Confer, *The Cherokee Nation in the Civil War*, 195.

76. Perdue, *The Cherokee Nation and the Trail of Tears*, Kindle ed., location 858.

77. Perdue, *The Cherokee Nation and the Trial of Tears*, Kindle ed., location 618.

78. Confer, *The Cherokee Nation in the Civil War*, 196.

79. Thornton, "Boundary Resolution and Revitalization Movements," 369.

80. Perdue, "The Conflict Within," 487.

81. Confer, *The Cherokee Nation in the Civil War*, 193; Malone, "The Cherokee Phoenix," 167.

82. Perdue, "The Conflict Within," 486.

83. Young, "The Cherokee Nation," 519.

84. Patrick Minges, "Beneath the Underdog: Race, Religion, and the Trail of Tears," *American Indian Quarterly*, Vol. 25, No. 3 (Summer 2001), 468.

85. Perdue, "The Conflict Within," 486.

86. Thornton, "Boundary Resolution and Revitalization Movements," 369.

87. McLoughlin, *After the Trail of Tears*, 4, 6.

88. McLoughlin, *After the Trail of Tears*, 6.

89. McLoughlin, *After the Trail of Tears*, 19.

90. McLoughlin, *After the Trail of Tears*, 4; Perdue, *The Cherokee Nation and the Trail of Tears*, Kindle ed., location 1715.

91. McLoughlin, *After the Trail of Tears*, 10; Perdue, *The Cherokee Nation and the Trail of Tears*, Kindle ed., Location 1710.

92. McLoughlin, *After the Trail of Tears*, 17; Perdue, *The Cherokee Nation and the Trail of Tears*, Kindle ed., Location 1710.

93. Perdue, *The Cherokee Nation and the Trail of Tears*, Kindle ed., location 1762.

94. McLoughlin, *After the Trail of Tears*, 27; Perdue, *The Cherokee Nation and the Trail of Tears*, Kindle ed., location 1820.

95. Young, "The Cherokee Nation," 505.

96. Confer, *The Cherokee Nation in the Civil War*, 22.

97. McLoughlin, *After the Trail of Tears*, 16.

98. Blackburn, "From Blood Revenge to the Lighthorsemen," 56.

99. McLoughlin, *After the Trail of Tears*, 12.

100. Confer, *The Cherokee Nation in the Civil War*, 28.

101. Thornton, "Boundary Dissolution and Revitalization Movements," 370.

102. Young, "The Cherokee Nation," 514–515; Confer, *The Cherokee Nation in the Civil War*, 38.

103. Perdue, *The Cherokee Nation and the Trail of Tears*, Kindle ed., location 1772.

104. Perdue, *The Cherokee Nation and the Trail of Tears*, Kindle ed., location 1719–1720.

105. Perdue, *The Cherokee Nation and the Trail of Tears*, Kindle ed., location 1720.

106. Perdue, *The Cherokee Nation and the Trail of Tears*, Kindle ed., location 1758.

107. McLoughlin, *After the Trail of Tears*, 33.

108. McLoughlin, *After the Trail of Tears*, 47.

109. McLoughlin, *After the Trail of Tears*, 55.

110. Perdue, *The Cherokee Nation and the Trail of Tears*, Kindle ed., location 1801.

111. McLouglin, *After the Trail of Tears*, 22.

112. McLoughlin, *After the Trail of Tears*, 37–38; Perdue, *The Cherokee Nation and the Trail of Tears*, Kindle ed., location 1782.

113. McLoughlin, *After the Trail of Tears*, 35.

114. Perdue, *The Cherokee Nation and the Trail of Tears*, Kindle ed., location 1692.

115. Perdue, *The Cherokee Nation and the Trail of Tears*, Kindle ed., location 1663.

116. Perdue, *The Cherokee Nation and the Trail of Tears*, Kindle ed., location 1786.

117. McLoughlin, *After the Trail of Tears*, 38.

118. McLoughlin, *After the Trail of Tears*, 51.

119. McLoughlin, *After the Trail of Tears*, 56, 57; Perdue, *The Cherokee Nation and the Trail of Tears*, Kindle ed., location 1840.

120. McLoughlin, *After the Trail of Tears*, 60, 64, 67–68.

121. McLoughlin, *After the Trail of Tears*, 60; Perdue, *The Cherokee Nation and the Trail of Tears*, Kindle ed., location 1786.

122. McLoughlin, *After the Trail of Tears*, 88.

123. Devon Mihesuah, "Out of the 'Graves of Polluted Debauches': The Boys of the Cherokee Male Seminary," *American Indian Quarterly*, Vol. 15, No. 4 (Autumn 1991), 504.

124. Mihesuah, "Out of the 'Graves of Polluted Debauches,'" 505–507.

125. McLoughlin, *After the Trail of Tears*, 93.

126. Mihesuah, "Out of the 'Graves of Polluted Debauches,'" 505.

127. Mihesuah, "Out of the 'Graves of Polluted Debauches,'" 508.

128. McLoughlin, *After the Trail of Tears*, 68, 75, 77, 85.

129. McLoughlin, *After the Trail of Tears*, 96–97, 101.

130. Confer, *The Cherokee Nation in the Civil War*, 41, 45.

131. Yarbrough, *Race and the Cherokee Nation*, 41.

CHAPTER 4

1. John D. Unruh, *The Plains Across: The Overland Emigrants and the Trans-Mississippi West, 1840–1890* (Urbana: University of Illinois Press, 1979), 91.

2. Robert Wooster, *The American Military Frontiers: The United States Army in the West, 1783–1900* (Albuquerque: University of New Mexico Press, 2009), 119.

3. Unruh, *The Plains Across*, 81, 98, 120.

4. Marysville *Daily Herald*, April 2, 1856, as cited in Unruh, *The Plains Across*, 86.

5. Unruh, *The Plains Across*, 93, 120.

6. Thomas Garth, "Waiilatpu after the Massacre," *The Pacific Northwest Quarterly*, Vol. 38, No. 4 (October 1947), 316.

7. Milton E. Holtz, "Old Fort Kearny, 1846–1848: Symbol of a Changing Frontier," *Montana: The Magazine of Western History*, Vol. 22, No. 4 (Autumn 1972), 53.

8. Frank Heywood Hodder, "The Railroad Background of the Kansas-Nebraska Act," *The Mississippi Valley Historical Review*, Vol. 12, No. 1 (June 1925), 5.

9. Shirley Ann Wilson Moore, "'We Feel the Want of Protection': The Politics of Law and Race in California, 1848–1878," *California History*, Vol. 81, No. 3/4, Taming the Elephant: Politics, Government, and Law in Pioneer California (2003), 97.

10. John Carlos Rowe, "Highway Robbery: 'Indian Removal,' the Mexican-American War, and American Identity in The Life and Adventures of Joaquín Murieta," *NOVEL: A Forum on Fiction*, Vol. 31, No. 2, 30th Anniversary Issue: II (Spring 1998), 151.

11. Elizabeth Hass, "War in California, 1846–1848," *California History*, Vol. 76, No. 2/3, Contested Eden: California before the Gold Rush (Summer/Fall 1997), 333.

12. Rowe, "Highway Robbery," 155.

13. Hass, "War in California," 333.

14. Hass, "War in California," 330–333.

15. Hass, "War in California," 349.

16. James J. Rawls, "Gold Diggers: Indian Miners in the California Gold Rush," *California Historical Quarterly*, Vol. 55, No. 1 (Spring 1976), 38.

17. Rowe, "Highway Robbery," 151.

18. Eugene Berwanger, *The Frontier against Slavery: Western Anti-Negro Prejudice and the Slavery Extension Controversy* (Urbana: University of Illinois Press, 1967), 60.

19. Huping Ling, "The Family and Marriage in Late-Nineteenth and Early-Twentieth Century Chinese Immigrant Women," *Journal of American Ethnic History*, Vol. 19, No. 2 (Winter 2000), 53.

20. Moore, "'We Feel the Want of Protection,'" 104.

21. Berwanger, *The Frontier against Slavery*, 63.

22. Berwanger, *The Frontier against Slavery*, 61.

23. Moore, "'We Feel the Want of Protection,'" 103.

24. Berwanger, *The Frontier against Slavery*, 63.

25. Berwanger, *The Frontier against Slavery*, 67.

26. Moore, "'We Feel the Want of Protection,'" 104.

27. Glen Sample Ely, "Gone from Texas and Trading with the Enemy: New Perspectives on Civil War West Texas," *The Southwestern Historical Quarterly*, Vol. 110, No. 4 (April 2007), 439, 445.

28. Ray C. Colton, *The Civil War in the Western Territories: Arizona, Colorado, New Mexico, and Utah* (Norman: University of Oklahoma, 1984), 3.

29. Ronald C. Woolsey, "The Politics of a Lost Cause: 'Secesher' and Democrats in Southern California during the Civil War," *California History*, Vol. 69, No. 4 (Winter 1990/1991), 373; W. H. Watford, "Confederate Western Ambitions," *The Southwestern Historical Quarterly*, Vol. 44, No. 2 (October 1940), 162.

30. James M. McCaffrey, *Army of Manifest Destiny: The American Soldier in the Mexican War, 1846–1848* (New York: New York University Press, 1992), 208.

31. Aurora Hunt, "The Far West Volunteers: The Army of the Pacific and the Unsung Valor of Its Men," *Montana: The Magazine of Western History*, Vol. 12, No. 2, Civil War in the West (Spring 1962), 49.

32. Colton, *The Civil War in the Western Territories*, 103.

33. Hodder, "The Railroad Background of the Kansas-Nebraska Act," 20.

34. Samuel Blessing, "Colorado Catastrophe," *Montana: The Magazine of Western History*, Vol. 11, No. 1 (Winter 1961), 13.

35. Hodder, "The Railroad Background of the Kansas-Nebraska Act," 5.

36. Cameron Addis, "The Whitman Massacre: Religion and Manifest Destiny on the Columbia Plateau, 1809–1858," *Journal of the Early Republic*, Vol. 25, No. 2 (Summer 2005), 240.

37. Addis, "The Whitman Massacres," 222; Garth, "Waiilatpu after the Massacre," 315.

38. Richard Van Alstyne, "International Rivalries in the Pacific Northwest," *Oregon Historical Quarterly*, Vol. 46, No. 3 (September 1945), 204.

39. Wooster, *The American Military Frontiers*, 140.

40. Berwanger, *The Frontier against Slavery*, 78.

41. Frederick Merk, "The Oregon Pioneers and the Boundary," *Oregon Historical Quarterly*, Vol. 28, No. 4 (December 1927), 380.

42. Wilfrid Schoenberg, "Frontier Catholics in the Pacific Northwest," *U.S. Catholic Historian*, Vol. 12, No. 4, Frontier Catholicism (Fall 1994), 66; Berwanger, *The Frontier against Slavery*, 78–79.

43. James Perry, Richard H. Chused, and Mary DeLano, "The Spousal Letters of Samuel R. Thurston, Oregon's First Territorial Delegate to Congress: 1849–1851," *Oregon Historical Quarterly*, Vol. 96, No. 1 (Spring 1995), 9.

44. Thomas C. Hogg, "Negroes and Their Institutions in Oregon," *Phylon*. Vol. 30, No. 3 (3rd Quarter 1969), 273; Berwanger, *The Frontier against Slavery*, 78.

45. Hogg, "Negroes and Their Institutions in Oregon," 274; Berwanger, *The Frontier against Slavery*, 80–81.

46. Walter Carlton Woodward, "The Rise and Early History of Political Parties in Oregon-III," *The Quarterly of the Oregon Historical Society*, Vol. 12, No. 2 (June 1911), 125.

47. Berwanger, *The Frontier against Slavery*, 81–83.

48. Rawls, "Gold Diggers," 38, 40.

49. Hogg, "Negroes and Their Institutions in Oregon," 272.

50. Schoenberg, "Frontier Catholics in the Pacific Northwest," 76.

51. *Oregon Statesmen*, January 13, 1857, as cited in Berwanger, *The Frontier against Slavery*, 83.

52. R. R. Russell, "A Revaluation of the Period before the Civil War: Railroads," *The Mississippi Valley Historical Review*, Vol. 15, No. 3 (December 1928), 348.

53. Rhoda Gilman, "Territorial Imperative: How Minnesota Became the 32nd State," *Minnesota History*, Vol. 56, No. 4, Making Minnesota Territory, 1849–1858 (Winter 1998/1999), 156.

54. Russell, "A Revaluation of the Period before the Civil War: Railroads," 125.

55. Hogg, "Negroes and Their Institutions in Oregon," 275.

56. Perry, "The Spousal Letters of James R. Thurston," 8.

57. Woodward, "The Rise and Early History Political Parties in Oregon," 126; Berwanger, *The Frontier against Slavery*, 85.

58. Woodward, "The Rise and Early History Political Parties in Oregon," 153.

59. *Oregon Argus*, February 21 and April 11, 1857, as cited in Berwanger, *The Frontier against Slavery*, 86.

60. *Oregon Argus*, October 14 and 17, 1857, as cited in Berwanger, *The Frontier against Slavery*, 91.

61. Woodward, "The Rise and Early History Political Parties in Oregon," 156; Schoenberg, "Frontier Catholics in the Pacific Northwest," 76; Berwanger, *The Frontier against Slavery*, 93.

62. Berwanger, *The Frontier against Slavery*, 93, 95.

63. *Oregon Argus*, December 1, 1855, as cited in Berwanger, *The Frontier against Slavery*, 88.

64. Berwanger, *The Frontier against Slavery*, 93–94.

65. Wooster, *The American Military Frontiers*, 145, 149.

66. Tom Generous, "Over the River Jordan: California Volunteers in Utah during the Civil War," *California History*, Vol. 63, No. 3 (Summer 1984), 206.

67. Newell Bringhurst, "The Mormons and Slavery—A Closer Look," in *African Americans on the Western Frontier*, ed. Monroe Lee Billington and Roger D. Hardaway (Niwot: University of Colorado Press, 1998), 29.

68. Gary Vitale, "Abraham Lincoln and the Mormons: Another Legacy of Limited Freedom," *Journal of the Illinois State Historical Society*, Vol. 101, No. 3/4 (Fall-Winter 2008), 266.

69. *Deseret News*, May 20, 1857, as cited in Bringhurst, "The Mormons and Slavery," 30.

70. Bringhurst, "The Mormons and Slavery," 31–33.

71. *Deseret News*, October 23, 1861, 189, as cited in Generous, "Over the River Jordan," 206.

72. Generous, "Over the River Jordan," 206; Vitale, "Lincoln and the Mormons," 260.

73. Bringhurst, "The Mormons and Slavery," 24–27.

74. Carol Higham and William Katerberg, *Conquests and Consequences: The American West from Frontier to Region* (Wheeling: Harlan Davidson, 2009), 137.

75. Colton, *The Civil War in the Western Territories*, 162–164, 208.

76. Watford, "Confederate Western Ambitions," 162.

77. Elliott West, "Reconstructing Race," *The Western Historical Quarterly*, Vol. 34, No. 1 (Spring 2003), 12.

78. Wooster, *The American Military Frontiers*, 127.

79. Berwanger, *The Frontier against Slavery*, 98; Edward Everett Dale, "Those Kansas Jayhawkers: A Study in Sectionalism," *Agricultural History*, Vol. 2, No. 4 (October 1928), 169.

80. Annie Heloise Abel, "The Indians in the Civil War," *The American Historical Review*, Vol. 15, No. 2 (January 1910), 281.

81. Berwanger, *The Frontier against Slavery*, 99.

82. Colton, *The Civil War in the Western Territories*, 11.

83. Gerald Wolff, "The Slavocracy and the Homestead Problem of 1854," *Agricultural History*, Vol. 40, No. 2 (April 1966), 102.

84. Hodder, "The Railroad Background of the Kansas-Nebraska Act," 16.

85. Hodder, "The Railroad Background of the Kansas-Nebraska Act," 18.

86. Granville Davis, "Arkansas and the Blood of Kansas," *The Journal of Southern History*, Vol. 16, No. 4 (November 1950), 436.

87. Little Rock, *True Democrat*, September 2, 1856, as cited in Davis, "Arkansas and the Blood of Kansas," 440.

88. Berwanger, *The Frontier against Slavery*, 100.

89. Davis, "Arkansas and the Blood of Kansas," 436–437.

90. Berwanger, *The Frontier against Slavery*, 99.

91. Albert Castel, "Civil War Kansas and the Negro," *The Journal of Negro History*, Vol. 51, No. 2 (April 1966), 125.

92. Dale, "Those Kansas Jayhawkers," 169.

93. Andreas Dorpalen, "The German Element and the Issues of the Civil War," *The Mississippi Valley Historical Review*, Vol. 29, No. 1 (June 1942), 69.

94. Davis, "Arkansas and the Blood of Kansas," 126.

95. Berwanger, *The Frontier against Slavery*, 98.

96. Berwanger, *The Frontier against Slavery*, 101; Davis, "Arkansas and the Blood of Kansas," 126.

97. Berwanger, *The Frontier against Slavery*, 110.

98. William Philips, *Conquest of Kansas*, 134–137, as cited in Berwanger, *The Frontier against Slavery*, 111.

99. Berwanger, *The Frontier against Slavery*, 112, 115.

100. Wooster, *The American Military Frontiers*, 143–144.

101. Wooster, *The American Military Frontiers*, 152.

102. Clarissa Confer, *The Cherokee Nation in the Civil War* (Norman: University of Oklahoma Press, 2007), 37.

103. Confer, *The Cherokee Nation in the Civil War*, 28–29, 32.

104. Davis, "Arkansas and the Blood of Kansas," 436.

105. Berwanger, *The Frontier against Slavery*, 107.

106. Elliott West, *The Contested Plains: Indians, Goldseekers, and the Rush to Colorado* (Lawrence: University of Kansas Press, 1998), 132–135.

107. Anne J. Bailey, *Invisible Southerners: Ethnicity in the Civil War* (Athens: University of Georgia Press, 2006), 26.

108. Bailey, *Invisible Southerners*, 26.

109. Wooster, *The American Military Frontiers*, 156–157.

110. Glen Sample Ely, "Gone to Texas and Trading with the Enemy: New Perspectives on Civil War West Texas," *The Southwestern Historical Quarterly*, Vol. 110, No. 4 (April 2007), 440.

111. Wooster, *The American Military Frontiers*, 121, 125, 134.

112. W. H. Timmons, "American El Paso: The Formative Years, 1848–1854," *The Southwestern Historical Quarterly*, Vol. 87, No. 1 (July 1983), 3, 18.

113. Andrés Resendez, "National Identity on a Shifting Border: Texas and New Mexico in the Age of Transition, 1821–1848," *The Journal of American History*, Vol. 86, No. 2, *Rethinking History and the Nation-State: Mexico and the United States as a Case Study: A Special Issue* (September 1999), 681.

114. Dorpalen, "The German Element and the Issues of the Civil War," 58.

115. Walter Kamphoefner, "New Perspectives on Texas Germans and the Confederacy," *The Southwestern Historical Quarterly*, Vol. 102, No. 4 (April 1999), 441.

116. Dorpalen, "The German Element and the Issues of the Civil War," 60.

117. George Woolfolk, "Turner's Safety-Valve and Free Negro Westward Migration," *The Journal of Negro History*, Vol. 50, No. 3 (July 1965), 189.

118. Sean Kelley, "'Mexico in His Head': Slavery and the Texas-Mexico Border, 1810–1860," *Journal of Social History*, Vol. 37, No. 3 (Spring 2004), 709–710.

119. Kamphoefner, "New Perspectives on Texas Germans and the Confederacy," 444.

120. Dale, "Those Kansas Jayhawkers," 170.

121. Dorpalen, "The German Element and the Issues of the Civil War," 59–60.

122. R. R. Russell, "A Revaluation of the Period before the Civil War: Railroads," *The Mississippi Valley Historical Review*, Vol. 15, No. 3 (December 1928), 353.

CHAPTER 5

1. Anne J. Bailey, *Invisible Southerners: Ethnicity in the Civil War* (Athens: University of Georgia Press, 2006), 2.

2. Bailey, *Invisible Southerners*, 26.

3. Glen Sample Ely, "Gone from Texas and Trading with the Enemy: New Perspectives on Civil War West Texas," *The Southwestern Historical Quarterly*, Vol. 110, No. 4 (April 2007), 451; Gary Clayton Anderson, *The Conquest of Texas: Ethnic Cleansing in the Promised Land, 1820–1875* (Norman: University of Oklahoma, 2005), 330.

4. Bailey, *Invisible Southerners*, 26.

5. Ely, "Gone from Texas," 442.

6. Ely, "Gone from Texas," 441.

7. Anderson, *The Conquest of Texas*, 362.

8. Ely, "Gone from Texas," 444; Anderson, *The Conquest of Texas*, 333.

9. Anderson, *The Conquest of Texas*, 327–328.

10. Ely, "Gone from Texas," 463.

11. Alvin Josephy, Jr., *The Civil War in the American West* (New York: Vintage Books, 1991), 21.

12. Bailey, *Invisible Southerners*, 33.

13. Bailey, *Invisible Southerners*, 11–12.

14. Ely, "Gone from Texas," 463.

15. Josephy, *The Civil War in the American West*, 22, 24–26.

16. Anderson, *The Conquest of Texas*, 333.

17. Josephy, *The Civil War in the American West*, 28.

18. Anderson, *The Conquest of Texas*, 332–333.

19. W. H. Watford, "Confederate Western Ambitions," *The Southwestern Historical Quarterly*, Vol. 44, No. 2 (October 1940), 161.

20. Watford, "Confederate Western Ambitions," 163, 174.

21. Baylor to S. B. Davis, November 2, 1861, 0. R., S., 1, IV, 149, as cited in Watford, "Confederate Western Ambitions," 178.

22. Watford, "Confederate Western Ambitions," 181.

23. G. R. Paul, Report, March 11, 1862, 0. R., S., 1, IX, 654, as cited in Watford, "Confederate Western Ambitions," 183.

24. Clarissa Confer, *The Cherokee Nation in the Civil War* (Norman: University of Oklahoma Press, 2007), 46.

25. William McLoughlin, *After the Trail of Tears: The Cherokee Struggle for Sovereignty* (Chapel Hill: The University of North Carolina Press, 1993), 176.

26. Confer, *The Cherokee Nation in the Civil War*, 45; McLoughlin, *After the Trail of Tears*, 136.

27. Confer, *The Cherokee Nation in the Civil War*, 46.

28. McLoughlin, *After the Trail of Tears*, 178.

29. Confer, *The Cherokee Nation in the Civil War*, 46.

30. McLoughlin, *After the Trail of Tears*, 177–178.

31. Annie Eloise Abel, "The Indians in the Civil War," *The American Historical Review*, Vol. 15, No. 2 (January 1910), 283.

32. Confer, *The Cherokee Nation in the Civil War*, 43, 45, 47.

33. McLoughlin, *After the Trail of Tears*, 123, 151.

34. Confer, *The Cherokee Nation in the Civil War*, 49.

35. McLoughlin, *After the Trail of Tears*, 145.

36. Confer, *The Cherokee Nation in the Civil War*, 49; McLoughlin, *After the Trail of Tears*, 177.

37. McLoughlin, *After the Trail of Tears*, 125.

38. Henry Rector to John Ross, January 29, 1861, in U.S. War Department, *The War of Rebellion: A Compilation of the Official Records of the Union and Confederate Armies*, ser. 1, Vol. 1, 683, as cited in Confer, *The Cherokee Nation in the Civil War*, 43.

39. John Ross, *The Papers of John Ross*, Vol. 2, 430–431, as cited in McLoughlin, *After the Trail of Tears*, 183.

40. McLoughlin, *After the Trail of Tears*, 184, 186.

41. McLoughlin, *After the Trail of Tears*, 187.

42. McLoughlin, *After the Trail of Tears*, 187–188.

43. McLoughlin, *After the Trail of Tears*, 130.

44. Confer, *The Cherokee Nation in the Civil War*, 57, 60.

45. McLoughlin, *After the Trail of Tears*, 182.

46. Also spelled Opothleyoholo.

47. Confer, *The Cherokee Nation in the Civil War*, 50, 59; McLoughlin, *After the Trail of Tears*, 191.

48. Confer, *The Cherokee Nation in the Civil War*, 59.

49. McLoughlin, *After the Trail of Tears*, 192–194.

50. Confer, *The Cherokee Nation in the Civil War*, 59.

51. Confer, *The Cherokee Nation in the Civil War*, 64.

52. Confer, *The Cherokee Nation in the Civil War*, 51.

53. Bailey, *Invisible Southerners*, 41.

54. McLoughlin, *After the Trail of Tears*, 197.

55. Confer, *The Cherokee in the Civil War*, 64, 66.

56. Robert Wooster, *The American Military Frontiers: The United States Army in the West, 1783–1900* (Albuquerque: University of New Mexico Press, 2009), 161.

57. Ray Colton, *The Civil War in the Western Territories: Arizona, Colorado, New Mexico, and Utah* (Norman: University of Oklahoma, 1984), 9.

58. Colton, *The Civil War in the Western Territories*, 11.

59. Tom Generous, "Over the River Jordan: California Volunteers in Utah during the Civil War," *California History*, Vol. 63, No. 3 (Summer 1984), 202.

60. Colton, *The Civil War in the Western Territories*, 180; Generous, "Over the River Jordan," 201.

61. War Dept. *WOR*, Vol. L, Part 2, 119, as cited in Generous, "Over the River Jordan," 203.

62. Colton, *The Civil War in the Western Territories*, 180.

63. Generous, "Over the River Jordan," 206.

64. Colton, *The Civil War in the Western Territories*, 180.

65. Generous, "Over the River Jordan," 207.

66. Wooster, *The American Military Frontiers*, 164.

67. Colton, *The Civil War in the Western Territories*, 180, 182.

68. Generous, "Over the River Jordan," 207.

69. Gary Vitale, "Abraham Lincoln and the Mormons: Another Legacy of Limited Freedom," *Journal of the Illinois State Historical Society*, Vol. 101, No. 3/4 (Fall-Winter 2008), 267–268.

70. Gary Clayton Anderson, *Kinsmen of Another Kind: Dakota-White Relations in the Upper Missouri Valley, 1650–1862* (St. Paul: Minnesota Historical Society Press, 1997), 261.

71. William Lass, "The Eden of the West," *Minnesota History*, Vol. 56, No. 4, Making Minnesota Territory, 1849–1858 (Winter 1998/1999), 204.

72. Lass, "The Eden of the West," 211–212.

73. Anderson, *Kinsmen of Another Kind*, 240.

74. Anderson, *Kinsmen of Another Kind*, 262–270; Dee Brown, *Bury My Heart at Wounded Knee: An Indian History of the American West* (New York: Henry Holt and Company, 1991), 37–67.

75. William D. Green, "Minnesota's Long Road to Black Suffrage, 1849–1868," *Minnesota History*, Vol. 56, No. 2 (Summer 1998), 70.

76. Green, "Minnesota's Long Road to Black Suffrage," 70, 72–73.

77. Carol Higham and William Katerberg, *Conquests and Consequences: The American West from Frontier to Region* (Wheeling, IL: Harlan Davidson, 2009), 196.

78. Confer, *The Cherokee and the Civil War*, 58.

79. Higham and Katerberg, *Conquests and Consequences*, 197.

80. Jeff Lalande, " 'Dixie' of the Pacific Northwest: Southern Oregon's Civil War," *Oregon Historical Quarterly*, Vol. 100, No. 1, *The Civil War in Oregon* (Spring 1999), 33.

81. Thomas Hogg, "Negroes and Their Institutions in Oregon," *Phylon*, Vol. 30, No. 3 (3rd Quarter 1969), 274.

82. Hogg, "Negroes and Their Institutions in Oregon," 272, 274.

83. Lalande, " 'Dixie' of the Pacific Northwest," 36, 38.

84. Lalande, " 'Dixie' of the Pacific Northwest," 36, 38–40.

85. Hogg, "Negroes and Their Institutions in Oregon," 275; Josephy, *The Civil War in the American West*, 19.

86. Hogg, "Negroes and Their Institutions in Oregon," 275.

87. Lalande, " 'Dixie' of the Pacific Northwest," 43.

88. *Oregonian*, October 12, 1861, as cited in Lalande, " 'Dixie' of the Pacific Northwest," 44.

89. Josephy, *The Civil War in the American West*, 19.

90. *Oregon Sentinel*, June 1, 1861, as cited in Lalande, " 'Dixie' of the Pacific Northwest," 45.

91. Lalande, " 'Dixie' of the Pacific Northwest," 49.

92. R. E. Stratton to Gen. E. V. Sumner (August 15, 1861) in *The War of the Rebellion: A Compilation of the Official Records of the Union and Confederate Armies*, Set. 1, Vol. 50, Pt. 1 (Washington, DC, 1897), 571, as cited in Lalande, " 'Dixie' of the Pacific Northwest," 50.

93. Lalande, " 'Dixie' of the Pacific Northwest," 54.

94. B. Sacks, "The Origins of Fort Buchanan: Myth and Fact," *Arizona and the West*, Vol. 7, No. 3 (Autumn 1965), 207–226.

95. Jacqueline Dorgan Meketa, *Louis Felsenthal, Citizen-Soldier of Territorial New Mexico* (Albuquerque: University of New Mexico Press, 1982), 19, as cited in Josephy, *The Civil War in the American West*, 41.

96. Josephy, *The Civil War in the American West*, 42, 53.

97. Josephy, *The Civil War in the American West*, 18–19.

98. Josephy, *The Civil War in the American West*, 34–35.

99. Josephy, *The Civil War in the American West*, 48.

100. Josephy, *The Civil War in the American West*, 49–51.

101. Josephy, *The Civil War in the American West*, 51; Colton, *The Civil War in the Western Territories*, 123.

102. Josephy, *The Civil War in the American West*, 56.

103. Josephy, *The Civil War in the American West*, 76–85.

104. Josephy, *The Civil War in the American West*, 85.

105. Josephy, *The Civil War in the American West*, 89–90.

106. Maurice Baxter, "Encouragement of Immigration to the Middle West during the Era of the Civil War," *Indiana Magazine of History*, Vol. 46, No. 1 (March 1950), 31.

107. Baxter, "Encouragement of Immigration to the Middle West during the Era of the Civil War," 41.

108. Baxter, "Encouragement of Immigration to the Middle West during the Era of the Civil War," 31.

109. Charles Plante and Ray Mattison, "The 'First' Homestead," *Agricultural History*, Vol. 36, No. 4 (October 1962), 186.

110. Lillian Schlissel, *Women's Diaries of the Westward Journey* (New York: Schocken Books, 1981), 24.

BIBLIOGRAPHIC ESSAY

From the beginning of this project, it became clear that American history has grown increasingly compartmentalized over the past 20 years. Southern, Western, and Civil War historians draw finite lines between regions and topics, often cutting off debate between fields because of these lines. Take, for example, the idea of the antebellum period. Southern and Civil War historians use this term and categorize studies that way. Western historians do not. The West was neither anticipating a war nor a full region of the United States until just before the war. Consequently, many of the books with "West" and "Civil War" in the title do not discuss the trans-Mississippi West as much as the debates about it, including: Michael Morrison, *Slavery and the American West: The Eclipse of Manifest Destiny and the Coming of the Civil War* (Chapel Hill: University of North Carolina Press, 1997). On the other hand, Eugene Berwanger's *The Frontier against Slavery: Western Anti-Negro Prejudice and the Slavery Extension Controversy* (Urbana, IL: University of Illinois Press, 1967) examines how settlers in the West viewed slavery and African Americans. Other books actually discuss the Civil War in the trans-Mississippi West from the military's point of view: Donald Frazier, *Blood and Treasure: Confederate Empire in the Southwest* (College Station, TX: Texas A & M University Press, 1995); Alvin Josephy, Jr., *The Civil War in the American West* (New York, NY: Vintage Books, 1991); and Ray Colton, *The Civil War in the Western Territories: Arizona, Colorado, New Mexico and Utah,*

(Norman, OK: University of Oklahoma, 1984). Robert Utley's *The Indian Frontier of the American West, 1846–1890* (Albuquerque, NM: University of New Mexico Press, 1984) provides an overview of the largest period, whereas Josephy and Colton begin just a few years before the Civil War, and it remains the bible of military policy toward the Indians. Several articles address the Confederate presence in the West: James Thane, "The Myths of Confederate Sentiment in Montana," *Montana: The Magazine of Western History*, Vol. 17, No. 2 (Spring 1967), 14–19; W. H. Watford, "Confederate Western Ambitions," *The Southwestern Historical Quarterly*, Vol. 44, No. 2 (October 1940), 161–187; and Stanley Davison and Dale Tash, "Confederate Backwash in Montana Territory," *Montana: The Magazine of Western History*, Vol. 17, No. 4 (Autumn 1967), 50–58.

Those overviews, though, failed to explore the West before the territories became states. When first beginning this project, it quickly became clear that other than the broad overviews provided by Ray Allen Billington and Martin Ridge, *Westward Expansion: A History of the American Frontier*, 6th ed. (Albuquerque, NM: University of New Mexico Press, 2001); and Carol Higham and William Katerberg, *Conquests and Consequences: The American West from Frontier to Region* (Wheeling, IL: Harlan Davidson, 2009), most books about the pre-war period focus on individual states, territories, or populations. Much more needs to be done by Western historians to integrate the history of the pre-war West as a region rather than increasingly smaller studies of moments in that history and development.

It, therefore, became necessary to subdivide the West into regions and examine the types of history regionally. Oregon presented the first dichotomy. There exists literature on the international tensions surrounding Oregon, including Stuart Anderson, "British Threats and the Settlement of the Oregon Boundary," *The Pacific Northwest Quarterly*, Vol. 66, No. 4 (October 1975), 153–160; and Norman Graebner, "Politics and the Oregon Compromise," *The Pacific Northwest Quarterly*, Vol. 52, No. 1 (January 1961), 7–14. Or there exists literature on the conflict between the settlers and the Indians: Cameron Addis, "The Whitman Massacre: Religion and Manifest Destiny on the Columbia Plateau, 1809–1858," *Journal of the Early Republic*, Vol. 25, No. 2 (Summer 2005), 221–258; Robert Boyd, "The Pacific Northwest Measles Epidemic of 1846–1848," *Oregon Historical Quarterly*, Vol. 95, No. 1, Early Contacts between Euro-Americans and Native Americans (Spring 1994), 6–47; Robert Burns, "Missionary Syndrome: Crusader and Pacific Northwest Religious Expansionism," *Comparative Studies in History and Society*, Vol. 30, No. 2 (April 1988), 271–285; and Wilfrid Schoenberg, "Frontier Catholics in the Pacific Northwest," *U.S. Catholic Historian*, Vol. 12, No. 4, *Frontier Catholicism* (Fall 1994), 65–68. Even more interesting are the articles about Confederates in Oregon: Jeff LaLande, "'Dixie' of the Pacific Northwest: Southern Oregon's Civil War," *Oregon Historical Quarterly*, Vol. 100, No. 1, *The Civil War in Oregon* (Spring 1999), 32–81; and Walter Carlton Woodward,

"The Rise and Early History of Political Parties in Oregon—III," *The Quarterly of the Oregon Historical Society*, Vol. 12, No. 2 (June 1911), 123–163.

The Mexican-American War created another region ripe with resources. Overviews include Jack Bauer and Robert Johansen's *The Mexican-American War, 1846–1848* (Lincoln, NE: Bison Books, 1992); Paul Foos's *A Short, Offhand, Killing Affair: Soldiers and Social Conflict during the Mexican-American War* (Chapel Hill: University of North Carolina Press, 2002); and James McCaffrey's *Army of Manifest Destiny: The American Soldier in the Mexican War, 1846–1848* (New York: New York University Press, 1992). Specific histories of units provide social history insight: Kent Barnett Germany's study "Patriotism and Protest: Louisiana and General Edmund Pendleton Gaines's Army of Mexican-American War Volunteers, 1845–1847," *Louisiana History: The Journal of the Louisiana Historical Association*, Vol. 37, No. 3 (Summer 1996), 325–335; and Samuel Watson's "Manifest Destiny and Military Professionalism: Junior U.S. Army Officers' Attitudes toward War with Mexico, 1844–1846," *The Southwestern Historical Quarterly*, Vol. 99, No. 4 (April 1996), 467–498.

Work on New Mexico and its inhabitants' reaction to the Mexican-American War exists in several small important articles: Phillip Gonzales, "Struggle for Survival: The Hispanic Land Grants of New Mexico: 1848–2001," *Agricultural History*, Vol. 77, No. 2, *Minority Land and Community Security* (Spring 2003), 293–324; Janet Lecompte, "The Independent Women of Hispanic New Mexico, 1821–1846," *The Western Historical Quarterly*, Vol. 12, No. 1 (January 1981), 17–35; and William Lyon, "Americans and Other Aliens in the Navajo Historical Imagination in the Nineteenth Century," *American Indian Quarterly*, Vol. 24, No. 1 (Winter 2000), 142–161. Darlis Miller's overview of the situation, "Hispanos and the Civil War in New Mexico: A Reconsideration," *New Mexico Historical Review*, Vol. 54, No. 2 (April 1979), 105, gives background on the region and its response as does Andrés Resendez's "National Identity on a Shifting Border: Texas and New Mexico in the Age of Transition, 1821–1848," *The Journal of American History*, Vol. 86, No. 2, *Rethinking History and the Nation-State: Mexico and the United States as a Case Study: A Special Issue* (September 1999), 668–688; John Carlos Rowe's "Highway Robbery: 'Indian Removal,' the Mexican-American War, and American Identity in 'The Life and Adventures of Joaquin Murieta,'" *NOVEL: A Forum on Fiction*, Vol. 32, No. 2, 30th Anniversary Issue: II (Spring 1998), 149–173; and Shelby Streeby's "American Sensations: Empire, Amnesia, and the US-Mexican War," *American Literary History*, Vol. 13, No. 1 (Spring 2001), 1–40.

In addition to military and social histories, several geographers helped explain the physical map changes and their consequences during the period surrounding the Mexican-American War: Gertrude Cunningham, "The Significance of 1846 to the Pacific Coast," *The Washington Historical Quarterly*, Vol. 8, No. 2 (Summer 1949), 95–114; Richard Nostrand, "The Borderlands in Perspective," *Conference of Latin Americanist Geographers*, International Aspects of Development in Latin America: Geographic Aspects, Vol. 6 (1977), 9–28; Louis Bernard Schmidt, "Manifest Opportunity and the Gadsden Purchase," *Arizona and the West*, Vol. 3, No. 3 (Autumn 1961), 245–264; and Malcolm Comeaux, "Attempts to Establish and Change a Western Boundary," *Annals of the Association of American Geographers*, Vol. 72, No. 2 (June 1982), 254–271. These geographers help point out how small changes on a map lead to big political or social changes in Washington or in the territory itself.

California deserves its own category, as historians of California treat it as having its own unique experiences. While that may be true, through the gold rush and its link to Asian markets, it weakens the literature on the Mexican-American War and its immediate aftermath. Several articles on California during and after the Mexican-American War exist: Elizabeth Haas, "War in California, 1846–1848," *California History*, Vol. 76, No. 2/3, *Contested Eden: California before the Gold Rush* (Summer-Fall 1997), 331–355; Howard Bell, "Negroes in California, 1849–1859," *Phylon*, Vol. 28, No. 2 (2nd Quarter 1967), 151–160; Shirley Ann Wilson Moore, "'We Feel the Want of Protection': The Politics of Law and Race in California, 1848–1878," *California History*, Vol. 81, No. 3/4, *Taming the Elephant: Politics, Government and Law in Pioneer California* (2003), 96–125; Michael Magliari, "Free Soil, Unfair Labor: Cave Johnson Counts and the Binding of Indian Workers in California, 1850–1867," *Pacific Historical Review*, Vol. 73, No. 3 (August 2004), 349–389; and Ronald Woolsey, "The Politics of a Lost Cause: 'Secesher' and Democrats in Southern California during the Civil War," *California History*, Vol. 69, No. 4 (Winter 1990/1991), 372–383.

The Gold Rush seems almost inseparable from California history. In some cases, like Haas and Moore, they are almost one and the same. For gold rush specific articles see: Patricia Limerick, "The Gold Rush and the Shaping of the American West," *The Western Historical Quarterly*, Vol. 77, No. 1, *National Gold Rush Symposium* (Spring 1998), 30–41; Sucheng Chan, "A People of Exceptional Character: Ethnic Diversity, Nativism and Racism in the California Gold Rush," *California History*, Vol. 79, No. 2, *Rooted in Barbarous Soil: People, Culture, and Community in Gold Rush California* (Summer 2000), 44–85; James J. Rawls, "Gold Diggers: Indian Miners in the California Gold Rush," *California Historical Quarterly*, Vol. 55, No. 1 (Spring 1976), 28–45; and Kevin Starr, "Rooted in Barbarous Soil: An Introduction to Gold Rush Society and Culture," *California History*, Vol. 79, No. 2, *Rooted in Barbarous Soil: People, Culture, and Community in Gold Rush California* (Summer 2000), 1–24.

Texas represents another state that has produced its own history that often exists without comparison to other regions of the country. One of the best and most amusing overviews would be Randolph Campbell's *Gone to Texas: A History of the Lone Star State* (New York: Oxford University Press, 2004). A refreshingly critical take on Texas history and settlement comes from Gary Clayton Anderson's *The Conquest of Texas: Ethnic Cleansing in the Promised Land, 1820–1875* (Norman: University of Oklahoma Press, 2005). Articles on the German population and the problems they faced exist: Andreas Dorpalen, "The German Element and the Issues of the Civil War," *The Mississippi Valley Historical Review*, Vol. 29, No. 1 (June 1942), 55–76; Walter Kamphoefner, "New Perspectives on Texas Germans and the Confederacy," *The Southwestern Historical Quarterly*, Vol. 102, No. 4 (April 1999), 440–455; and Anne Bailey, *Invisible Southerners: Ethnicity in the Civil War* (Athens: University of Georgia Press, 2006). Histories on the turbulent role of West Texas include: Glen Sample Ely, "Gone from Texas and Trading with the Enemy: New Perspectives on Civil War West Texas," *The Southwestern Historical Quarterly*, Vol. 110, No. 4 (April 2007), 438–463; Sean Kelley, " 'Mexico in his Head': Slavery and the Texas-Mexico Border, 1810–1860," *Journal of Social History*, Vol. 37, No. 3 (Spring 2004), 709–723; Mabelle Eppard Martin, "California Emigrant Roads through Texas," *The Southwestern Historical Quarterly*, Vol. 28, No. 4 (April 1925), 287–301; and W. H. Timmons, "American El Paso: The Formative Years, 1848–1854," *The Southwestern Historical Quarterly*, Vol. 87, No. 1 (July 1983), 1–36. A better understanding of how German populations in Texas and their response to the Civil War differed from those in other parts of the West or looking at how the need for forts compares with other states' fears about the withdrawal of federal troops would be useful.

The rise of the Church of Latter-day Saints presents a wealth of topics that need to be explored more fully, including attitudes within Utah toward the Civil War, toward African Americans, and toward Manifest Destiny. A comparison of the Mormon experience to those of other forced migrants would also help us understand the more nuanced experiences of western migrants and states' rights. Currently, several strong works examine Mormons in the West: Todd Kerstetter, *God's Country, Uncle Sam's Land: Faith and Conflict in the American West* (Urbana: University of Illinois Press, 2008); James Christensen, "Negro Slavery in the Utah Territory," *The Phylon Quarterly*, Vol. 18, No. 3 (3rd Quarter 1957), 298–305; Tom Generous, "Over the River Jordan: California Volunteers in Utah during the Civil War," *California History*, Vol. 63, No. 3 (Summer 1984), 200–211; Malise Ruthven, "The Mormons' Progress," *The Wilson Quarterly*, Vol. 15, No. 2 (Spring 1991), 22–47; and Gary Vitale, "Abraham Lincoln and the Mormons: Another Legacy of Limited Freedom," *Journal of the Illinois State Historical Society*, Vol. 101, No. 3/4 (Fall-Winter, 2008), 260–271.

Early on, it became clear that one of the most challenging aspects of this project would be finding sources on African Americans in the West. The recent overview by Albert Broussard, *Expectations of Equality: A History of Black Westerners* (Wheeling, IL: Harlan Davidson, Inc., 2012) argues that blacks migrated west for many of the same reasons as whites and provided a guide to cases and names that would yield more information. From that point, though, it became a painful territory by territory search of resources. In addition to Berwanger's book, which really looks at anti-Negro attitudes more than African Americans themselves, Monroe Lee Billington and Roger D. Hardaway's *African Americans on the Western Frontier* (Niwot, CO: University of Colorado, 1998) attempts to correct this problem, but contains only a couple of essays prior to the Civil War. State by state examinations include: Albert Castel, "Civil War Kansas and the Negro," *The Journal of Negro History*, Vol. 51, No. 2 (April 1966), 125–138; William Green, "Minnesota's Long Road to Black Suffrage, 1849–1868," *Minnesota History*, Vol. 56, No. 2 (Summer 1998), 68–84; Thomas Hogg, "Negroes and Their Institutions in Oregon," *Phylon*, Vol. 30, No. 3 (3rd Quarter 1969), 272–285; Mamie Oliver, "Idaho Ebony: The African American Presence in Idaho State History," *The Journal of African American History*, Vol. 91, No. 1, *The African American Experience in the Western States* (Winter 2006), 41–54; Christine Farnham Pope, "Southern Homesteads for Negroes," *Agricultural History*, Vol. 44, No. 2 (April 1970), 201–212; and George Woolfolk, "Turner's Safety-Valve and Free Negro Westward Migration," *The Journal of Negro History*, Vol. 50, No. 3 (July 1965), 185–197. A better synthesis of attitudes toward African Americans in the West and their own ideas about their place in the West needs to be done to help develop an understanding of how these populations settled there.

Another group that receives short shrift, but in a different way, would be the Indian nations of the West. Over the past 20 years, the study of Western Indian nations has exploded, but mainly as individual studies and mainly through ethnohistory. The pendulum now needs to swing back and historians need to revisit western Indian groups as international players who made choices. Some of the more helpful ones include: Kim Allen and Ken Kempke, "A Journey to the Heart of Darkness: John W. Wright and the War Against the Sioux, 1863–1865," *Montana: The Magazine of Western History*, Vol. 50, No. 4, *Frontier Military History Issue* (Winter 2000), 2–17; Mark Brown, "A New Focus on the Sioux War," *Montana: The Magazine of Western History*, Vol. 11, No. 4, *Cowboy and Cattleman's Issue* (Autumn 1961), 76–85; and Jane Davis, "Two Sioux War Orders: A Mystery Unraveled," *Minnesota History*, Vol. 41, No. 3 (Fall 1968), 117–125.

The history of the Cherokee has exploded over the past 20 years, much of it thanks to Theda Perdue and her students. This new literature and knowledge raises new and interesting questions about the experiences before, during, and after the Civil War, and the Cherokees relationship to their Southern and Western neighbors. Two of Perdue's books provide strong overviews: *The Cherokee Nation and the Trail of Tears* (New York: Penguin/Viking, 2007); and *Cherokee Women* (Lincoln: University of Nebraska Press, 1998). Only one book explores the period between the Trail of Tears and the Civil War, William McLoughlin's *After the Trail of Tears: The Cherokee Struggle for Sovereignty* (Chapel Hill: University of North Carolina Press, 1993). More research is emerging on Cherokee institutions in the West after the removal: Devon

Mihesuah, "Out of the 'Graves of the Polluted Debauches': The Boys of the Chero-kee Male Seminary," *American Indian Quarterly*, Vol. 15, No. 4 (Autumn 1991), 503–521. One of the most exciting books to appear in the last few years explores the relationship between racial attitudes in the South and the Cherokee's attempt to establish sovereignty through a constitution: Faye Yarbrough, *Race and the Cherokee Nation: Sovereignty and the Cherokee Nation* (Philadelphia: University of Pennsyl-vania Press, 2008). And sadly, only two histories exist that explore the Cherokee in the Civil War: Annie Heloise Abel, "The Indians in the Civil War," *The American Historical Review*, Vol. 15, No. 2 (January 1910), 281–296; and Clarissa Confer, *The Cherokee in the Civil War* (Norman: University of Oklahoma Press, 2007). Little exists on the other Five Civilized Tribes and their role in the Civil War. In addition to the overviews, articles on the Cherokee experience in the West before removal provide context, if on a microlevel: Brad Agnew, "The Cherokee Struggle for Lovely's Purchase," *American Indian Quarterly*, Vol. 2, No. 4 (Winter 1975–1976), 347–361; Scerial Thompson, "The Cherokee Cross Egypt," *Journal of the Illinois State Histori-cal Society*, Vol. 44, No. 4 (Winter 1967), 289–304; Edward Dale, "Arkansas and the Cherokee," *The Arkansas Historical Quarterly*, Vol. 8, No. 2 (Summer 1949), 95–114; Sheri Marie Shuck-Hall, "Borderlands and Identities in Imperial Texas: The Ala-bamas and Coushattas in the Anti-Comanche Union, 1820–1840," *The International History Review*, Vol. 25, No. 3 (2003). 563–591; and Ernest William Walker, "The Cherokee Indians in Texas," *The Quarterly of the Texas State Historical Association*, Vol. 7, No. 2 (October 1903), 95–165. Explorations of how the Cherokee trans-formed over the course of the first half of the 19th century include: Bob Blackburn, "From Blood Revenge to the Lighthorsemen: Evolution of Law Enforcement Institu-tions among the Five Civilized Tribes to 1861," *American Indian Law Review*, Vol. 8, No. 1 (1980), 49–63; Theda Perdue, "Clan and Court: Another Look at the Early Cherokee Republic," *American Indian Quarterly*, Vol. 24, No. 4 (Autumn 2000), 562–569; Henry Malone, "The Cherokee Phoenix: Supreme Expression of Cherokee Nationalism," *The Georgia Historical Quarterly*, Vol. 34, No. 3 (September 1950), 163–188; Tim Gammon, "Black Freedmen and the Cherokee Nation," *Journal of American Studies*, Vol. 11, No. 2 (December 1977), 357–364; Circe Sturm, "Blood Politics, Racial Classification, and Cherokee National Identity: The Trials and Tribu-lations of the Cherokee Freedmen," *American Indian Quarterly*, Vol. 22, No. 1/2 (Winter/Spring 1998), 230–258; Theda Perdue, "The Conflict Within: The Chero-kee Power Structure and Removal," *The Georgia Historical Quarterly*, Vol. 73, No. 3, *Special Issue Commemorating the Sesquicentennial of Cherokee Removal, 1838–1839* (Fall 1989), 467–491; Russell Thornton, "Boundary Dissolution and Revitalization Movements: The Case of the Nineteenth-Century Cherokees," *Ethnohistory*, Vol. 40, No. 3 (Summer 1993), 359–383; Russell Thornton, "Nineteenth-Century Cherokee History," *American Sociological Review*, Vol. 50, No. 1 (February 1985), 124–127;

H. David Williams, "Gambling Away the Inheritance: The Cherokee Nation and Georgia's Gold and Land Lotteries of 1832–1833," *The Georgia Historical Quarterly*, Vol. 73, No. 3, *Special Issue Commemorating the Sesquicentennial of Cherokee Removal 1838–1839* (Fall 1989), 519–539; and Mary Young, "The Cherokee Nation: Mirror of the Republic," *American Quarterly*, Vol. 33, No. 5. Special Issue: American Culture and the American Frontier (Winter 1981), 502–524, and Yarbrough treat the Cherokee as peoples who have fluid cultural borders and recognize that fact. Patrick Minges's "Beneath the Underdog: Race, Religion, and the Trail of the Tears," *American Indian Quarterly*, Vol. 25, No. 3 (Summer 2001), 453–479, explores racial conflict within the Cherokee during the course of removal.

The military history of the West presents another field, with a surprising number of new interpretations. Durwood Ball's *Army Regulars on the Western Frontier, 1848–1861* (Norman, OK: University of Oklahoma Press, 2001) and Robert Wooster's *The American Military Frontiers: The United States Army in the West, 1783–1900* (Albuquerque: University of New Mexico Press, 2009) present new interpretations of life on the military frontier. As helpful as they were, more social histories of army life in the West, like Sherry Smith's *The View from Officers' Row: Army Perceptions of Western Indians* (Tucson: University of Arizona Press, 1991), would help us understand the motivations and perceptions of the military in the West. A. B. Bender's "The Soldier in the Far West, 1848–1860," *Pacific Historical Review*, Vol. 8, No. 2 (June 1939), 159–178, remains a classic about the basic roles of soldiers.

New histories of specific forts or units helped spur an interest in the interactions between units and populations through the constabulary and the peacekeeping missions. These works include: Fairfax Downey, "From Plumes to Buckskin: High-Hatted Dragoons of the Revolution Became our Hard-Bitten Indian Wars Cavalrymen," *Montana: The Magazine of Western History*, Vol. 13, No. 1 (Winter 1963), 18–24; Alison Hoagland, "Village Constructions: U.S. Army Forts on the Plains, 1848–1890," *Winterthur Portfolio*, Vol. 34, No. 4 (Winter 1999), 215–237; Aurora Hunt, "The Far West Volunteers: The Army of the Pacific and the Unsung Valor of Its Men," *Montana: The Magazine of Western History*, Vol. 12, No. 2, *Civil War in the West* (Spring 1962), 49–61; Karen Merrill, "In Search of the 'Federal Presence' in the American West," *The Western Historical Quarterly*, Vol. 30, No. 4 (Winter 1999), 449–473; and Milton Holtz, "Old Fort Kearney, 1846–1848: Symbol of a Changing Frontier," *Montana: The Magazine of Western History*, Vol. 22, No. 4 (Autumn 1972), 44–55. Other works look specifically at units in the Civil War: William Burton, " 'Title Deed to America' Union Ethnic Regiments in the Civil War," *Proceedings of the American Philosophical Society*, Vol. 124, No. 6 (December17, 1980), 455–463; Dora Costa and Matthew Kahn, "Cowards and Heroes: Group Loyalty in the American Civil War," *The Quarterly Journal of Economics*, Vol. 118, No. 2 (May 2003), 519–548; and James McPherson, "Was Blood Thicker Than Water? Ethnic and Civic

Nationalism in the American Civil War," *Proceedings of the American Philosophical Society*, Vol. 143, No. 1, *Papers Delivered at a Joint Meeting with the Royal Swedish Academy of Sciences*, Stockholm, May 24–26, 1998 (March 1999), 102–108.

Finally, several theoretical articles influenced the interpretations presented here. Gary Kornblith's "Rethinking the Coming of the Civil War: A Counterfactual Exercise," *The Journal of American History*, Vol. 90, No. 1 (June 2003), 76–108, helped me reconceptualize my understanding of the Mexican-American War and the Civil War. Elliott West's "Reconstructing Race," *The Western Historical Quarterly*, Vol. 34, No. 1 (Spring 2003), 6–26, reconfirmed my idea that the history of the West remains separate from that of the Civil War.

Other topics need to be explored as the West and the Civil War become more integrated into a history of the greater United States. Comparisons between the West and the South over issues related to the Civil War would broaden our understanding of how Americans viewed these issues. A large percentage of the population went west just prior or during the Civil War, and their ideals represent American ones just as the Southern and Northern ones do. Comparisons of how the Mormons conceptualized squatter and popular sovereignty with Kansas and Southern interpretations might help underline the unintended consequences of a debate so tightly focused around one issue: slavery. More comparison between the tensions within the Cherokee, Chickasaw, and Creek nations over slavery and secession and those in the South, particularly in the Border States, might help delineate the diversity of opinions and better illustrate class and racial tensions within groups. It might also shake the idea that all yeoman farmers in the South sided with the planter class and open the door for a more nuanced interpretation of this issue. More work needs to be done to understand the West and the South as part of the same country but with different points of view. The Civil War cannot continue to be studied as a stand-alone event. It, too, must be integrated into the other events and conflicts of the 19th century.

INDEX

Abolitionists, 10, 60–61, 81–82
African Americans: in California, 18–19, 70–71, 101; exclusion of, 19, 72, 73, 78, 87, 107; German immigrants and, 84–85; Mormons and, 10, 78
Alabama, 57
Alabama-Coushatta Indians, 50, 83
Amador, Jose Marie, 13
Anderson, Gary Clayton, 88
Apache, 31, 34, 88, 90, 104–5
Arizona, 2, 14, 71; in Civil War, 89–90, 103–6; Fort Buchanan in, 31, 34, 39
Arkansas, 25, 27, 109; in Civil War, 96; Indian frontiers and, 48–49, 51–52, 61–62, 64–65
Army of the West: Civil War and, 103; as constabulary, 36–38; evolution of, 39–41; expansion of, 109–10; formation of, 22–23; forts and, 30–34, 36, 38–39, 40, 45; on frontier, 27–32; Indian nations and, 22–25, 27–41, 64–65; Manifest Destiny and, 25–26, 32, 36; Mexican-American War and, 23–26, 33–36, 38–40; as militia, 22–27; protection by, 40–41, 110; role of, 27–39, 108; Texas and, 21–22, 24–25, 30, 34; in trans-Mississippi West, 19–41
Atkinson, Henry, 29
Austin, Stephen, 50–51

Bannocks, 9, 76
Baylor, John, 89–90, 104–5
Bear Flag Revolt, 13
Bender, A. B., 32
Benton, Thomas Hart, 24
BIA. See Bureau of Indian Affairs
Boudinot, Elias, 58, 60, 63, 93–94
Boudinot, Elias C., 94–95
Britain. See England
Brown, John, 60

Bureau of Indian Affairs (BIA), 36, 38, 41, 65, 92

Calhoun, John C., 77
California, 13–14, 45; African Americans in, 18–19, 70–71, 101; Civil War and, 71–72, 104; gold rush, 17–20, 30, 68–69, 71, 101; slavery and, 70–72, 112; statehood of, 68–72, 69, 87
Californios, 13–14, 18–19, 70
Canby, Edward, 105
Carter, R. C., 9
Cass, Lewis, 28–29, 33, 44–45, 79
Catholicism, 4–8, 14, 16
Cayuse, 5, 19, 45
Charbonneau, Toussaint, 3–4
Cherokee nation: Christianity and, 48, 52, 55, 60–61; Civil War and, 43, 46, 52, 64–65, 91–96, 111; Comanche and, 50; conflict with, 30, 56–59; Constitution, 53–57, 59–60, 65; Eastern, 48, 52–65, 67; in Indian frontiers, 43–44, 46–52, 67, 110–11; in international frontier, 7–9; Mormons and, 63, 77; National Party of, 59–62, 65, 67, 110–11; removal of, 43–45, 52, 56–59, 67; Ross in, 58–65, 67, 92–95; schools, 63–64; as settlers, 59–65; slavery and, 49, 52–53, 58, 60–62, 82, 92–95; sovereignty of, 44, 46, 51, 54, 56, 59, 64–65, 92, 95–96; Spain and, 50–51; Trail of Tears of, 59; Treaty Party of, 58–62, 64–65, 67, 93–94, 110–11; Western, 48–50, 52–53, 55–65, 67
Chickasaw, 43, 46, 49, 96
Chivington, John, 105
Choctaw Indians, 9, 22, 43, 46, 96
Christianity: Catholicism, 4–8, 14, 16; Cherokee and, 48, 52, 55, 60–61; slavery and, 82; in trans-Mississippi West, 2, 4–5, 8–12, 14, 16. *See also* Mormons
Church of Latter-day Saints, 77–78, 96, 98

Civil War, U.S.: Arizona in, 89–90, 103–6; Arkansas in, 96; Army of the West and, 103; as background noise, 112; California and, 71–72, 104; Cherokee and, 43, 46, 52, 64–65, 91–96, 111; Dakota War and, 98–101; enlistments extended during, 26; Five Civilized nations and, 43, 46, 52, 64–65, 92–96, 100; generals, training of, 14; Homestead Act and, 106–8; Indian nations and, 43–46, 49, 52, 58, 62, 64–65, 90–96, 100–101, 104–5; Kansas and, 90–91, 94; New Mexico and, 89–91, 103–6; Oregon in, 101–2; statehood and, 68; Texas and, 84, 87–91, 94–96, 104; trans-Mississippi West response to, 87–108; Utah in, 96–97, 100. *See also* Confederacy; Union
Clark, Edward, 89
Clark, William, 3–4
Colorado, 89–90, 104, 106
Columbia Plateau Indians, 2, 4–5, 8
Comanche: Cherokee and, 50; conflict with, 7, 9, 30, 50–51, 62, 83, 88, 90
Confederacy, 84, 87–90, 97, 101–6; Indian nations and, 64, 91–96, 100; westward migration and, 111
Connor, Patrick Edward, 97
Constabulary, Army of the West as, 36–38
Constitution, Cherokee, 53–57, 59–60, 65
Coushatta, 50, 83
Creek Indians, 43, 46, 49, 56, 94–96

Dakota War of 1862, 98–101
Davis, Jefferson, 34, 71, 92
Delaware Indians, 44, 49, 80
Deseret, 11, 22, 37, 76–78
Douglas, Stephen, 72, 77, 80
Drew, John, 94–95

Eastern Cherokee, 48, 52–65, 67
Eastern Indians, 7–9, 22, 28, 43–44, 68
East Texas, 83–84
El Paso garrison, 34–35

England: in French and Indian War, 46; in international frontier, 1–5, 8, 15, 22, 35, 107, 109

Extractive frontier, 44

Filibusters, 35

Five Civilized nations: Chickasaw, 43, 46, 49, 96; Choctaw, 9, 22, 43, 46, 96; Civil War and, 43, 46, 52, 64–65, 92–96, 100; Creek, 43, 46, 49, 56, 94–96; in Indian frontiers, 43, 46–65; removal of, 7–9, 28, 43–44; Seminole, 43–44, 46, 96; as settlers, 59–65. *See also* Cherokee nation

Foreign Miners' Tax, 19, 72

Forts: Army of the West and, 30–34, 36, 38–39, 40, 45; Indian frontiers and, 45, 64, 69, 79, 83, 103–4; international frontier and, 31

Fox Indians, 7–8, 28, 44, 80

France: in French and Indian War, 46; in international frontier, 1, 3–4, 8, 15, 22

Fredonian Rebellion, 51

Freeman, Daniel, 107

Free Soil movement, 17, 80–81

Free State Letter, 75–76

Frémont, John C., 13, 33

French and Indian War, 46

Frontier: Army of the West on, 27–32; extractive, 44. *See also* Indian frontiers; International frontier

Gadsden Purchase, 15

Galbraith, Thomas, 99

Generals, training of, 14

Georgia, 56–58, 92

German immigrants: African Americans and, 84–85; in Texas, 23, 81, 84–85, 88–89

Glorieta Pass, 104–6

Gold rush, 17–20, 30, 68–69, 101

Grant, Ulysses, 14

Gratiot, Charles, 29, 83

Great American Desert, 8, 27–28

Great Plains Indians, 52, 68–69, 80; Army of the West and, 23, 33–34; in international frontier, 4, 8–9, 18

Greeley, Horace, 103

Harney, William, 40

Harris, Carey, 28

Hispanics, 68, 103

Homestead Act, 106–8

Hopi, 2

Hudson's Bay Company, 5, 35

Illinois, 10–12, 24, 49, 52, 65, 69

Indiana, 24

Indian frontiers: Arkansas and, 48–49, 51–52, 61–62, 64–65; Cherokee in, 43–44, 46–52, 67, 110–11; Civil War and, 43–46, 49, 52, 58, 62, 64–65; Five Civilized nations in, 43, 46–65; forts and, 45, 64, 69, 79, 83, 103–4; removal policy and, 43–45, 52, 56–59, 65; Texas and, 45, 49–52; of trans-Mississippi West, 43–65

Indian nations: Army of the West and, 22–25, 27–41, 64–65; Civil War and, 43–46, 49, 52, 58, 62, 64–65, 90–96, 100–101, 104–5; Confederacy and, 64, 91–96, 100; in Dakota War, 98–101; gold rush and, 18–20; Mexican-American War and, 14–17; in Rogue River Indian War, 30, 45, 101–2; Texas and, 45, 49–52, 62, 65, 83–84, 88, 91, 100, 104–5; Union and, 64–65, 91–92, 94–96, 100–101; in Utah, 76–79, 97. *See also specific nations*

Indian removal policy, 27, 33; Cherokee and, 43–45, 52, 56–59, 67; Five Civilized nations and, 7–9, 28, 43–44; Indian frontiers and, 43–45, 52, 56–59, 65

Indian Territory, 49, 58–59, 65, 82; Civil War and, 90–96; establishment of, 44–45

International frontier: Cherokee in, 7–9;
    end of, 113; England in, 1–5, 8, 15, 22,
    35, 107, 109; forts and, 31; France in,
    1, 3–4, 8, 15, 22; gold rush in, 17–20;
    Great Plains Indians in, 4, 8–9, 18;
    Manifest Destiny and, 13–15, 17–18;
    Mexican-American War and, 4–7,
    11–17, 23–26, 33–35; Mormons in,
    9–12, 17; New Mexico in, 2, 4, 13–14,
    16–17; Spain in, 1–4, 6–7, 14–15, 22,
    107, 109; Texas in, 6–7, 13, 15–17; of
    trans-Mississippi West, 1–20; U.S. in, 1,
    3–20, 109
Iowa, 28, 44
Iroquois, 22, 28, 43–44

Jackson, Andrew, 8, 58
Jefferson, Thomas, 3–4, 48
Johnston, Albert Sidney, 104

Kansas, 22, 28, 36–38, 41, 64; Civil War
    and, 90–91, 94; slavery and, 37, 79–82;
    statehood of, 68, 79–82
Kansas-Nebraska Act, 71, 77, 80
Karankawa Indians, 50
Kearney, Stephen, 29, 36
Kent, James, 14
Kentucky, 53, 69
Kickapoo, 44, 49
Kiowa, 88
Knights of the Golden Circle, 75, 102

Lamar, Mirabeau, 83
Land Bounty, 25–26
Latter-day Saints. *See* Mormons
Lee, Daniel, 5
Lee, Jason, 5
Lewis, Meriwether, 3–4
Lincoln, Abraham, 65, 97–98, 100–101,
    106
Little Crow, 99–100
Louisiana, 3–4, 8, 24–25, 27, 109
Lubbock, Francis, 89

Magoffin, James, 34
Manifest Destiny, 102, 109, 111; Army of
    the West and, 25–26, 32, 36; in interna-
    tional frontier, 13–15, 17–18; statehood
    and, 72, 76, 78, 83
McLoughlin, William, 63
Mexican-American War, 44, 68, 70, 74,
    83, 107; Army of the West and, 23–26,
    33–36, 38–40; decade before, 4–6;
    Indian nations and, 14–17; interna-
    tional frontier and, 4–7, 11–17, 23–26,
    33–35; legacies of, 17
Mexico: forts and, 31; as hybrid country,
    15–16, 18; Texas and, 6–7, 84–85,
    87–90, 104
Miami Indians, 28, 44
Michigan, 24
Military: gold rush and, 19–20; militia and,
    23. *See also* Army of the West
Militia, 22–27
Minnesota, 28, 98–101
Mississippi, 25, 27, 49–50, 52
Missouri, 4, 10–12, 24, 28, 109
Mormons: African Americans and, 10, 78;
    Cherokee and, 63, 77; Church of Latter-
    day Saints of, 77–78, 96, 98; in inter-
    national frontier, 9–12, 17; slavery and,
    10–11; in Utah, 11–12, 22, 36–37, 68,
    76–79, 87, 96–97
Morrill Anti-Bigamy Act, 97–98
Myrick, Andrew, 99

Napoleon Bonaparte, 3
National Party, 59–62, 65, 67, 110–11
Nativism, 16, 19, 74
Nauvoo, 10–11
Navajo, 2, 39
Nebraska, 11, 22, 28, 80
New Mexico, 30, 35–36; Civil War and,
    89–91, 103–6; in international frontier,
    2, 4, 13–14, 16–17
New Orleans, 3, 6
Nez Perce, 5, 45

North Carolina, 49, 53, 57–58
Northwest Coast, 1–4, 8

Oklahoma, 28, 100
Old Northwest, 24, 27, 49, 71, 107
Old Settlers. *See* Western Cherokee
Old Southwest, 27, 107
Omaha Indians, 38
Opothleyahola, 94
Oregon: in Civil War, 101–2; slavery and,
    72–76, 101; statehood of, 68–69,
    72–76, 87; Territory, 5–6, 21, 29–30,
    45, 68, 79, 113; Trail, 29–30, 37, 69, 82;
    Whitman Massacre in, 5–6, 9, 45, 72, 74
Osage Indians, 9, 30, 49, 62
Otoe, 38

Paiute, 9, 34, 39, 76
Palouse, 19
Paul, G. R., 90
Pawnee, 38, 43
Pea Ridge, 95–96
Pig War, 35
Pike, Zebulon, 8, 27
Plains Indians. *See* Great Plains Indians
Polk, James, 5, 13, 24
popular sovereignty, 75, 77, 79–80
Proclamation Line, 46
Provencher, Joseph, 4–5
Pueblo, 2
Pyron, Charles, 105–6

Railroad, 15–16, 33–34, 103, 106–7
Removal policy. *See* Indian removal policy
Ridge, John, 52, 60, 63
Ridge, John Rollin, 52
Rogue River Indian War, 30, 45, 101–2
Ross, John, 58–65, 67, 92–95
Russell, R. R., 74
Russia, 2–3

Sac Indians, 7–8, 28, 44, 80
Schools, Cherokee, 63–64

Scott, Winfield, 26
Scurry, William, 105–6
Seminole Indians, 43–44, 46, 96
Seminole Wars, 24–25
Sequoyah, 52, 54
Settlement, of trans-Mississippi West,
    59–65, 67–69, 106–11
Settlers: Five Civilized nations as, 59–65;
    Homestead Act and, 106–8; westward
    migration of, 67–69, 111
Sevier, John, 16
Shawnee, 43, 49–50, 79–80
Shoshone, 34, 39, 76
Sibley, Henry Hopkins, 90
Sioux, 23, 38–39, 98–101
Slavery, 17, 87, 107, 109–11; abolition-
    ists, 10, 60–61, 81–82; California and,
    70–72, 112; Cherokee and, 49, 52–53,
    58, 60–62, 82, 92–95; Christianity and,
    82; Kansas and, 37, 79–82; Mormons
    and, 10–11; Oregon and, 72–76, 101;
    Texas and, 6–7, 21, 84–85, 88, 90, 112;
    Utah and, 77–78, 98, 112
Slough, John, 105
Smith, Hyrum, 10
Smith, Joseph, 9–10
Southern Rights Party, 93
Southwest Indians, 1–2
Southwest Texas, 84–85
Sovereignty: Cherokee, 44, 46, 51, 54, 56,
    59, 64–65, 92, 95–96; popular, 75, 77,
    79–80; squatter, 77, 98, 107
Spain: Cherokee and, 50–51; in interna-
    tional frontier, 1–4, 6–7, 14–15, 22,
    107, 109
Spalding, Henry Harmon, 5
Squatter sovereignty, 77, 98, 107
Statehood: of California, 68–72, 69, 87;
    Civil War and, 68; of Kansas, 68, 79–82;
    Manifest Destiny and, 72, 76, 78, 83;
    of Oregon, 68–69, 72–76, 87; of Texas,
    68, 83–85; in trans-Mississippi West,
    67–85, 110; of Utah, 68, 76–79, 98

Steen, Enoch, 31
Stratton, R. A., 102
Sumner, Edwin "Bull Head," 36, 40, 102
Sutter, John, 17

Temperance, 61
Tennessee, 49, 53, 57–58, 69
Texas: Army of the West and, 21–22,
    24–25, 30, 34; Civil War and, 84,
    87–91, 94–96, 104; East, 83–84; Ger-
    man immigrants in, 23, 81, 84–85,
    88–89; Indian nations and, 45, 49–52,
    62, 65, 83–84, 88, 91, 100, 104–5; in
    international frontier, 6–7, 13, 15–17;
    Mexico and, 6–7, 84–85, 87–90, 104;
    slavery and, 6–7, 21, 84–85, 88, 90,
    112; Southwest, 84–85; statehood of,
    68, 83–85; voice of, 109
Tonkawa Indians, 50
Trail of Tears, 59
Transcontinental railroad, 15–16, 33–34
Trans-Mississippi West: Army of the West in,
    19–41; as canvas, 109; Christianity in,
    2, 4–5, 8–12, 14, 16; Civil War response
    of, 87–108; Indian frontiers of, 43–65;
    international frontier of, 1–20; racial
    makeup of, 110; settlement of, 59–65,
    67–69, 106–11; statehood in, 67–85,
    110; Western Indians in, 1–2, 38–39
Treaty of 1846, 62–63
Treaty of Guadalupe-Hidalgo, 13, 34, 70
Treaty of Hopewell, 47
Treaty of New Echota, 58–59, 62
Treaty of San Ildefonso, 3
Treaty Party: Cherokee and, 58–62, 64–65,
    67, 93–94, 110–11; overview of, 110–11

Turner, Frederick Jackson, 28, 45, 110
Twiggs, David E., 89
Tyler, John, 13

Umatilla, 5
Union, 72, 88–90, 97, 102; Glorieta Pass
    and, 104–6; Indian nations and, 64–65,
    91–92, 94–96, 100–101
United States, in international frontier, 1,
    3–20, 109. *See also* Civil War, U.S.
Utah: in Civil War, 96–97, 100; as De-
    seret, 11, 22, 37, 76–78; Indians in,
    76–79, 97; Mormons in, 11–12, 22,
    36–37, 68, 76–79, 87, 96–97; slavery
    and, 77–78, 98, 112; statehood of, 68,
    76–79, 98
Ute, 9, 76

Vallejo, Mariano, 13

Wagon trains, guarding, 32, 34
Washington, 35, 87
Watie, Stand, 93–95
West. *See* Trans-Mississippi West
Western Cherokee, 48–50, 52–53,
    55–65, 67
Western Indians, 1–2, 38–39
West Point, 22, 25–27, 33
White Path, 56
Whitman, Marcus, 5, 29
Whitman Massacre, 5–6, 9, 45, 72, 74
Williams, George H., 75
Wisconsin, 24
Worcester v. Georgia, 57, 65

Young, Brigham, 11, 37, 76–78, 97

ABOUT THE AUTHOR

CAROL L. HIGHAM is an independent scholar. She is coauthor of *Conquests and Consequences: The American West from Frontier to Region* (Harlan Davidson, Inc., 2009) and coeditor of *One West, Two Myths, Volumes 1 and 2* (University of Calgary Press, 2001, 2004). Additionally, she wrote *Noble, Wretched, and Redeemable* (University of New Mexico/University of Calgary, 2000). Her articles have appeared in the *Pacific Historical Review* and the *Canadian Review of American Studies*.